FOR LOVE OF COUNTRY

For Love of Country

AN ESSAY ON PATRIOTISM
AND NATIONALISM

MAURIZIO VIROLI

CLARENDON PRESS · OXFORD

Oxford University Press, Great Clarendon Street, Oxford OX2 6DP
Oxford New York
Athens Auckland Bangkok Bogota Bombay
Buenos Aires Calcutta Cape Town Dar es Salaam
Delhi Florence Hong Kong Istanbul Karachi
Kuala Lumpur Madras Madrid Melbourne
Mexico City Nairobi Paris Singapore
Taipei Tokyo Toronto Warsaw
and associated companies in
Berlin Ibadan

Oxford is a trade mark of Oxford University Press

Published in the United States
by Oxford University Press Inc., New York

First published 1995
First issued as paperback 1997

British Library Cataloguing in Publication Data
Data available

Library of Congress Cataloging in Publication Data
Data available

ISBN 0–19–827952–3
ISBN 0–19–829358–5 (Pbk.)

Printed in Great Britain
on acid-free paper by
Bookcraft (Bath) Ltd
Midsomer Norton, Somerset

For
Norberto Bobbio

Acknowledgements

I WISH first of all to thank my colleagues the political theorists at Princeton University: George Kateb, Amy Gutmann, Alan Ryan, Elizabeth Kiss, and Oliver Avens. To all of them goes my deepest gratitude for the friendly and stimulating intellectual environment that they have created and kept alive over the years. I also wish to express my most sincere thanks to Professor Ezra Suleiman and to the Committee for European Studies for their very generous support.

I owe special thanks to Quentin Skinner for his encouragement and for his precious comments and criticisms on earlier versions of the manuscript, and to Michael Walzer, for his important theoretical remarks. I also wish to thank Benjamin Barber, Daniel Dudney, and Gareth Stedman Jones for having given me the opportunity to discuss my ideas in lively and challenging seminars.

My most sincere gratitude also goes to Tim Barton for the enthusiasm with which he has supported my project since the beginnings, and to Dorothy McCarthy and Rowena Anketell for their excellent job in copy-editing the typescript.

I reserve the last words for my wife Nadia, who has discussed with me many times of *patria* and *amor di patria* and suggested to me many precious sources, including the quote from John Stuart Mill that I have chosen as epigraph for the book.

This book is dedicated to Norberto Bobbio, who has taught me that political commitment must go together with moral integrity and intellectual rigour.

M. V.

Contents

We need scarcely say that we do not mean [by principle of nationality] a senseless antipathy to foreigners; or a cherishing of absurd peculiarities because they are national; or a refusal to adopt what has been found good by other countries. In all these senses, the nations which have had the strongest national spirit have had the least nationality. We mean a principle of sympathy, not of hostility; of union, not of separation. We mean a feeling of common interest among those who live under the same government, and are contained within the same natural or historical boundaries. We mean, that one part of the community shall not consider themselves as foreigners with regard to another part; that they shall cherish the tie which holds them together; shall feel that they are one people, that their lot is cast together, that evil to any of their fellow-countrymen is evil to themselves, and that they cannot selfishly free themselves from their share of any common inconvenience by severing the connexion.

John Stuart Mill, *A System of Logic*, VI. 10. 5

Introduction

IN scholarly literature and common language, 'love of country' and 'loyalty to the nation', patriotism and nationalism, are used as synonyms.[1] And yet, as I hope to show in this study, they can and must be distinguished.[2] The language of patriotism has been used over the centuries to strengthen or invoke love of the political institutions and the way of life that sustain the common liberty of a people, that is love of the republic; the language of nationalism was forged in late eighteenth-century Europe to defend or reinforce the cultural, linguistic, and ethnic oneness and homogeneity of a people. Whereas the enemies of republican patriotism are tyranny, despotism, oppression, and corruption, the enemies of nationalism are cultural contamination,

---

[1] An interesting example is E. J. Hobsbawm, *Nations and Nationalism since 1870* (Cambridge, 1992); pp. 46 and 75, he uses the term 'national patriotism' and describes the 'proto-nationalism' of Tudor England as something close to 'modern patriotism'; on p. 78 he speaks of 'national or state patriotism'; in other instances (e.g. p. 90), he distinguishes 'nationalism as a political force' from state patriotism. See also B. C. Shafer, 'Bourgeois Nationalism in the Pamphlets on the Eve of the French Revolution', *Journal of Modern History*, 10 (1938), 31–50, and H. Kohn, *The Idea of Nationalism* (New York, 1944).

[2] 'The blurring of patriotism into nationalism, or even the acknowledgement of nationalism as a "species" of patriotism reveals that we have literally lost touch with history, with a very real past in which real patriots held to a particular set of political principles and their associated practices—to a conception of citizenship that bears scant resemblance to modern nationalism': M. G. Dietz, 'Patriotism', T. Ball *et al.* (eds.) *Political Innovation and Conceptual Change* (Cambridge, 1989), 191. 'We need to stop confusing patriotism with simple conservatism, or smothering it with damning and dismissive references to chauvinism and jingoism. Quite as much as any other human activity, the patriotism of the past requires flexible, sensitive and above all, imaginative reconstruction': L. Colley, *Britons. Forging the Nation 1707–1837* (London, 1994), 372. On the importance of separating patriotism from nationalism see also J. Lukacs, 'Nationalism and Patriotism', *Freedom Review*, 25 (1994), 78–9.

heterogeneity, racial impurity, and social, political, and intellectual disunion.

This does not mean that the champions of patriotism neglected
or despised the culture, the ethnic background, the language, or
the traditions of peoples. Even the theorists who wanted to make
the distance between the political values of the republic and the
sphere of ethnicity and culture as wide as possible, always meant
the republic as it was expressed by the common liberty of a
particular people with its particular background and its particular culture. The crucial distinction lies in the priority or the
emphasis: for the patriots, the primary value is the republic and
the free way of life that the republic permits; for the nationalists,
the primary values are the spiritual and cultural unity of the
people. In the writings of the founders of modern nationalism,
the republic is either repudiated or regarded as an issue of sec-
ondary importance. Patriots and nationalists have not only recommended different ideals as objects of our love: the republic,
in the case of the patriots, the nation as a cultural and spiritual
unity in the case of the nationalists; they have also endeavoured
to instil or strengthen in us different types of love: a charitable
and generous love in the case of patriotism, an unconditional
loyalty or an exclusive attachment in the case of the nationalists.

The long history of the languages of patriotism and nationalism is of course much more complicated than this. Historically,
patriotism has also meant loyalty to the monarch and the language of patriotism has also been used to oppress, discriminate,
and conquer, while the ideal of the nation and the cultural and
spiritual unity of a people have been invoked to sustain struggles for liberty. The distinction that I suggest is a poor repres-
entation of a rich intellectual and political story made up of many
localized and highly contextualized stories told over the centuries on love of country. However, in spite of all the similarities
and nuances, one can identify a language of patriotism that has
been a language of common liberty, which is substantially different from the nationalist language of oneness, uniqueness, and
homogeneity.

Efforts to separate patriotism and nationalism have been made,
but have failed to express the distinction adequately. Here is
George Orwell's attempt:

Nationalism is not to be confused with patriotism. Both words are normally used in so vague a way that any definition is liable to be challenged, but one must draw a distinction between them, since two different and even opposing ideas are involved. By 'patriotism' I mean devotion to a particular place and a particular way of life which one believes to be the best in the world but has no wish to force upon other people. Patriotism is of its nature defensive, both militarily and culturally. Nationalism, on the other hand, is inseparable from the desire for power. The abiding purpose of every nationalist is to secure more power and more prestige, *not* for himself but for the nation or other unit in which he has decided to sink individuality.[3]

Orwell's definitions identify important features of patriotism and nationalism, but they are also misleading. Patriotism has not been understood by its champions as a form of devotion; they spoke rather of respect, charity, and compassion. The difference is not purely terminological, but involves a different interpretation of the passions that constitute the core of patriotism: the object of compassion and love for the patriot was the republic and the ability to live in freedom in a particular place. As for nationalism, to define it as desire for power for the nation surely holds true for many nationalist thinkers, but would be inappropriate, for instance, for a prominent nationalist like Herder.[4]

Similar observations can also be applied to the distinction suggested by Karl Deutsch.

Patriotism is an effort or readiness to promote the interests of all the persons born or living with the same *patria*, i.e., country, whereas nationalism aims at promoting the interests of all those of the same *natio*, i.e., literally a group of common descent and upbringing, that is

[3] 'Notes on Nationalism', in *The Collected Essays, Journalism and Letters of George Orwell* (New York, 1968), iii. 362.
[4] In a similar vein Louis L. Snyder wrote that 'Nationalism is primarily concerned with the independence and unity of the nation, whereas patriotism is more specifically the passion that influences the individual to serve the object of his devotion—his country, either in defending it from invasion, or in protecting its rights, or in maintaining its laws and institutions in vigor and purity. Nationalism is inseparable from the idea of power; patriotism, on the other hand, is by nature defensive, both culturally and militarily. But so ambivalent is the character of patriotism that it can easily be used to justify aggression. *German Nationalism: The Tragedy of a People* (Harrisburg, Ill., 1952), 148; another curious definition of nationalism and patriotism is in C. J. H. Hayes, *Essays on Nationalism* (New York, 1926), 29.

to say, of complementary habits of communication. Patriotism appeals
to all residents of an ethnic group, regardless of their ethnic background. Nationalism appeals to all members of an ethnic group, regardless of their country of residence. Patriotism based on residence,
often appears at an earlier stage of economic and social mobilisation,
such as was found in Europe during the later Mercantilist era, and up
to the middle of the nineteenth century. As mobilisation progresses
and comes to involve larger masses of the population in more intense
competition and greater political insecurity, patriotism is replaced by
nationalism which is based on far more intimate and slow-changing
personal characteristics and communication habits of each individual.[5]

To situate patriotism in the period between the later mercantilist
era and the middle of the nineteenth century, and to present
nationalism as connected to a later stage marked by more intense competition and greater political insecurity is a historical
mistake, since texts defending and urging patriotism were also
written in times of great political insecurity and, as I shall show,
much later than the middle of the nineteenth century.

Like Proteus, the prophetic sea god of Greek mythology capable of changing his shape at will, nationalism and patriotism
seem to possess a particular ability to avoid the conceptual tools
that scholars have tenaciously been forging.[6] Understandably, a
tone of dissatisfaction or even frustration is easily detected in
the literature: like Proteus, patriotism and nationalism have a lot
to tell us about our past, our present, and our future, but we
cannot find the way to convince them to reveal their secrets.

Instead of aiming at forging scientific definitions of the nature
of patriotism and nationalism, we should aim at understanding
what scholars, agitators, poets, and prophets have meant when

[5] *Nationalism and Social Communication: An Inquiry into the Foundations
of Nationality* (New York, 1953), 232 n. 40.

[6] Herder himself spoke of 'this Proteus, which is usually called national
character': *Kleine Schriften 1791–1796*, in *Sämmtliche Werke*, ed. B. Suphan
(Berlin, 1883), xviii. 57–8. See also L. Greenfeld: 'The national populations—
diversely termed "peoples", "nations" and "nationalities"—are defined in many
ways, and the criteria of membership in them vary. The multiformity which
results is the source of the conceptually evasive, Protean nature of nationalism
and the cause of perennial frustration of its students.' *Nationalism: Five Roads
to Modernity* (Harvard, Mass. 1992), 7.

they spoke of love of country. We need historical interpretation rather than scientific theories, to uncover and understand the meaning of the themes, metaphors, allusions, exhortations, and invectives that the language of patriotism has been crafting over the centuries to sustain or repeal, damper, inflame, or rekindle a rich and colourful universe of passions. The historical approach can, of course, only help us to uncover localized meanings. At best, it may allow us to outline a tradition based upon recurrent terms with similar meanings. Though fragmented and incomplete, stories of love of country, love of liberty, and love of unity, of patriots narrating experiences of moral and political exile, of historians attempting to reconstruct the past in order to reshape the nation's cultural identity, of philosophers investigating possible alchemic transformations of the passions of love and pride, respect, compassion, charity, hatred, fear, and resentment tell us more than models, theories, and definitions.

The lack of a historically accurate distinction between patriotism and nationalism negatively affects even the best studies on modern nationalism. An example is Benedict Anderson's *Imagined Communities*, an essay which does not attempt to provide scientific or objective definitions of nation but rightly interprets nation and nationalism as 'cultural artefacts of a particular kind' that have to be studied from a historical perspective to understand 'in what ways their meanings have changed over time, and why, today, they command such a profound emotional legitimacy'.[7]

Instead of treating nationalism as a 'pathology of modern developmental history', he approaches it with an anthropological spirit and treats it as if it belonged with kinship and religion, rather than liberalism or Fascism. Anderson rejects the idea that nationalism is rooted 'in fear and hatred of the Other'; he refuses to consider nationalism as a form of racism. He connects, instead, nationalism with love. It is useful, he stresses, to remind ourselves that nations inspire love, and often profoundly self-sacrificing

---

[7] *Imagined Communities: Reflections on the Origin and Spread of Nationalism* (London, 1991).

love.[8] Nationalistic poetry, prose, fiction, music, plastic arts express love, rarely fear and loathing. As an example, he quotes *Ultimo adíos*, a poem written by José Riza, the 'father of Filipino Nationalism':

> Farewell, dear Land, beloved of the sun,
> Pearl of the Orient seas, lost Paradise!
> Gladly, I will to you this life undone;
> Were it a fairer, fresher, fuller one,
> I'd cede it still, your will to realize . . .
>
> What matters then that you forget me, when
> I might explore your ev'ry dear retreat?
> Be as a note, pulsing and pure; and then,
> Be scent, light tone; be song or sign, again;
> And through it all, my theme of faith, repeat.
>
> Land I enshrine, list to my last farewell!
> Philippines, Love, of pains my pain extreme,
> I leave you all, whom I love so well,
> To go where neither slaves nor tyrants dwell,
> Where Faith kills not, and where God reigns supreme.
>
> Farewell to all my soul does comprehend—
> O kith and kin in my home dispossessed;
> Give thanks my day oppressive is at end;
> Farewell, sweet stranger, my delight and friend;
> Farewell, dear ones. To die is but to rest.[9]

Rizal's words poignantly express a generous, embracing patriotism. But other nationalist texts speak of hatred and enemies.[10] 'Fatherland' can mean the native soil pervaded by common memories, bonds of fellowship, and ideals of liberty, but it can also mean a community bound by language and blood; love of country can be generous, compassionate, and intelligent, but it can also be exclusive, deaf, and blind. These differences have to be addressed; to speak of 'love of country' or 'nationalism' in general is like melting bright colours into an insipid mixture.

The confusion between patriotism and nationalism leads to

---

[8] Ibid. 141.   [9] Ibid. 143.
[10] See e.g. the texts quoted by H. Kohn, 'Arndt and the Character of German Nationalism', *American Historical Review*, 54 (1949), 791 and 795.

misunderstandings about the historical meaning of the origin of the language of nationalism. The specificity of nationalism, argues Liah Greenfeld, for example, in her excellent study, 'derives from the fact that nationalism locates the source of individual identity within a "people", which is seen as the bearer of sovereignty, the central object of loyalty, and the basis of collective solidarity'.[11] Contrary to the conventional wisdon, she argues that *nationalism is not necessarily a form of particularism*', since it is historically rooted not in the late eighteenth-century vindication of the importance of attachment to one's own particular language, culture, and ethnic background, but on the creation of the concept of the sovereign people in the early sixteenth century.

National identity in its distinctive modern sense is, therefore, an identity which derives from membership in a 'people', the fundamental characteristic of which is that it is defined as a 'nation'. Every member of the 'people' thus interpreted partakes in its superior, elite quality, and it is in consequence that a stratified national population is perceived as essentially homogeneous, and the lines of status and class as superficial. This principle lies at the basis of all nationalisms and justifies viewing them as expressions of the same general phenomenon.[12]

As Greenfeld perceptively remarks, in sixteenth-century England terms like 'publike weale' and 'country'—both direct derivations from the Latin words *respublica* and *patria*—were used as equivalents of 'nation'. This suggests that when political writers spoke of 'nation' understood as a sovereign people united in an independent political comunity, they meant 'republic' or 'country' in the classical sense. But the appearance of the word 'nation' used in this sense does not mark the beginning of the history of modern nationalism; it is, rather, another chapter in the long history of patriotism. Not only in England, but also in France, Italy, Spain, and the United States, those who committed themselves to the ideal of nation—in the sense of republic—called themselves and were called patriots, not nationalists. Like the great majority of scholars, Greenfeld distinguishes between a civic nationalism that identifies nationality with citizenship and

[11] *Nationalism*, 3.   [12] Ibid. 7.

an ethnic nationalism that treats nationality as a genetic or cultural characteristic. She also separates individualistic-libertarian (civic) nationalism from collectivistic-authoritarian (civic or ethnic) nationalism. All these distinctions and subdivisions are useful, but they tend to approach nationalism as a single intellectual stream that originated in sixteenth-century England (or in classical antiquity, if we accept Hans Kohn's thesis) and presented a different face in different times and places. As I hope to be able to show in this book, the historical picture looks quite different. The language of modern nationalism came about as a transformation or adaptation of the language of patriotism, by which words like 'country' and expressions like 'love of country' were given new meanings, while a number of themes like cultural or ethnic unity and purity that republican patriotism did not address at all or treated as minor compared to the main question of common liberty, assumed a central role. To understand nationalism, we must then begin with patriotism and think in terms of two languages, not a single language unfolding and changing over the centuries.

In addition to being historically wrong, the confusion between patriotism and nationalism has pernicious practical effects. Properly understood, the language of republican patriotism could serve as a powerful antidote to nationalism. Like the language of nationalism it is eminently rhetorical; it aims at resuscitating, strengthening, and directing the passions of a particular people with a specific cultural and historical identity rather than at attaining the reasoned approval of impersonal rational agents. It endeavours to reinforce bonds, such love of the common liberty of a people, which are as particularistic as the love of, or pride in, the cultural tradition or the shared destiny of a people. Precisely because it competes with nationalism on the same terrain of passions and particularity and uses rhetorical rather than purely rational arguments, patriotism is a formidable opponent for nationalism. It works on bonds of solidarity and fellowship that like feels toward like to transmute them into forces that sustain liberty instead of fomenting exclusion or aggression. It does not say to the Italians or the Germans who want to remain Italian or German, that they should think and act as citizens of the world, or as lovers of an anonymous liberty and justice; it tells them that they should become Italian or German *citizens* committed to defend and improve their own republic, and to live freely in their own way, and it says so by using poignant images that refer to shared memories and by telling meaningful stories that give colour and warmth to the ideal of the republic.

Patriotic stories have morals to tell, but do not offer a moral argument as to why we have the obligation to commit ourselves to the common liberty of our people. The answer that republican thinkers have been giving to this question is well known: we have a moral obligation toward our country because we are indebted to it. We owe our country our life, our education, our language, and, in the most fortunate cases, our liberty. If we want to be moral persons, we must return what we have received, at least in part, by serving the common good.

Many lists of benefits and obligations are possible; all of them are open to question; not one has ever commanded, or shall ever command, general agreement. This does not imply that arguments on the individual's moral obligations toward his or her country are irrelevant. We need to define the boundaries of the obligation; we have to be able to say in public arguments which demands our country makes on us must be rejected, and which must be accepted. If our obligation toward our country is an obligation to protect the common liberty, the boundaries of the obligation are defined with sufficient precision, with as much precision as is possible in moral arguments. If we are patriots in this sense, we have to fight against anyone who attempts to impose a particular interest over the common good; we have to oppose discrimination and exclusion, but we have no obligation to impose cultural, or ethnic, or religious homogeneity, nor to foster self-aggrandizement at the expense of other peoples' liberty, nor to deny civil and political rights to any of our fellow patriots.

To be committed to the common liberty of our people means that if our country is unfree we have to work to make it free instead of leaving to look for liberty elsewhere, and if we are forced to leave, we have to continue to work in order to be able to go back to live in freedom with our fellows. 'Why', one may ask, 'should I suffer for the liberty of my own people instead of looking for my own liberty elsewhere? If my country treats me injustly, I owe her nothing, I have no obligation.' One possible answer is that the liberty that we may enjoy in another country is necessarily less rich, less complete than the liberty that we would be able to enjoy with our own people. In another country we might, in the best possible case, enjoy civil or even political liberties, but we would not be able to live freely according to our culture. Liberty among our own people has a sweeter taste; we would enjoy it as our own liberty, as a liberty that is distinctively ours.

This argument has its weaknesses: the reward may well appear too remote and uncertain; one may still find liberty in another country more attractive. To move our compatriots to commit themselves to the common liberty of their people we have to appeal to feelings of compassion and solidarity that are— when they are—rooted in bonds of language, culture, and history. The work to be done is to translate these bonds into love of common liberty. To make this alchemy of passions possible we surely need moral arguments that appeal to reason and interests, but we must also be able to resort, as good rhetoricians do, to stories, images, and visions.

Hard as it is, we cannot disregard the task of working to encourage patriotism: to survive and flourish, political liberty needs civic virtue, that is citizens capable of committing themselves to the common good, to stand up for the defence of common liberty and rights. Contemporary political philosophers, however (at least many of them), regard civic virtue as a hopelessly obsolete vestige of antiquity or as a dangerous political myth that irresponsible nostalgics are trying to retrieve. What we can reasonably expect to have in contemporary democratic multicultural society, wrote Michael Walzer, is a 'balance of civility and civic virtue' in which civility is the predominant component. If we wanted to redress the balance in favour of civic virtue, patriotism, and political activism, we have to be aware that this might be done at the expense of civility and toleration. Patriotism and political activism make for passion and excitement, which are both dangerous enemies of orderliness, tranquillity, and tolerance.[13] Without a vocation for politics, with no significant ethnic or religious or national commonality, entirely absorbed by the pleasures of private life, modern citizens do not and cannot find the ideal of civic virtue appealing. What they really care about is not civic virtue but liberty, or, to use Benjamin Constant's famous distinction, they want the liberty of the moderns, not that of the ancients. Collective and direct exercise of several parts of complete sovereignty, which the ancients regarded as the highest expression of civic virtue and the most ennobling part of citizens' life, is of little interest to the moderns.[14]

Contemporary advocates of 'a politics of civic virtue', on the other hand, stress that civic virtue can only be sustained by a 'vision of the good' and the attachment to a particular community, to a particular culture. The devotion to the public good, they say, must be rooted in the love of the country, a love of what makes each country unique: its language, its ethnic background, and its history.[15] The identification with this sort of patriotism, however, damages rather than helps the cause of civic

---

[13] 'Civility and Civic Virtue in Contemporary America', in *Radical Principles* (New York, 1980), 61–2 and 67–8. Like the other sources I am quoting in this article, Walzer explicitly refers to the USA. I am, however, discussing the problem of civic virtue from a broader perspective. I take Walzer's and others' view to be representative of an intellectual position that has been playing a central role in contemporary political culture since Benjamin Constant's speech on 'The Liberty of the Ancients Compared with that of the Moderns'.

[14] 'The right to be subjected only to the laws, and to be neither arrested, detained, put to death or maltreated in any way by the arbitrary will of one or more individuals. It is the right of everyone to express their opinion, choose a profession and practise it, to dispose of property, and even to abuse it; to come and go without permission, and without having to account for their motives or undertakings.' Constant, 'Of the Liberty of the Ancients compared with that of the Moderns', in *Political Writings*, ed. Biancamaria Fontana (Cambridge, 1988), 310–11.

[15] M. Sandel, 'Morality and the Liberal Ideal', *New Republic*, 7 May 1984, 17. See also id. 'The State and the Soul', *New Republic*, 10 June 1985, 39. The kind of patriotism that can be a virtue, indeed a central virtue, writes Alasdair MacIntyre, is a loyalty to a particular community. 'The patriot does not value similar merits and achievements of some nation other than his or hers. For he or she—at least in the role of the patriot—values them not just as merits and achievements, but as the merits and achievements of this particular nation': 'Is Patriotism a Virtue?', Lindley Lecture, University of Kansas, 26 Mar. 1984.

virtue. If to love one's country means to love common ethnic and linguistic characteristics, a shared conception of the good life, or the vision of a common national destiny, such a love no doubt sustains commitment to the common good. It also encourages, however, contempt and intolerance for cultural, racial, and political diversity both at home and abroad. Examples abound of civic-minded citizens who are prepared to give their blood for their country but who are also prepared to deny religious liberty, minority rights, and cultural pluralism; and the narrowness of their patriotism reflects the exclusive character of their love of country.

Civic virtue seems then to be either impossible or dangerous; it cannot and must not become an important concept in our political language and a shared value among contemporary citizens. But a decent republic needs citizens who are not just interested but capable of love and attachments; and love and attachments belong with particular peoples, and ways of life. One must find ways of encouraging and sustaining the right sort of passions and love; one must enter into the dangerous world of particularity and confront the dangers of exclusive and intolerant loves. Civic virtue has to be particularistic to be possible and yet we do not want it to be dangerous or repugnant.

To find a solution to this dilemma, we should re-examine the works of republican political theorists who define civic or political virtue as love of country understood not as attachment to the cultural, ethnic, and religious unity of a people, but as love of common liberty and the institutions that sustain it. It is a particularistic love, as it is love of the common liberty of a particular people, sustained by institutions that have a particular history which has for that people a particular meaning, or meanings, that inspire and are in turn sustained by a particular way of life and culture. Because it is a love of the particular it is possible, but because it is a love of a particular liberty it is not exclusive: love of the common liberty of one's people easily extends beyond national boundaries and translates into solidarity.[16]

---

[16] For this reason it is not necessarily true that 'Attachment to the group is at once an act of solidarity and an act of exclusion', as T. Todorov remarks in *On Human Diversity* (Harvard, Mass., 1993), 173.

Historically, arguments about country and love of country have been made with either liberty or unity in mind as the goal. My only concern is liberty, or, more precisely, equal liberty, by which I mean the possibility for all the members of the republic to live their lives as citizens without being oppressed through the denial of political, civil, or social rights. I consider cultural, ethnic, religious oneness and homogeneity as vices. They do not make the republic stronger, nor do they help to forge citizens committed to liberty. On the contrary, they make the republic asphyxiatingly dull, soporific, and oppressive, and citizens narrow-minded bigots, intolerant, and boring. A good republic that really wants to be the city of all does not need cultural or moral or religious unity; it needs another sort of unity, namely a political unity sustained by the attachment to the ideal of the republic. Here I must emphasize that I do not mean love of the republic in general or attachment to an impersonal republic based on universal values of liberty and justice. I mean the attachment to a particular republic with its particular way of living in freedom. A purely political republic would be able to command the philosopher's consent, but would generate no attachment, no love, no commitment. To generate and sustain these sorts of passions one needs to appeal to the common culture, to shared memories. But if the appeal has liberty as a goal, one must resort to the culture that grows out of the practice of citizenship and is sustained by shared memories of commitment to liberty, social criticism, and resistance against oppression and corruption. There is no need to strengthen moral or religious unity, ethnic homogeneity, or linguistic purity.

Projects of social and political reform inspired by the ideal of the republic need commitment, solidarity, and the working together of many men and women over a long period. There has to be some sense of belonging and membership; to perform one's share, one must feel part of something. All that is a matter of rhetoric: one must be able to say the right words and say them properly. The language of republican patriotism offers the right rhetoric to help create or reinforce the sort of commitment that a project of social and political reform inspired by the ideal of the city of all demands. Its effectiveness derives from the fact that it works on the already existing ethnic and cultural bonds that somehow connect members of the same people to transform them into a generous commitment against oppression, political corruption, and discrimination. It appeals to shared, though often dormant, feelings to work together for purposes that are common to all and yet close to each one. Speaking of country, it brings the republic closer to the hearts and minds of the citizens and gives the ideals of equal liberty and justice that are embodied in the notion of the republic the colours and warmth that motivate action and commitment.

As history has often shown, when a nation faces a moral and political crisis, either the language of patriotism or that of nationalism is likely to attain intellectual hegemony. Those languages seem to possess a unifying and mobilizing force that others lack. A rhetoric that tells citizens that they should above all regard themselves as individuals endowed with a number of rights against the intrusions of other individuals or of the government, is unlikely to generate the commitment and the solidarity that is needed to make many individuals work together to regenerate a nation. More effective, perhaps, would be words that tell citizens of multicultural liberal societies that beyond particular group loyalty they, as rational moral individuals, ought to share allegiance to the common values of liberty and justice. The argument is powerful, as it appeals to common universal principles and values. The commonality based on shared universal values, however, is too distant and too general. If this sort of liberal language were to be opposed to a nationalist language that appeals to less rational but closer common values like religion, ethnicity, language, culture, and memory, its chances of winning a rhetorical contest do not seem high. Political languages cannot be assessed in absolute terms; they should be evaluated for what they can do against other languages that sustain different or alternative political projects. What is needed is a language capable of countering nationalistic and communitarian languages that give priority to the quest for cultural purity and distinctiveness. The language of republican patriotism is perhaps the right antidote because it is as particularistic as the languages of nationalism and communitarianism, but it is particularistic in the sense that it makes the republic particular; it does not fly the field of particular loyalties on which nationalism flourishes, but works on it to make citizenship grow.

The need to confront nationalism seriously both intellectually and politically is particularly urgent for the democratic left. Nationalist rhetoric has been and still is very powerful on the poor, the unemployed, frustrated intellectuals, and the declining middle class. Socially humiliated and discontented people find in the membership of the nation a new sense of pride, a new dignity: 'I am poor, but at least I am American (or German or Italian).' As a result important social forces that ought to contribute to the cause of a democratic socialist left have often passed into the camp of the right.

And yet, although the political costs have been very high, the left has allowed the right to have the monopoly over the language of patriotism. Historically, socialists have been either internationalists or champions of solidarity within the unions or the party, or both.[17] With a few laudable exceptions, socialist intellectuals have made little or no effort to construct a patriotism of the left capable of countering nationalism.[18] The democratic left has to fight nationalism on its own ground; it must

[17] Walzer has written that 'Solidarity is the patriotism of the left; often it replaces the sense of citizenship and even love of country', in *Obligations: Essays on Disobedience, War and Citizenship* (Harvard, Mass. 1970), 191.

[18] Reflecting upon the defeat of American political radicalism of the 1960s, John Schaar made an important observation concerning the importance of patriotism for American radical politics; 'The radicals of the 1960s did not persuade their fellow-Americans, high or low, that they genuinely cared for and shared a country with them. And no one who has contempt for others can hope to teach those others. A revived radicalism must be a patriotic radicalism. It must share and care for the common things, even while it has a "lovers quarrel" with fellow-citizens.' See *Legitimacy in the Modern State* (New Brunswick, NJ, 1981), 287. Another important exhortation to socialists to take the issue of patriotism seriously can be found in Hugh Cunningham's seminal essay 'The Language of Patriotism, 1750–1915', *History Workshop*, 12 (1981), 27. 'The question socialists need to ask is whether it is possible to divest the language of patriotism of those right-wing accretions which became so much part of its essence in the age of imperialism; whether indeed it is possible to differentiate sharply enough from the patriotism largely devoid of history which Conservatives now invoke.' For a recent and powerful argument against leftists' dismissal of patriotism see R. Rorty, 'The Unpatriotic Left', *New York Times*, 13 Feb. 1994, 15.

have an answer to the need for national identity, and yet its answer must be different from that of nationalism; it must not flee the battleground, yet it must not join the ranks of the enemy. The intellectual task is not easy: it requires a lot of research and much serious discussion; a first step might be to critically reconsider the tradition of patriotism.

Over the centuries, in different political and intellectual contexts, the language of political patriotism has been used to motivate individuals to work together to make their communities more similar to republics in which each and every one may live the sort of life they wish to as free and equal citizens. At times, the language of patriotism has been used as a call to unite all those who want to live as citizens against those who find civil and political equality unbearable; in other circumstances it has been invoked by the excluded to claim full recognition and denounce political and social oppression. If properly used, the language of patriotism focused on the ideal of the republic can still sustain different forms of emancipatory collective action; it can work again, as it did in the past, as a powerful intellectual tool to rediscover and learn to practice politics at its best.

The language of the patriotism of liberty can be an alternative to theories that aim at transcending politics by some sort of ethical foundation which aspires to create criteria for settling political conflicts through procedures defined from the point of view of disinterested, culturally neutral, dispassionate individuals, and it can be an alternative to theories that confine political action within pre-political spheres of culture, ethnicity, and religion. Against the former, the language of patriotism invites individuals to remain culturally defined, interested, and passionate, and tries to instil in them a culture of liberty, an interest in the republic, a love of the common good; it does not aim to dictate what rational moral individuals ought to do, but to make those who love liberty stronger than the champions of oppression and discrimination. Against the latter—which can be defined as a nationalist or communitarian position—patriotism tries to translate a particular attachment between people who are culturally similar into commitment to a good—the republic—which is still particular as it is the republic of a particular people, although it encompasses cultural diversity. In the case of philosophical foundations of politics the work to be done is to avoid useless forays into rationality, remain well attached to the world of passions, and try to shape them through rethoric and political action; in the case of nationalism and communitarianism one must still conduct the intellectual and political fight at the level of passions and interests aiming to transform sordid and ignoble passions, again through rhetoric and political action, into higher and more generous ones that give strength and translate into solidarity with the victims of oppression. Between the ideal worlds of rational moral agents, impartial observers, and ideal speakers and the real world of exclusive and narrow passions there is space for a possible politics for the republic. The task of the language of patriotism is to keep this space open.

Though theoretically defensible, I believe that political patriotism lacks a language of its own; it does not look capable of making its own voice sound different from, and yet as powerful as, nationalistic exhortations to love of country. It seems prohibitively difficult to say convincingly that country means republic and common liberty; that to love the republic and common liberty is neither infatuation nor a greedy desire to possess but compassion and generosity. How can the distinctive combination of *this* country and *this* love be expressed? I do not know the answer, but the only patriotism that is worth being retrieved from the past must be one that speaks of compassion and republic: it has to be a patriotism of liberty.

1

The Legacy of Republican Patriotism

THE language of modern patriotism was built upon the legacy of the ancients. Modern philosophers, historians, and poets took from Greek and Roman sources both the religious and the political content of patriotism. As Fustel de Coulanges wrote, ancient patriotism, was a religious sentiment. The word 'country' signified *terra patria* (land of the fathers). The fatherland of every man was that part of the soil which his domestic or national religion had sanctified, the land where the remains of his ancestors were deposited, and which their souls occupied. His little fatherland was the family enclosure with its tomb and its hearth; his great fatherland was the city, with its *prytaneum* and its heroes, with its sacred enclosure and its territory marked out by religion. The fatherland was a sacred soil inhabited by gods and ancestors and sanctified by worship. For this reason the patriotism of the ancients was an energetic sentiment, the supreme virtue to which all other virtues tended. Whatever man held most dear was associated with the idea of country, for in it he found his property, his security, his laws, his faith, his god. To lose it, meant to lose everything.[1]

---

[1] *The Ancient City*, ed. W. Small (Boston, 1882), 264–7. Ancient culture also harboured beliefs in the superiority and uniqueness of one's own country, as Herotodus remarked in a well-known passage about the Persians: 'Of nations, they honour their nearest neighbours, whom they esteem next to themselves; those who live beyond these they honour in the second degree; and so with the remainder, the further they are removed, the less the esteem in which they hold them. The reason is, that they look upon themselves as very greatly superior in all respects to the rest of mankind, regarding others as approaching to excellence in proportion as they dwell nearer to them; whence it comes to pass that those who are the farthest off must be the most degraded of mankind'. (*Histories*, 1. 134)

Religious patriotism attaches man to his country by a sacred tie. He must love it as he loves his religion, and obey it as he obeys his gods. He must give himself to it entirely. It is a demanding love that admits no distinctions, no conditions. He must love his country, whether it is glorious or little-known, prosperous or unfortunate. He must love it for its generosity, and also for its severity.

In addition to and strictly intertwined with religious patriotism, however, classical antiquity transmitted to modernity a political patriotism based on the identification of *patria* with *respublica*, common liberty, common good. In the *Tusculanae disputationes*, to cite the most frequently quoted text, Cicero connects *patria* with liberty and laws.[2] Sallust in *De coniuratione Catilinae* sets *patria* and liberty against oligarchic government.[3] In a passage from *Ab urbe condita*, Livy, reporting an imaginary oration, speaks of sacred armies, *patria*, liberty, and lustral gods.[4] Quintilian, in the *Institutio oratoria* makes a distinction between *natio* which he takes to mean the customs of a people, and *patria*, understood as the laws and institutions of the city.[5] Finally, in *De civitate Dei*, Augustine condenses and transmits to the Middle Ages the republican equation between *patria*, republic, and common good: 'rem publicam, id est rem populi, rem patriae, rem communem'.[6]

The *patria*, understood as *respublica*, must commend a particular type of love, that is, *pietas* or *caritas*, which may be translated as respect and compassion. This was the other main feature Roman republican patriotism. Citizens owe to their *patria*, went the typical exhortation, a benevolent love similar to the affection that they feel for their parents and relatives, a love that expresses

---

[2] 'proelium rectum est hoc fieri, convenit dimicare pro legibus, pro libertate, pro patria.' 4. 43.

[3] 'Praeterea, milites, non eadem nobis et illis necessitudo impendet: nos pro patria, pro libertate, pro vita certamus; illis supervacuaneum est pro potentia paucorum pugnare.' 58. 11.

[4] 'Praebet sacra arma pro patria pro deum delubris pro libertate sese armanti-bus', 24. 21. 10–11.

[5] 'natio, nam et gentibus proprii mores sunt nec idem in barbaro, Romano, Graeco probabile est: patria, quia similiter etiam civitatium leges, instituta, opiniones habent differentiam': *Institutio Oratoria*, 5. 10. 24–6.

[6] 5. 18.

itselfs in acts of service (*officium*) and care (*cultus*).[7] *Pietas* and *caritas* involve no cupidity (*cupiditas*), no desire to possess the object of our love or our desire exclusively; they are, on the contrary, generous affections that extends beyond the family to embrace the republic and all fellow-citizens.[8] For the virtuous citizen, *pietas* is part of the duties that justice imposes on him; it is the specific way of behaving justly toward one's own country.[9] And it is also the particular passion that moves citizens to accomplish acts of benevolence and service not just for their parents and relatives but for the republic.[10] As Livy explains in his *History*,[11] where he narrates the earliest phases of consolidation of Roman liberty after the expulsion of Tarquinius Superbus, it was charity toward the republic (*caritas reipublicae*) that gave Brutus the moral strength to overcome his reluctance and accomplish the unpleasant but necessary task of speaking against Lucius Tarquinius, who had fought against Tarquinius Superbus, before the people of Rome.

Republic and compassion, the two key terms of Roman republican language of patriotism, are no longer to be found together in medieval patriotism. The word *patria* retained a flavour of the ancient meaning in the texts of the Fathers of the Church and the canonists.[12] They referred, however, to the *patria paradisii*, the celestial polity that commands the martyr's sacrifice just as the earthly republic of the ancients commended the heroic abnegation of the good citizen. Medieval jurists, too, continued to use the word *patria* and stressed the *patria* as the source of highest obligation; but they meant the *patria* embodied

---

[7] 'Pietatem quae erga patriam, aut parentes aut alios sanguine coniunctos officium conservare moneat': Cicero, *De inventione*, 22. 66.

[8] 'Omnes caritate cives . . . complexus': Livy, *Ab urbe condita*, 7. 40.

[9] 'Justitiam cole et pietatem, quae cum magna in parentibus et propinquis, tum in patria maxima est': Cicero, *De republica*, 6. 16.

[10] 'Nam aut caritate moventur homines, ut deorum, ut patriae, ut parentum, aut amore ut fratrum, ut coniugum, ut liberorum, aut honestate, ut virtutum maximeque earum quae ad communionem hominum et liberalitatem valent': Cicero, *Partitione oratoriae*, 16. 56.

[11] *Ab urbe condita*, 2. 2.

[12] See e.g. Augustine: 'Oportet in via laborare, ut in patria gaudeamus', in *Enarratio in Psalmum CII*, in *Opera Omnia*, ed. J. P. Migne (Patrologia Latina, 37; Paris, 1845), 1331.

in the monarch's public persona. Vassals and knights who fought and died for their lord were sacrificing themselves *pro domino*, not *pro patria*, to honour a bond of fidelity or faith (*fidelitas* or *fides*), not to discharge a civic duty.[13] Even when it was portrayed and exalted as an exemplary form of brotherly love, love of country never regained the sense of compassionate love for fellow-citizens.[14]

The idioms of Roman republican patriotism survived to a degree in the works of Scholastic philosophers. In his authoritative treatment in the *Summa Theologiae*, Aquinas refers in many instances to Cicero to stress that love of country is a form of piety that consists 'in acts of loving care and benevolent service for the fellow-citizens and the friends of the country' ('in cultu autem patriae intelligitur cultus concivium et omnium patriae amicorum').[15] It is an affection that 'comes from love' ('procedit ex amore') and drives citizens to serve the common good. For this reason it can be said that *pietas* for one's country is the same as justice ('idem esse cum iustitia legali, quae respicit bonum commune').[16] As long as it remains subordinate to our higher obligation to God, love of country is right and noble; it is a duty that our country—understood not as *republica* but as the place 'in which we were born and nurtured [*in qua nati et nutriti sumus*]'—can legitimately demand.

The interpretation of love of country as compassion appears also in the *De regimine principum* in a section surely written by Ptolemy of Lucca but wrongly attributed to Thomas Aquinas

[13] E. Kantorowicz, *The King's Two Bodies* (Princeton, 1957), 234.

[14] See e.g. the following exhortation addressed to the soldiers of the Crusades: 'Fight for your *patria* and suffer even death for her, if such should overwhelm you. Victory itself is a means of saving the soul. For whoever suffers death for his brothers, offers himself a living host to God, and unambiguously he follows Christ who for his brothers deigned to lay down his life [I John 3: 16]. If, therefore, one of you, be overcome by death in this war, let that death be atonement for and absolution of, all his sins'. Geoffrey of Monmouth, *Historia Regum Britanniae*, quoted ibid. 241.

[15] In *Sancti Thomae Aquinatis opera omnia* (Rome, 1897), 2a, 2ae, CI, a. I, p. 368. The Cicero text that Aquinas discusses is *De inventione*, 2. 53: 'Pietas, per quam sanguine coniunctis patriaeque benivolum officium et diligens tribuitur cultus.'

[16] *Summa theologiae*, 2–2ae, q. CI, a. III, p. 370.

and therefore regarded as holding a highly authoritative position. The crucial passage of Ptolemy's reasoning deserves to be quoted at length:

Love for the fatherland is founded in the root of charity [*Amor patriae in radice charitatis fundatur*] which puts not the private things before those held in common, but the things held in common before those of the private as the Blessed Augustine says, elucidating the words of the Apostles on charity. Deservedly, the virtue of charity precedes all other virtues because the merit of any virtue depends upon that of charity. Therefore *amor patriae* deserves a rank of honour above all other virtues.[17]

Ptolemy was referring to *Psalm* 121: 12 on which Augustine had remarked that although charity is a love that does not seek a particular advantage or interest ('non quaeret quae sua sunt'), but the common good, it is a powerful passion. 'Love is as strong as death'; these words, writes Augustine, describe in the best way the force of that particular love that we call charity (*fortitudo caritatis*). Death is more powerful than kings, fire, water, iron, and yet charity is equally powerful because, like death, it destroys what we are so that we may become what we were not.[18] Understood as a form of charity, love of country has a transformative and empowering effect: it generates, through the death of the soul who was attached to private goods, a different soul which puts public things before private and longs for sharing and unity. The new soul is larger and more powerful than the old one; so powerful that it challenges death because it makes the individual part of a larger unity that outlives him.

Ptolemy integrates the Christian doctrine with substantial borrowings from Aristotle's *Nicomachean Ethics* and above all Cicero's *De officiis* and Sallust's *De coniuratione Catilinae*, to

[17] *De regimine principum at regem Cipry*, in R. Spiazzi (ed.), *Divi Thomae Aquinatis, opuscula philosophice* (Turin, 1954), 299.

[18] 'Magnificentius exprimi non potuit fortitudo charitatis, quam ut diceretur, *Valida est sicut mors dilectio*. Quis enim resistit morti, fratres? Intendat Charitas vestra. Resistitur ignibus, undis, ferro; resistitur potestatibus, resistitur regibus: venit una mors, quis ei resistit? Nihil illa fortius. Propterea viribus ejus charitas comparata est, et dictum est, *Valida est sicut mors dilectio*. Et quia ipsa charitas occidit quod fuimus, ut simus quod non eramus; facit in nobis quamdam mortem dilectio.' *Enarratio in Psalmum CXXI*, in *Opera Omnia*, 1627.

elaborate a conception of love of country in which the theological virtue of charity is fused with the republican principle of commitment to the common good. As Augustine had written, the virtues that allowed the Romans to gain the favour of God and enlarge their empire even if they did not worship the true God, were love of country (*amor patriae*), zeal for justice, and enthusiasm for civil benevolence. Their love of country amply justifies domination (*dominium*) because it is a love of the common good, which is a divine good, as Aristotle writes in *Nicomachean Ethics*. The favour that the Romans received from God was then proportional to the excellence of their virtue, since God, Ptolemy remarks, rewards according to virtue.

To corroborate Augustine's point that love of country is a form of compassion which drives us to comprehend our love for our family within an ampler love for the republic, Ptolemy quotes a passage from Cicero's *De officiis* that condenses the republican conception of patriotism:

But when with a rational spirit you have surveyed the whole field, there is no social relation among them all more close, none more dear than that which links each one of us with our country [*re publica*]. Parents are dear; dear are the children, relatives, friends; but one fatherland [*patria*] embraces all our loves [*caritates*]; and who that is true would hesitate to give his life for her, if by his death he could render her a service?[19]

Though more comprehensive and higher, love of country retains for Ptolemy the essential feature of compassion. It is ampler and higher than love of parents, relatives, and friends, but it is still a love of concrete people whom we hold dear, with the difference that we include among the people who are dear to us our fellow-citizens. Though less natural and more political, love of country is still a love of particular people, not of impersonal entities: we do not know each of our fellow-citizens individually, but we know that whoever they are, they are citizens like

[19] 'Sed cum omnia ratione animoque lustraris, omnium societatum nulla est gravior, nulla carior quam ea, quae cum re publica est uni cuique nostrum. Cari sunt parentes, cari liberi, propinqui, familiares, sed omnes omnium caritates patria una complexa est, pro qua quis bonus dubitet mortem oppetere si ei sit profuturus?' *De officiis*, 1. 17. 57.

us; they are fellow-members of the same republic. When it embraces the common good, it becomes less natural and more political or, to put it more precisely, it becomes the political virtue *par excellence* because its object is the republic; that is, the only genuine political community. Through subtle combination, Ptolemy establishes an intellectual continuity between the theological virtue of charity and the pagan love of the republic. Love of country can now count on the blessing of both the Fathers of the Church and the authorities of Roman republicanism.

It was, however, in the intellectual context of the Italian city-republics that the classical Roman meaning of *patria* was fully recovered to form the basis for a distinctive republican language of patriotism. The works of the theorists of communal self-government and of the civic humanists offer examples of different arguments for patriotism: some stressed that love of the republic is a rational love; others that citizens should hold their republic dear because life in a free city is sweet; others still that citizens have the obligation to serve their country because they have contracted with her a debt that can never be fully repaid. An example of the first line of defence of patriotism is Remigio de Girolami's *Tractatus de bono communi*, composed in 1304. In this text Remigio uses the term 'fatherland' (*patria*) as the equivalent of the common good. Quoting Cicero's famous line from the first speech against Catiline: 'our country, which is much dearer to me than my life',[20] he stresses that love of country imposes upon those who rule the republic the obligation to care for the good of the whole community: the common good is the source of all the honour and glory of the citizens, because there is nothing nobler and more glorious than to be citizens of a free city in which the common good is properly realized. In addition, the common good is also the foundation of the most valuable good of civil life (*bonum civile*), which consists in living together in peace under the protection of just laws. The love for the common good is therefore virtuous and rational and we

[20] 'Patria, mihi vita mea multo carior est': *In Catilinam*, 1. 11; Engl. trans. L. E. Lord in *The Speeches* (London, 1937), 40–1.

should be devoted to it, as the political virtue of the pagans urges us to do.[21]

The love of *patria*—which is the basis of political virtue (*Politicam virtutem*)—is a rational love because it is a love for a good (the free city) that it is rational for each citizen to want to preserve. If the community is corrupted, the individual's life is also impoverished. Once the city is destroyed, the citizens can no longer cultivate the virtues that make them truly citizens. There remains only the external appearance, a statue or a painting, no longer the true and living citizen.[22] Whoever loses the quality of citizen, loses that of man too, since one cannot live a proper human life without being a the citizen.[23] For this reason, stresses Remigio, a citizen should never remain passive before the corruption of his city, but should instead fight it with the utmost vigour.

An example of emphasis on the moral and existential value of the free city is a lecture by Lapo of Castiglionchio delivered in 1438 in which he stresses that our *patria* is particularly dear if it is a republic or city. *Patria*, Lapo remarks, borrowing the words of the *Digest*, is the most holy and sweet name, particularly if the *patria* is a city in which one lives freely [*ubi libere vivitur*], because in a free republic citizens have many things in common: the laws, the forum, the senate, public honours, the magistrates, enemies, and hopes.[24] If they want to continue to enjoy such a precious good, they must devote their best energies to preserving it.

The most orthodox exhortation to serve our *patria* because we have a moral obligation toward it can be found in Matteo Palmieri's *Vita civile* composed between 1435 and 1440. Quoting from *De officiis*, he stresses that our obligation to our *patria* comes before our duties towards our parents. Every citizen

[21] *Tractatus de bono communi*, in M. C. De Matteis, *La teologia politica comunale di Remigio de' Girolami* (Bologna, 1977), 8.

[22] Ibid. 18.

[23] 'Et si non est civis non est homo, quia "homo est naturaliter animal civile", secundum philosophum in VIII *Ethic.* et in I *Polit*': ibid.

[24] 'Oratio domini Andreae magistri Hugonis de Senis', in *Reden und Briefe italienischer Humanisten* (Munich, 1970), 250.

should be totally committed to his *patria* because nothing is in fact more precious than the safety of our country. When we die, our last thoughts always go to our sons and our country. We would like to be sure that they will survive and flourish after our death; as long as our country and our descendants live, the memory of us lives with them.[25] Because the virtue of the civil man preserves a good which is eternal, its reward is accordingly perennial glory and eternal beatitude. As Plato and Cicero correctly explained, the souls of all the good rulers and the excellent civil men (*optimi civili*) return to heaven immediately after their death, and the reward is indeed proportional to the good that they did in their life.

In spite of the differences in the rhetoric they use to exhort men to serve the country, for all civic humanists *patria* means the common liberty of the city that has been conquered in the past and that can be preserved only through the citizens' civic spirit. As Alamanno Rinuccini wrote in the *Dialogue on Liberty*, written in 1479, since liberty is the property of a strong mind that refuses to obey another 'unless his commands are just and legitimate and serve a useful purpose', only he who possesses fortitude can put himself at risk for the good of the republic.[26] By contrast, the lack of fortitude and the base ambition of the citizens who do not dare to stand up to the tyrant and his partisans are the main causes of the city's servitude.

For the quattrocento humanists the opposite of the patriot who serves the common liberty is the corrupt citizen who favours his own or his party's interests. Whereas the 'men of state' (*statuali* or *staterecci*) use public institutions as their private possessions, the good citizen cares more for the common good than his own private or factional interest. As Leon Battista Alberti wrote in *The Book of the Family*, the 'civil man' is concerned with the concord, peace, and tranquillity of his own family, but he must be even more concerned with the concord and peace of the republic. The wise citizen knows that the good order of the

[25] *Vita civile*, ed. G. Belloni (Florence, 1982), 103–5.
[26] *Dialogus de libertate*, in *Atti e memorie dell'Accademia toscana di scienze e lettere La Colombaria*, 21 (1956), 265–303; Eng. trans. in Renée Neu Watkins, *Humanism and Liberty* (Columbia, SC, 1978), 202.

republic cannot be preserved if the citizens only care for their own domestic affairs.[27] Therefore, he completely takes to heart the old advice that urges us to devote ourselves to the service of the republic in order to prevent it falling into the hands of the ambitious citizens who would use power to corrupt both public and private life. Serving our own republic is not servitude; it is the discharge of our duty as citizens and should be praised as the most noble activity.[28] A good citizen should indeed serve the republic without, however, neglecting his private life and business: political life cannot be a substitute for domestic and private business; it is, rather, an additional burden to be shouldered in order to enjoy the good of private liberty.[29]

Florentine fifteenth-century patriotism, however, was not just commitment to the republic and common liberty, but also celebration of the city's military and cultural superiority, of the nobility of its ancestors, and the purity of the language. Models of Greek and Roman rhetoric were skilfully employed to instil in citizens a love mixed with pride and haughtiness.[30] The most obvious example is Leonardo Bruni's *Laudatio florentinae urbis*, composed in 1403–4. Florence, he remarks in the conclusion of the eulogy, is a republic devoted to justice and liberty, because without justice 'there can be no city, nor would Florence even be worthy to be called a city', and without liberty a great people 'would not even consider that life worth living'.[31] The principles of justice and equality that inform the institutions of the republic also affect the way of life of the citizens, encouraging habits of toleration and humanity: since all are equal as citizens, no one

---

[27] *I primi tre libri della famiglia*, in *Opere volgari*, ed. C. Greyson (Bari, 1960), 281.

[28] Ibid. 282.   [29] Ibid. 284.

[30] Love of country could also be used to demand inhuman ferocity: 'Thou knowest not how sweet is the *amor patriae*: if such would be expedient for the fatherland's protection or enlargement, it would seem neither burdensome and difficult nor a crime to thrust the axe into one's father's head, to crush one's brothers, to deliver from the womb of one's wife the premature child with the sword': Salutati, *Epistolario di Coluccio Salutati*, ed. F. Novati (Rome, 1891), quoted in Kantorowicz, *King's Two Bodies*, 245.

[31] In Hans Baron (ed.), *From Petrarch to Leonardo Bruni* (Chicago, 1968), 259; trans. in G. Groffith, *et al.*, *The Humanism of Leonardo Bruni* (Binghamton, NY, 1987), 169.

can be 'prideful or disparage others'.[32] Fair to its citizens, Florence is also fair to the foreigners who come to live there. All those who have been exiled from their country either by seditious plots or by the envy of their compatriots can find another homeland in Florence: 'as long as Florence continues to exist, no one will ever really lack a homeland [*ne quisquam patria se carere put donec Florentinorum supersit urbs*]'.[33] Hence, Florence is not only a true *patria* for the Florentines; it is also a *patria* for all victims of misfortune and injustice.

Along with the celebration of republican political principles, the *Laudatio* exalts Florence's superiority based on the purity of its language and its unique splendour: 'Florence is of such a nature that a more distinguished or more splendid city cannot be found on the entire earth.'[34] The city's extraordinary splendour is a claim for domination: everyone, stresses Bruni, must surely recognize that she is 'worthy of attaining dominion and rule over the entire world'.[35] Moreover, Florence's origin is nobler than that of any other city, since it was founded by the Romans when Rome was still a republic.

Since Florence has as its founders those who were obeyed everywhere by everyone and dominated by their skill and military prowess, and since it was founded when a free and unconquered Roman people flourished in power, nobility, virtues and genius, it cannot be doubted at all that this one city not only stands out in its beauty, architecture, and appropriateness of site (as we have seen), but that Florence also greatly excels beyond all other cities in the dignity and nobility of its origin.[36]

The combination of republican values and civic pride that characterizes Bruni's patriotism also appears in the *Oration for the Funeral of Nanni Strozzi*. Strozzi was a Florentine citizen who died in 1427 in battle against the forces of the Duke of Milan. Our *patria*, Bruni remarks, deserves the foremost honour, even above our parents, because she is 'the first and prerequisite basis of human happiness'.[37] And by *patria*, he means—again in

---

[32] Ibid. 262 (Eng. trans. 174).   [33] Ibid. 251 (Eng. trans. 159).
[34] Ibid. 232 (Eng. trans. 135).   [35] Ibid. 239 (Eng. trans. 143).
[36] Ibid. 248 (Eng. trans. 154).

[37] Id., 'Oratio in funere Johannis Strozzae', in E. Baluze and G. Manzi, *Miscellanea novo ordine digesta . . . et aucta* (Lucca, 1764), 2–7; Eng. trans. in Groffith *et al.*, *The Humanism of Leonardo Bruni*, 123.

full agreement with the Roman republicans—the free republic. Florence, he remarks, has a popular constitution designed to protect the liberty and equality of all citizens. She deserves the citizens' devotion because she allows each and all of them to live 'free from the fear of men' and to pursue the highest public honours.[38]

To the Florentines gathered for the funeral of Nanni Strozzi, Bruni says that not only ought they to love their republic because it allows them to live in freedom, they ought also to be proud to belong to the most noble of all cities which possesses a wide dominion and commands universal respect. They are descendants from the Etruscans and the Romans, two of the most glorious peoples of antiquity; no city can claim a nobler origin, no people has more illustrious ancestors. They are not only entitled to live in freedom; they are also entitled to dominate the other cities of Tuscany. Bruni's *Oratio* is not only intended to instil in the Florentines a love of common liberty, but also on this solemn occasion, to resuscitate in their hearts a love more exclusive than the political love for the republic, a love combined with pride in being citizens of a unique and extraordinary republic.

In Bruni's rhetoric, republican patriotism is used in an ambiguous way: it is the language of political and civil liberty set against domestic tyranny and foreign conquest, but also of exclusion and aggression abroad; of virtue, but of a virtue mixed with pride and the feeling of being a unique city; of the republic, but of a republic dominated by a social and political élite strongly attached to its privileges.

It took a patriot who did not belong to the Florentine élite, Niccolò Machiavelli, to elaborate a different version of republican patriotism. Unlike Bruni, he was not interested in the celebration of Florence's superiority and historical mission. The magnificent palaces that Bruni had mentioned in the *Laudatio* as symbols of the city's splendour, were for Machiavelli 'proud and regal' symbols of the power and wealth of the great families. To build his magnificent palace, he writes in the *Istorie fiorentine*, Luca Pitti did not refrain from using illegal means, and once it

---

[38] Ibid. (Eng. trans. 124).

was completed, it became the centre of seditious gatherings of the enemies of the republic.[39] The theme of the origins of the city that had received great attention from Florentine historians, was for him of little interest. In the *Istorie fiorentine* he settles the issue with few words: 'it was born under the Roman Empire; and in the times of the first emperors it began to be recorded by historians'.[40] Its origins were therefore servile; a mark that affected the subsequent history of the city. All the wars that Florence fought to enlarge its territory, Bruni had claimed, were justified because the Florentine were the descendants of the Romans and therefore the heirs of the territories that belonged to the Roman Republic. But the wars Florence fought with King Ladislao and Duke Philip, remarked Machiavelli, 'were made to fill the citizens [with riches and power], not for necessity': they were therefore unjust.[41] Since the very beginnings of his political career he was more a critic of, than an apologist for, the Florentine Republic. He was devoted to it, he served it with all his energies and with impeccable honesty, but he did not fail to remark upon its injustice and imprudence. As his political enemies pointed out, he was even too ready to denounce Florence's faults. He admitted, 'it is true that I am contrary, as in many other things, to the opinion of [Florentine] citizens'.[42] His love of country shows no signs of parochialism and civic pride. It did not make him blind. It, rather, pushed him to try to understand the larger horizons of Italian and European politics, and to search into the past to find the roots for a possible regeneration of Italy: 'this land seems born to resuscitate dead things, as one has seen in poetry, painting, and sculpture'.[43]

Love of country was not only his deepest love; it was also the

---

[39] VII. 4, in *Opere di Niccolò Machiavelli*, ed. A. Montevecchi (Turin, 1986).

[40] Ibid. II. 2; *Discorsi sopra la prima deca di Tito Livio*, I. 49, in *Il principe e i Discorsi*, ed. S. Bertelli (Milan, 1983).

[41] 'e se questo modo si fosse trovato prima, non si sarebbe fatta la guerra con il re Ladislao, né ora si farebbe questa contro il duca Filippo; le quali si erano fatte per riempiere i cittadini e non per necessità', *Istorie fiorentine*, IV. 14.

[42] Letter to Francesco Guicciardini, 17 May 1521, in *Opere di Niccolò Machiavelli*, ed. F. Gaeta (Turin, 1984), iii. 520.

[43] *Arte della guerra*, in *Arte della guerra e scritti politici minori* (Milan, 1961), 519.

kind of love that he would like to see flourishing in the hearts of his compatriots. One of the goals of the *Discourses*, as he clearly states in the *proem* to book II, was to encourage the youth of the city to imitate the virtue of the Romans, and in the *Istorie fiorentine* he remarks that the central theme of his study is corruption and his goal is to explain the lack of virtue brought about the loss of liberty and the decline of Florence.[44] And when he speaks of *virtù*, what he means is patriotism; that is, in the republican sense of love of common liberty that makes men generous, capable of seeing their private and particular interests as part of the common good, and willing to fight vigorously for their republic. At the very outset of the *Discourses*, he calls 'the actions accomplished by captains for their country [*che si sono per la patria loro affaticati*] most virtuous [*virtuosissime*]'. Elsewhere, he mentions the common good (*bene comune*) together with the common fatherland (*patria comune*) as the distinctive aims of the virtuous founders.[45] To realize his virtuous goal Romulus needed to acquire complete authority for himself. The murder of his brother Remus and of Tatius Sabinus are therefore to be excused, Machiavelli tells us, because they were perpetrated for the common good, for the common fatherland.[46]

The patriotism of Rome's founders channelled the patriotism of the Roman people which for four hundred years 'were enemies to the very name of king, and lovers of glory and of the common good of their country [*amatore della gloria e del bene comune della sua patria*]'.[47] The love of the common good and love of country that Machiavelli portrays as being at the core of civic virtue is in fact love of liberty and of the laws that protect it. Manlio Capitolino, reports Machiavelli, was sentenced to death by the Roman people because he raised tumults 'against the senate and his country's laws [*contro il Senato e contro alle leggi patrie*]'.[48] The conduct of the Roman people was particularly remarkable because Manlio Capitolino was an enemy of the Senate, and the Roman people 'were sympathetic to projects which might thwart the nobility'. And yet, in spite of his

---

[44] *Istorie fiorentine*, Proem, in *Opere*, ed. Montevecchi, 281–2.
[45] *Discorsi*, I. 10.   [46] Ibid. 9.   [47] Ibid. 58.   [48] Ibid. III. 8.

hostility toward the Senate, the people of Rome put Manlio to death because, explains Machiavelli, 'for all of them the love of the country [*lo amore della patria*] weighed more than any other consideration'.⁴⁹ The love of country that inspired the verdict of the Roman people was a desire to stop an ambitious citizen who wanted to corrupt the laws and impose his own power over the city, thereby threatening the common liberty. In Machiavelli's interpretation of Livy's report, 'country' (*patria*) stands again for laws and common liberty. The civic virtue of the Roman people was, then, a love of liberty that gave them the courage and the strength to stand against powerful men who attempted to impose tyranny over the republic.

It was primarily because of their love of country that the Roman people succeeded in remaining free for centuries. The many good laws in favour of public liberty (*pubblica libertà*) that were passed under the Republic were the outcome of the plebeians' desire not to be oppressed and their determination to resist the insolence of the patricians.⁵⁰ The common good (or the country), as Machiavelli stresses, to which ancient peoples were so deeply devoted was their own individual liberty to pursue their own interests without being obstructed or having their rights infringed by powerful and arrogant men. The virtuous citizens whom Machiavelli extols in the *Discourses* serve the common good—the liberty and the laws of the city—because they are aware that the common good is the same as the individual interest of each.⁵¹

Like the humanists, Machiavelli repeats the Ciceronian theme that to serve his country is the honest's man highest moral obligation. 'I have always gladly served my country,' he remarks at the outset of the *Discorso o dialogo intorno alla nostra lingua*, 'even when it was onerous and dangerous, because no obligation is greater than that that we owe to our country.' Even if a citizen is offended by his country, it would be most ignominious for him to turn into an enemy of his country.⁵² He should forgive

---

⁴⁹ Ibid.   ⁵⁰ Ibid. I. 37.

⁵¹ 'Onde ne nasce che gli uomini a gara pensano a' privati e publici commodi, e l'uno e l'altro viene maravigliosamente a crescere': ibid. II. 2.

⁵² 'Sempre ch'io ho potuto onorare la patria mia, eziamdio con mio carico e

and forget because his obligation toward his country is not extinguished by the hardships that he has received. If the voice of duty is not powerful enough, love of country will give him the strength to forgive and forget.

Both the moral obligation and love of country have, however, their limits which are defined by the very nature of the obligation and by the nature of the love: the citizen has an obligation toward his *patria* because he owes it all the goods of life, and he loves his *patria* because it is the place where he can enjoy sweet freedom. If the *patria* dissolves into a tyranny of arrogant men, the obligation ceases and love turns into hatred. There is no reason and no motivation to forgive and forget. Rinaldo degli Albizzi, the enemy of Cosimo de' Medici who joined the Duke of Milan, is reported by Machiavelli in the *Istorie fiorentine* to have said the following words:

I shall always esteem it little to live in a city where the laws can do less than men. For that fatherland is desirable in which property and friends can be safely enjoyed, and not that in which property can be taken from you, nor friends, out of fear for their own, abandon you in your greatest necessities.[53]

The patriot Machiavelli has no words of comment to add; and we know that in the *Istorie*, commissioned by the Medici pope Clement VII, he put in the mouth of the opponents of the Medici the words that he himself would have wished to say.

For Machiavelli love of country gives the strength to accomplish great and generous deeds in exceptional times, but it also

pericolo, l'ho fatto volentieri: perchè l'uomo non ha maggiore obligo nella vita sua che con quella, dependendo prima da essa l'essere e di poi tutto quello che di buono la fortuna e la natura ci hanno conceduto; e tanto viene a essere maggiore in coloro che hanno sortito patria più nobile. E veramente colui il quale con l'animo e con l'opera si fa nimico della sua patria, meritatamente si può chiamare parricida, ancora che da quella fussi suto offeso': *Discorso o dialogo intorno alla nostra lingua*, in *Opere letterarie*, ed. L. Blasucci (Milan, 1964), 212.

[53] 'Io stimerò sempre poco vivere in una città dove possino meno le leggi che gli uomini: perchè quella patria è desiderabile nella quale le sustanze e gli amici si possono sicuramente godere, non quella dove ti possino essere quelle tolte facilmente, e gli amici per paura di loro propri nelle tue maggiori necessità t'abbandonono'. IV. 33.

nurtures habits of civility in ordinary circumstances; it expands the soul and gives it the correct order and measure that a good republic needs. As examples of a virtuous citizenry he mentions the Roman people who revolted against the young aristocrats who had 'no respect for any civility [*sanza avere rispetto ad alcuna civilità*]'[54] and the citizens of the German free republics who hated the nobles because they were antagonistic to civil life.[55] He stresses also that as long as the Republic was uncorrupted, the Roman people were both virtuous and respectful of the norms of civil life. Even when they fought against the enemies of the common liberty they did not exceed the bounds of legality. Coriolanus tried to use famine to diminish the people's authority and make them more docile. Having discovered his nepharious intentions, the plebeians were ready to lynch him but in the end accepted the tribunes' proposal to bring him to a regular trial. This episode, Machiavelli remarks, reveals once again the goodness of Roman republican institutions. If the plebeians had lynched Coriolanus, they would have acted as private individuals and would not have done justice but committed a crime. If the magistrates of the Republic had tolerated a summary execution of Coriolanus the citizens would have begun to feel insecure and would have tried to protect themselves by forming sects and factions which would have spelt disaster for the republic. A virtuous people that wants to preserve its liberty must always respect the laws and norms of civil life, it must live in an orderly way, and love of country makes it easier.

When love of country fades, virtue remains, but it becomes brute force, courage, and resolution; it becomes a virtue that no longer sustains liberty but destroys it. As an example, Machiavelli mentions the conflicts between the plebeians and the senate over the Agrarian Laws. For more than three hundred years the conflicts between the plebeians and the senate were remarkably civilized: no more than eight or ten citizens were exiled; very few were put to death or fined. The city had known havoc—the masses would run helter-skelter about the streets, shops would be closed, the plebeians would troop out of Rome *en masse*—but

---

[54] *Discorsi*, I. 2.   [55] Ibid. 55.

this was never a threat to liberty. The conflicts over the Agrarian Laws, however, went far beyond the boundaries of civility and for this reason were one of the causes of the end of Roman liberty.

The Roman people, Machiavelli says, deserve then to be extolled as an example for the moderns because they were virtuous and civilized. They loved their common liberty and were capable of resisting the ambitious and the insolent; but they were also a law-abiding people, obedient to their magistrates, respectful of morality and religion. They hated servitude, but had no desire to oppress.[56] Civic virtue and civility go hand in hand also in the German free cities, one of the few surviving examples of civil life in Machiavelli's time. The citizens were prepared to kill the lazy [*oziosi*] noblemen because they regarded them as a source of corruption and scandal; but they paid their taxes and obeyed their magistrates with the most remarkable discipline.[57]

The point that Machiavelli stresses again and again in the *Discourses* is that love of country not only protects liberty but also sustains orderly and decent customs. Because of their patriotism, the Roman people succeeded in imposing good laws in favour of the common liberty which in turn stimulated good customs. But when the republic became corrupt and the citizens were no longer virtuous, the wicked citizens managed to pass laws that were not designed to protect the common liberty but to enhance their own power. Bad laws in turn corrupted both public and private life and brought about the decline of the republic. The weakening of patriotism was then the cause of the loss of liberty and also of the decay of morals.[58]

The ideal of civic virtue that Machiavelli derived from his Roman republican sources, and which he recommended to his Florentine fellow-citizens stressed that sovereign authority should be entrusted to the citizenry as a whole, to the nobility and the

---

[56] 'Mentre durò la Republica incorrotta, non serví mai umilmente, nè mai dominò superbamente; anzi con li suoi ordini e magistrati tenne il suo grado onorevolmente. E quando era necessario commuoversi contro a un potente, lo faceva; come si vide in Manlio, nei Dieci ed in altri che cercorono opprimerla: e quando era necessario ubbidire a' Dittatori ed a' Consoli per la salute pubblica, lo faceva': Ibid. 58.

[57] Ibid. 55.   [58] Ibid. 10.

people, and that the people must have its place in the institutional arrangements of the republic, though not a monopoly of power. He never advocated, however, full-time political participation.[59] The virtue that he wanted to see flourish was the love of liberty that gives the citizens the will and the strength to stand against ambitious men and factions attempting to impose their domination over the city. It was, in other words, love of the republic.

While *patria* is a central word, 'nation' (*nazione*) was of negligible importance in the works of Machiavelli. As Federico Chabod has convincingly shown in a seminal essay, Machiavelli rarely uses the term 'nation' at all.[60] In the *Discourses* he speaks of nation with reference to France, Spain, and Italy to indicate common customs, and specifically corrupt ones.[61] In the same chapter he uses as a synonym for *nazione* the old Roman term *provincia* that indicated in origin the administrative subunits of the Empire. A few lines earlier, he stresses the same point regarding the corruption of France, Spain, and Italy, calling them this time 'provinces' instead of nations.[62]

The distinctive characters of provinces or nations are for Machiavelli customs and forms of life. The title of chapter 43 in book III of the *Discorsi*, for instance, reads: 'That Men who are born in the same Country [*provincia*], display throughout the Ages much the same Characteristics'. As he clarifies in the same chapter, each province has its own mode of life.[63] In addition to customs and forms of life, other distinctive features of provinces or nations are their particular tongues and political orderings, as Machiavelli indicates in *The Prince*:

---

[59] Ibid. 5 and 58; *Discursus florentinarum rerum, post mortem iunioris Laurentii Medice*, in *Arte e scritti politici minori*, 272.

[60] *L'idea di nazione* (Bari, 1962), 60.

[61] '[German free cities] non hanno possuto pigliare i costumi né franciosi né spagnuoli né italiani; le quali nazioni tutte insieme sono la corruttela del mondo.' *Discorsi*, I. 55.

[62] 'E veramente dove non è questa bontà non si può sperare nulla di bene; come non si può sperare nelle provincie che in questi tempi si veggiono corrotte, come è la Italia sopra tutte l'altre; ed ancora la Francia e la Spagna di tale corrozione ritengono parte.' Ibid.

[63] 'vero è che le sono le opere loro, ora in questa provincia piú virtuose che in quella, ed in quella piú che in questa, secondo la forma della educazione nella quale quegli popoli hanno preso il modo del vivere loro': ibid. III. 43.

I say, then, that the territories a conqueror annexes and joins to his own well-established state [*stato antiquo*] are either in the same country [*provincia*] with the same language, or they are not. If they are, it is extremely easy to hold them, especially if they are not used to governing themselves [*usi a vivere liberi*] ... But considerable problems arise if territories are annexed in a country [*provincia*] that differs in language, customs and institutions.[64]

The customs of nations are to be studied and understood since customs are of fundamental political importance; they are not to be loved. Love goes to the *patria*, understood as the political institutions and the particular way of life of the republic. He is not concerned at all with the protection of the cultural homogeneity of the republic and even less so with the protection of the purity of its language. He regards the assimilation of alien words as an enrichment, not as a corruption of the language, as he writes in his *Discorso o dialogo intorno alla nostra lingua*, which was composed to defend the honour of Florence against those who claimed that Dante wrote the *Divina commedia* in Italian, not in Florentine.[65]

For Machiavelli, political institutions and political values cannot be separated from customs and ways of life. He speaks in fact of the *vivere libero*, or *vita libera*, a particular way of life, a culture, as opposed to the *vivere servo*, another way of life and culture. *Patria*, like nation, is a way of life and a culture; it is a particular way of life inspired by liberty. In the famous sentence that Machiavelli wrote to his friend Vettori in one of his last letters—'I love my country more than my soul'—one could replace *patria* with *vivere libero* without altering the meaning of the sentence; to replace *patria* with *nazione* would make it absurd.

Love of country is a love that stimulates sharing. It makes

[64] *Il principe*, ch. 3; Eng. trans. in *The Prince*, ed. Q. Skinner and R. Price (Cambridge, 1988).

[65] 'Oltra di questo, io voglio che tu consideri come le lingue non possono essere semplici, ma conviene che sieno miste con l'altre lingue. Ma quella lingua si chiama d'una patria, la quale convertisce i vocaboli ch'ella ha accattati da altri nell' uso suo, ed è si potente che i vocaboli accattati non la disordinano, ma ella disordina loro; perchè quello ch'ella reca da altri, lo tira a sé in modo che par suo.' *Discorso*, p. 223.

men subordinate their attachment to goods that are distinctively their own to their attachment to goods that they have in common with others. No good can be more individual than one's soul; yet love of country makes us subordinate it to the common liberty; that is, to a liberty which is ours as much as anyone else's. It is a love that only magnanimous souls experience, such as Cosimo Rucellai, the dedicatee of the *Arte della guerra*: 'I do not know what thing could be so much his (not excepting even his soul) that would not be spent by him willingly for his friends; nor do I know what undertaking would ever have dismayed him once he knew it to be for the good of his country.'[66] Or like the brave citizens who defied the Pope's interdict and defended Florence's liberty: 'they were called Saints even though they had little regard for censures, had despoiled the churches of their goods and had compelled the clergy to celebrate the offices—so much more did those citizens then esteem their country [*patria*] than their souls'.[67]

To love one's country more than one's soul means that one ought to be ready to sacrifice his or her own soul for the life and liberty of the city.

For when the safety of one's country wholly depends on the decision to be taken, no attention should be paid either to justice or injustice, to kindness or cruelty, or to its being praiseworthy or ignominious. On the contrary, every other consideration being set aside, that alternative should be wholeheartedly adopted which will save the life and preserve the freedom of one's country.[68]

One's soul versus one's country. But the country is not one's own in the same sense in which the soul is. The country is one person's as it is everyone's. However important the soul is, its sacrifice for the common liberty is still a sacrifice of an individual good for a common one. God, said the Fathers of the Church,

---

[66] *Arte*, 328.

[67] 'Ed erano chiamati Santi, ancora che gli avessino stimate poco le censure, e le chiese de' beni loro spogliate, e sforzato il clero a celebrare gli uffici: tanto quelli cittadini stimavono allora più la patria che l'anima', *Istorie fiorentine*, III. 7; Eng. trans. *Florentine Histories*, trans. L. Banfield and H. L. Mansfield (Princeton, 1988).

[68] *Discorsi*, III. 41; Eng. trans. *The Discourses*, ed. B. Crick (London, 1970), 515.

holds commonwealths very dear; he must then look favourably at those great men who have been able to sacrifice their soul for their country.[69] The saviours and redeemers of countries can count on God's friendship. If judged like the others, they would be damned; but God can exempt them from judgement. A man who has saved his country deserves to be saved in turn. His deed was extraordinary; the reward must be accordingly extraordinary. During their life on earth the founders and redeemers of countries were most happy (*felicissimi*) and 'made their country happy and noble [*la loro patria ne fu nobilitata e felicissima*]'. When they die, they are admitted to enjoy perennial beatitude through God's special intervention.

Love of country is a moral strength that makes ordinary citizens capable of doing great deeds against tyranny and corruption worth being recorded in the memory of the city, like the Florentine citizens mentioned in the *Istorie* who offered the Signori of the Republic their help to restore the rule of law against the factions of the Albizzi and the Ricci. Machiavelli says 'they were moved by love of country [*mossi dall' amore della patria*]' and they spoke as patriots: 'The love that we bear, magnificent Signori, for our fatherland [*alla patria nostra*] first made us gather and now makes us come to you to reason about the evil that one sees already great and yet keeps frowning in this republic of ours, and to offer ourselves ready to help to eliminate it.'[70] When ambition and avarice are destroying civil life, love of country is the only passion to which political leaders can appeal, as did Lorenzo de' Medici speaking to the most prominent citizens gathered in his house: 'Nor I do believe that in all Italy are there so many examples of violence and avarice as in this city. Then did this fatherland of ours give us life so that we might take life from it? Make us victorious so that we might destroy it? Honour us so that we might insult it?'[71]

---

[69] 'Io credo che il maggiore onore che possono avere gli uomini sia quello che voluntariamente è loro dato dalla loro patria: credo che il maggiore bene che si faccia, e il più grato a Dio sia quello che si fa alla sua patria.' *Discursus florentinarum rerum*, 220.

[70] *Istorie fiorentine*, III. 5 (Eng. trans. 109).

[71] Ibid. VII. 23 (Eng. trans. 302).

For Machiavelli, a citizen who loves his country is one who feels compassion for her, who shares her sufferings, and takes care of her. He wants to see his own people living freely because they are dear to him. Italy, as he wrote in the Exhortation that ends *The Prince*, is 'beaten, overrun, lacerated'; she is waiting for someone 'to heal her wounds'. Only a great and compassionate soul can answer her call and be, out of love, her liberator and 'rescue her from the cruel and arrogant domination of the foreigners'.[72] Machiavelli's patriotism, as has rightly been said, was a 'bewildered sentiment', infused with 'love of life and people, of language and woman, of God and heroes'.[73] But the core of it was love of liberty and respect, as the Roman masters and Christian religion too, if correctly interpreted, had taught.[74]

[72] *Il principe*, ch. 36. (Eng. trans. 88).

[73] Sebastian de Grazia, *Machiavelli in Hell* (Princeton, 1990), 21.

[74] 'though it looks as if the world were become effeminate and as if heaven were powerless, this undoubtedly is due rather to pusillanimity of those who have interpreted our religion according to idleness, not in terms of virtue. For, had they borne in mind that religion permits us to exalt and defend the fatherland, they would have seen that it also wishes to love and honour it, and to train ourselves to be such that we may defend it.' *Discorsi*, II. 2 (Eng. trans. 278).

2

Decline and Revival

BEGINNING with the mid-sixteenth century, the language of republican patriotism underwent a series of declines and revivals. In the late sixteenth and seventeenth centuries, it burgeoned in the few republics still surviving in the Europe of monarchies and principalities, and was reborn in those countries where significant experiences of rebellion against foreign domination took place. It remained alive where political liberty still existed; it was retrieved from the past where political liberty had to be regained. Its history became one with the history of liberty.

An example of the survival of the language of republican patriotism is Paolo Paruta's *Della perfezione della vita politica libri tre*, one of the latest celebrations of patriotism and the republican idea of politics. Following classical teaching, Paruta stresses that love of country is the foundation of civil life.[1] He who longs to live a life of virtue cannot be concerned only with himself, but must serve his *patria* as obligation to our country is our highest duty.[2] The preservation of the good order and liberty of our republic is necessary not only for the safe enjoyment of our property and our domestic relationships, but also for the pursuance of virtue, the most precious of all goods. We are bound to civil life both by nature and by choice. To rescind

---

[1] 'Ma, come si sia, per certo non si deve permettere per alcun modo che violato sia questo santo e venerando nome della Patria ... non avendo la nostra umanità niuna cosa né più cara né più preziosa che la Patria ... perciocché, distrutto l'amor della Patria, cade tosto ogni dignità della vita civile, e vana riesce ogni nostra fatica di intorno alle virtù.' In *Opere politiche di Paolo Paruta* (Florence, 1852), i. 216.

[2] 'Troppo grande è l'obbligo che habbiamo alla patria': ibid. 215.

the bonds that link us to our country, admonishes Paruta, amounts to a degeneration of our condition as men.[3]

Other examples of the survival of the language of republican patriotism can be found in Holland among the theorists and pamphleteers of the revolt against the King of Spain that led to the institution of the 'Dutch Republic of the Seven United Provinces'.[4] Every man 'wishing to be a good Patriot', wrote Jacob Heyndrix in his treatise *Political Education* of 1582, must take a solemn oath to renounce by any means 'the King of Spain and his adherents' and promise 'Homage and Fidelity to the present Government, the Country and one another'.[5] To our fatherland, he stresses, quoting Cicero's *De officiis*, we owe a love that embraces the love for our parents and relatives.[6] Hence, Dutch youth must not 'tremble for the power of the enemy' nor value their own lives over that of the fatherland because, as Cicero said, 'one is not bound to anything so much as to the fatherland, and . . . one should prefer (if necessity requires it) the welfare of the fatherland to the welfare of the father'.[7]

The Dutch Revolt was not the only case in which the classical concept of *patria* was used to sustain claims of political independence. The Neapolitan rebels of 1647, too, resorted to the ideal of the *patria* to argue that their revolution was in fact the revolution of a loyal people, since they were loyal, as one should be, to their *patria* and not to the person of the sovereign. By appealing to the *patria* as the source of the highest political obligation, the intellectual leaders of the Neapolitan insurrection managed to separate the interests and the rights of the crown from those of the people or the nation; they provided the movement with a legal and political legitimacy and found in the old language of patriotism a powerful rhetoric of liberty.[8]

Though historically and politically important, the cases of Venice, Holland, and Naples, did not arrest the decline of the

---

[3] 'La natura, dunque, è quella che per salute degli uomini, sue creature, volse adunarli nelle città, e insegnar loro il comandare e l'ubbidire, l'amare i figliuoli, i parenti, gli amici; ma sopra tutte queste cose, la Patria': ibid. 219.
[4] See M. van Gelderen (ed.), *The Dutch Revolt* (Cambridge, 1993), introd.
[5] Quoted ibid. 165.   [6] Quoted ibid. 173.   [7] Quoted ibid. 224.
[8] See R. Villari, *Per il re o per la patria* (Bari, 1994), 70.

language of republican patriotism in the broader context of six-
teenth- and seventeenth-century continental Europe. Its eclipse
was primarily due to the unfavourable political context: in absolute monarchies or principalities, there was not much encouragement for using a language that spoke of common liberty and
commitment to the common good. It was also due, however, to
the ideological affirmation of a language of politics—the language of reason of state—that claimed, against the main tenet of
republicanism, that man's highest obligation is not to the *patria*
but to the state personified by the sovereign.

The critics of republicanism equated loyalty to the *patria* with
loyalty to the king or stressed that *patria* was not necessarily the
same as republic. They meant to disassociate *patria* and liberty.
An important text that reflects this ideological tendency is the
Dialogo del reggimento di Firenze in which Francesco Guicciardini argues that love of country is not necessarily love of liberty,
in the sense of love for the republican form of government. The
celebrated virtue of the ancients, he wrote, came not from the
love of liberty but from the love of country. 'Country' (*patria*)
therefore, means more than republican institutions and common
liberty. There are in fact many examples of virtuous deeds
accomplished, for love of their country, by subjects of princes.[9]

Another equally powerful argument against the republican
conception of patriotism was that modern men were incapable of
virtuous deeds and therefore unfit for republican self-government.
In a memorandum addressed to the Medici, for instance,
Guicciardini stresses that their regime had a good chance of
lasting, because Florence, unlike Rome and Athens, was no longer
inhabited by generous souls seeking the glory which is the
reward of citizens defending the common liberty.[10] The love of
liberty and the hatred of tyranny, observes Guicciardini, are in

---

[9] 'Si può dire più tosto che questi simili abbino fatto per amore della patria
che della libertà; la patria abbraccia in sè tanti beni, tanti affetti dolci, che
eziandio quegli che vivono sotto e' prìncipi amano la patria, e se ne sono trovati
molti che per lei si sono messi a pericoli'; in *Dialogo e discorsi del reggimento
di Firenze*, ed. R. Palmarocchi (Bari, 1932), 39.
[10] *Del modo di riformare il Governo, per meglio assicurare lo Stato alla Casa
dei Medici*, in *Opere inedite*, ed. F. Canestrini (Florence, 1858), ii. 323–4.

his times much weaker because contemporary Florentines are concerned only with their particular interest.[11]

In seventeenth-century continental Europe the language of patriotism gradually lost its republican content. Love of country was taken to mean no longer love of the republic and common liberty, but loyalty to the state or the monarch. Trajano Boccalini, in his *Advertisements from Parnassus*, offers us a valuable insight into the changes in the meaning of the language of patriotism. With typical irony, he tells the instructive story of Marcus Cato, the symbol of republican patriotism and alleged author of the famous distich 'pro patria pugna', which he promptly engraved in gold letters upon the portal of his house in Parnassus. A few days later he realizes that the original distich recites 'pro patria libera pugna', not just 'pro patria pugna', and promptly changes the inscription. Noticing the motto, the princes of Parnassus vehemently protest to Apollo, stressing that these words might set all the world afire. Cato must hence be severely punished as a seditious man who wants to appear to the vile plebeians as a lover of truth and teach them 'an impertinent Liberty'.[12] Apollo summons Cato and reproaches him bitterly for having provoked the legitimate resentment of the princes. To Apollo's charges, Cato fiercely responds that good men do what their conscience tells them and do not care about the threats of princes. He added the word *libera*, he states, because it was necessary to explicate the full significance of the sentence. Without *libera* the sentence could be used to make the common people understand that they have to give their lives and faculties to defend their country 'as a thing properly belonging to them', whereas they do not in fact have the least interest in it. To that, Apollo replies that good princes have the power to make their subjects fight for the state of the prince (*lo Stato del Prencipe*)[13] with the same undaunted valour as if they were defending their own private

[11] 'moverebbeli sopra ogni cosa lo interesse loro particulare, che è lo maestro che ne mena tutti gli uomini': ibid. 333.

[12] *Ragguagli di Parnaso e pietra del paragone politico*, ed. G. Rua (Bari, 1910), 2 vols. C. II, Adv. 31; Eng. trans. *The New-found Politicke*, ed. W. Vaughan (London, 1626).

[13] Ibid.

patrimony because love of country is not love of liberty but loyalty to the sovereign. *Patria* and liberty part company.

Another line of criticism regarding patriotism in general was generated around the same time by neo-Stoic philosophers. Patriotism, they argued, is not so much useless or, in its republican version, dangerous to the stability of monarchies; it is above all else unreasonable. The main proponent of this line of thought was Justus Lipsius. In his work *De constantia*, composed in 1584, he stresses that love of country is a passion that contradicts the rule of reason and must therefore be fought with the utmost resolution to attain the tranquillity of soul and the complete self-mastery that is the supreme goal of the wise man.[14]

Constancy, which Lipsius defines as 'a right and immovable strength of the mind, neither lifted up, nor pressed down with external or casual accidents', is threatened by false goods and false evils, namely those goods and evils that 'are not in us but about us' and therefore cannot hurt the 'inner man', even though the judgement of common people believes they do.[15] Patriotism belongs to the rank of false evils. Examined through right reason it clearly shows itself to be based upon a false opinion and to be, as such, a source of irrational distress of the mind.

Lipsius' argument on the irrationality of love of country is a radical critique of the philosophical foundations of republican

---

[14] Other neo-Stoic philosophers, however, had different views on patriotism. Guillaume du Vair, for instance, argued that reason commands us to revere our country because it encompasses all the goods of life and because love of country is the source of men's noblest actions: 'En cet androit [*of the channels through which we enter in this world*] nous trouvons la patrie toute la première, qui, sous un nom feint et composé, comprend une vraie et naturelle charité. Nous lui devons par raison plus d'affection qu'à tout le reste des choses de ce bas-monde, pour ce qu'elle enveloppe en soi tout le reste, et contient en son salut tout ce que nous aimons et chérissons; et, au contraire, avec elle tout le reste se perd. De cette généreuse affection sont sorties tant de belles actions et si glorieuses de ceux qui ont employé leur vie pour la conservation de leur pays, de ceux qui ont oublié leur propres injures de peur de les venger aux dépens du public, de ceux qui ont volontairement choisi une dure et misérable vie pour mettre leur pays en repos'; *De la sainte philosophie: Philosophie morale des stoïques* (1599), ed. G. Michaut (Paris, 1946), 103–4. On late Renaissance neo-Stoic philosophy see R. Bodei, *Geometria delle passioni* (Milan, 1991).

[15] Lipsius, *De constantia*, ed. Lucien du Bois (Brussels, 1873), 164; Eng. trans. *Two Books of Constancie*, ed. R. Kirk (New Brunswick, NJ, 1939), 85.

patriotism which had always claimed that to love and serve our *respublica* is the most rational behaviour of man, not only because it is a duty prescribed by right reason, but also because it is the best means of sustaining liberty, which alone allows us to live in accordance with reason. As republican political writers have repeated over the centuries, a citizen who refuses to discharge his share of public service is not only immoral but also a fool. For Lipsius, on the contrary, the wise man must use reason to erase from his soul the passion of patriotism because it is in fact 'a vice, a note of intemperance, a deposing of the mind from his right seat'.[16]

Through the rhetorical technique of the dialogue, Lipsius presents a contrast between a natural and a political conception of patriotism. We are tied to our country, says the supporter of natural patriotism, 'by a secret bond of nature' which is a particular affection for the native soil

which we first touched with our bodies, and pressed with our feet: where we first drew our breath: where we cryed in our infance, played in our childhood, and exercised our selves in manhood. Where our eyes are acquainted with the firmament, clouds, and fields: where have been by long continuance of descents our kinsfolk, friends and companions, and too many occasions of joy besides, which I may expect in vaine in another part of the world.[17]

Natural patriotism is an attachment to the native soil understood as a place of memory. No other place has the same meaning. We may conceive of ourselves as citizens of the world, but that particular corner of the world excites in us feelings that we cannot experience anywhere else. The rigid wisdom of the Stoics may well treat this as vulgar opinion, but it remains none the less true that men are so attached to their native place that 'whoever bears the face of a man will never refuse to die for it and in it'. Rightly, hence, Euripides said that

> Necessity forces every wight
> To love his country with all his might.[18]

---

[16] Ibid. 184 (Eng. trans. 93).　　[17] Ibid. (Eng. trans. 93).
[18] Ibid. 186 (Eng. trans. 93).

To the claims of natural patriotism, Lipsius opposes the republican conception of *patria* as a political community and a way of life. At this stage of his argument, he simply reports the conventions of republican language. Men, remark the advocates of Stoicism, decided to abandon their savage and wild manner of living in order to to defend themselves and to attack enemies. For this purpose they gathered in cities surrounded by walls and shared the same territory. He then proceeds to repeat and paraphrase the famous passage from *De officiis* that had been quoted over and over by civic humanists. 'Over time a certain communion necessarily began among them, and a social participation of divers things. They parted the earth between them with certain limits and bounds: They had temples in common: also market places, treasuries, seats of judgement: and principally ceremonies, rites, laws.'[19]

Fatherland is not a natural reality but an institution: it is 'a new erected state [*novi status*] which now we call properly the Commonwealth [*Rempublicam*], or our Country [*Patriam*]'. Like one common ship under the direction of a pilot, our country is 'a certain common state [*unus aliquis status*]' under one prince or one law.[20] Our love and charity (*amor et caritas*) for our country comes therefore from the persuasion that our own safety and the safety of our property rests upon the safety of our country. For this reason we rejoice at the good of the commonwealth and we suffer at its miseries. Love of country is then essentially a love of the common good inspired in us by God's hidden plan and nurtured by the words and deeds of our ancestors.[21]

Political patriotism too, however, is unattractive for the wise man. As citizens we are fully entitled to love our country, to defend it, and to die for it; as men, however, we are not entitled to wail, lament, and despair for it like children and women. All forms of patriotism must cede to our obligations as men. Terrestrial countries are meaningful only for the body, but do not affect man's soul, whose true country is in the heavens from

---

[19] Ibid. 190 (Eng. trans. 96). [20] Ibid. 196 (Eng. trans. 97).
[21] Ibid. 192 (Eng. trans. 96).

where it comes. The example to be followed is then that of Anaxagoras who, asked why he had no affection for his country, pointed his finger to the heavens and said: 'my country is there'.[22]

The Stoic argument holds if we are prepared to concede that attachment to a particular place affects only the body and consists of passions and emotions that are less important than the life of the mind. Both concessions are quite onerous. Attachment to a particular place comes from images, from colours, from flavours that we experience or have experienced through the senses; they live with us through memory and become meaningful through imagination. Both memory and imagination are part of spiritual life; to rescind our bonds with places causes in fact spiritual suffering. If forced or if we decide for any reason so to do, we can certainly live without the feelings and the passion that come from our attachment to a particular place, but it would remain a life spiritually impoverished.

For Lipsius, if we analyse patriotism through the light of reason, we cannot fail to see that under solemn declarations of love of country, there is nothing but vainglorious dissimulation (*ambitiosa simulatio*), misplaced compassion (*pietas*), commiseration (*miseratio*), three affections equally pernicious to constancy. Men claim that they are afflicted by the calamities that plague their country, but their words are insincere, since they are only concerned by their private evils. The world, says Marcus Aurelius, is a stage play, and when men speak like patriots, they speak like actors.[23] Public evils like tyranny, war, and corruption are inevitably private evils. Patriotism, concludes Lipsius, is simply a prudent line of conduct, in spite of its rhetorical pretensions to virtue.

If fire should happen to be kindled in this city, we should have a general outcry: the lame and almost the blind would hasten to help quench it. What think you? For their country's sake? Ask them and you shall see, it was, because the loss would have redounded to all, or at the least, the fear thereof. So falleth it out in this case. Public evils do move and disquiet many men, not for that the harm touches a great number, but because themselves are of that number.[24]

[22] Ibid. 198 (Eng. trans. 98).   [23] Ibid. 175 (Eng. trans. 89).
[24] Ibid. 175 (Eng. trans. 98).

In saying that patriotism is not a virtue at all but a form of intelligent selfish behaviour, Lipsius was addressing a powerful critique to republican patriotism. Equally powerful was his attack against the other typically republican theme of love of country as a form of *caritas* (compassion). Compassion, he remarks, is an excellent virtue which, properly speaking, consists of a lawful and due love and honour (*legitimum debitumque honorem et amorem*) to God and our parents. Although the country is often said to be the most ancient and holiest common mother, the wise man cannot accept this 'popular opinion'. Our country did not receive us into this world more than taverners and innkeepers did. Nor did she cherish us more than maids and nurses. She does not nourish us; cattles, trees, and corn do. There is then no reason to call our country 'common mother', and the attachment that we feel for her 'compassion'.[25] What men feel when they are touched and tormented by the calamities of their country and their countrymen is commiseration; that is, 'the fault of an abject and base mind, cast down at the shew of another mishap'.[26] Unlike mercy, which is an inclination to succour our countrymen, compassion does not translate into commitment and action.

Lipsius' interpretation of patriotic feelings as a form of compassion, however, applies only to false or insincere patriotism. It would be totally irrelevant to the true patriotism depicted and recommended by republican thinkers. For them, love of country is a passion that gives strength to the soul and pushes men to act even in situations of great danger, not simply to commiserate with the victims of injustice and oppression.

Lipsius' critique of patriotism is meant to offer a spiritual refuge in times of great calamities. His exhortation to patriots

[25] According to du Vair our country can legitimately claim our pity: 'Représentez-vous donc tous les jours que votre pays, qui vous a mis en ce monde et vous y a conservé, vous redemande les droits de piété, exige de vous le devoir d'un bon et fidèle citoyen, et vous y conjure par la terre de votre naissance, par les lois de votre ville, par la foi de la société civile, par le salut de vos pères, de vos enfants, de vos amis, de vous-memes. Ayez donc soin de votre pays plus que tout le reste du monde; ne préférez jamais votre profit particulier à son bien, et, pour éviter le mal que vous menace, ne le rejetez point sur lui': *De la sainte philosophie*, 104.

[26] Lipsius, *De constantia*, 200 (Eng. trans. 99).

not to indulge themselves in sorrow and affliction for their country's disaster is addressed against patriotic lamentations or, more precisely, against indulging in sorrow and affliction for one's own country's calamities when it is clear that nothing can be done. The patriot's sorrow is pointless because it neither helps the country nor has any moral worth whatsoever, and it is impious because it attempts to combat God's eternal intelligence which governs the universe. The wise man knows that public calamities are imposed upon us 'by God himself', that they are necessary, and, finally, that they are 'neither grievious, nor strange'.[27] If we believe, as all men who are in possesion of right reason must, that necessity 'is naturally borne together with public evils', we may find some solace in our sorrow.[28]

Lipsius invokes the Stoic's theory of necessity as a relief that reason offers to the afflicted soul. As public evils can neither be avoided nor opposed, the last resort is to provide the soul with a powerful armoury against the sorrow that they induce in us. 'War, tyrannie, slaughter, and death hang over your head, which things truly are sent from above, and do not in any wise appertain to thy will or pleasure. Thou maist fear, but not prevent: fly, but not avoid. Arm yourself against them, and take this fatal weapon in your hand, which will not only pricke but wholly unlode you of them.'[29]

Unlike Machiavelli's *Fortuna*, Stoic necessity cannot be mastered or charmed into submission. God's necessary plan can be understood, not changed. If we understand that we are the means through which destiny carries out its plan, we can better heal our soul in times of calamity.

It is destiny you should have children: yet first you must sow the seeds in your wife's garden. To be cured of your disease: but so as you use the physician and good nourishment. So likewise if it be destiny that this weather-beaten ship of your country shall be saved from drowning, it is destiny with all that that she be aided and defended. If you will attain the haven, you must play the oares, and hoyse your sayles, and not idly expect wind at will from heaven. Contrarily, if it be destiny that your country shall be brought to confusion, such things shall come to pass by destiny, as will bring her to desolation by human means.[30]

---

[27] Ibid. 200 (Eng. trans. 101).   [28] Ibid. 266 (Eng. trans. 124).
[29] Ibid. 266 (Eng. trans. 124).   [30] Ibid. 270 (Eng. trans. 126).

The wise man hopes until there is breath in the sick body, but if he sees that nothing can be done to prevent the dissolution of the country, he shall not 'fight against God'. In dark times, we must yield to God 'and give place to the time'. If you are a good citizen, reads the exhortation that ends the first part of the dialogue, 'preserve yourself to a better and happier end. The liberty which now is lost, may be recovered again hereafter; and your decayed country may flourish in another age: why do you lose all courage and fall into dispair?'[31]

The time for the language of patriotism to assume again a central place came some forty years after the publication of the *De constantia* during the English Revolution. Once again, when liberty was sought, the language of patriotism had powerful ideas and words to offer. Particularly in the Levellers' literature, 'love of country' came again to mean love of a free commonwealth, a charitable attachment to the common liberty of the people tempered by respect for the principles of natural law and *jus gentium* and religious liberty. It was understood, as Cicero had stressed in the *De inventione*, as a part or an aspect of justice.

An example of the presence of Ciceronian idioms in the seventeenth-century English language of patriotism can be seen in the *Manifestation* signed by the leaders of the Levellers John Lilburn, William Walwyn, Thomas Prince, and Richard Overton on 14 April 1649. The duty 'to employ our endeavours for the advancement of a communitive Happiness' and to pursue the freedom and the good of the nation, it reads, rests on the principle that 'no man is born for himself only', imposed on us by the laws of nature, of Christianity, and of 'Publick Societie and Government'.[32]

For the Levellers the patriot is the soldier who fights for the common right and liberty,[33] or the Member of Parliament

---

[31] Ibid. 274 (Eng. trans. 127).

[32] In W. Haller (ed.), *The Levellers Tracts* (New York, 1944), 277.

[33] 'And now (*right worthy patriots of the Army*) you your selves upon the *same principle*, for *recovery of common right* and *freedome*, have entered upon this your present honourable and *Solemne Engagement*, against the oppressing party at *Westminster*'; *An Appeale from the Degenerate Representative Body of the Commons of England Assembled at Westminster* (London, 1647), in D. M. Wolfe (ed.), *Leveller Manifestoes of the Puritan Revolution* (New York, 1944), 160.

devoted to the common good.[34] If the members of the English
Commonwealth want to preserve their common liberty, we read
in *The Just Defence of John Lilburn*, they must be sensitive to
the wrongs inflicted upon their fellows.

What is done to any one, may be done to every one: besides, being all
members of one body, that is, of the English Commonwealth, one man
should not suffer wrongfully, but all should be sensible, and endeavour
his preservation; otherwise they give way to an inlet of the sea of will
and power, upon all their laws and liberties, which are the boundaries
to keep out tyrany and oppression; and who assists not in such cases,
betrays his own rights, and is over-run, and of a free man made a slave
when he thinks not of it, or regards it not, and so shunning the censure
of turbulency, incurs in the guilt of treachery to the present and future
generations.[35]

In a similar vein John Milton, writing in 1660, calls 'our old
Patriots . . . the first Assertors of our religious and civil rights',
the Members of the Rump Parliament who 'judging kingship by
long experience a government burdensom, expensive, useless and
dangerous, justly and magnanimously abolished it'.[36] In the grand
council that ought to form the foundation of the commonwealth,
he writes in the second edition of *The Readie and Easie Way to
Establish a Free Commonwealth*, must be seated 'chosen Patriots [who] will be then rightly call'd the true keepers of our
libertie'.[37] The country that the patriot loves, and to which he
is committed, is the commonwealth; that is, the free political
community based upon the rule of law that republican writers
called *respublica* or *civitas*. It is a political value which rests
upon the laws of nature and the *jus gentium*. The country, or
commonwealth, can demand her offspring to offer her their best
energies and even their lives; but she cannot ask them to violate
the laws of nature and the *jus gentium* which constitute its
moral foundation. The very moment the country, through its

[34] See W. Walwyn, *England Lamentable Slaverie*, in W. Haller (ed.), *Tracts
on Liberty in the Puritan Revolution* (New York, 1934), iii. 317.
[35] In Haller (ed.), *Leveller Tracts*, 455.
[36] *The Readie and Easie way to Establish a Free Commonwealth* (1660), in
Complete Prose Work of John Milton (New Haven, 1980), vii. 355–6.
[37] Ibid. 443.

representatives, asks them to commit injustice, it ceases to be a country and turns into a gang of wicked men that can neither command obedience nor gain the citizens' affection. Samson's words to his wife Dalila in the poem *Samson Agonistes*, published in 1671 under the Restoration, powerfully expresses Milton's view that devotion to one's own country cannot transgress the boundaries set by the law of nature:

> If aught against my life
> Thy countrey sought of thee, it sought unjustly,
> Against the law of nature, law of nations,
> No more thy countrey, but an impious crew
> Of men conspiring to uphold thir state
> By worse then hostile deeds, violating th'ends
> For which our countrey is a name so dear;
> Not therefore to be obey'd.[38]

In Milton's language, love of country is a compassionate love of liberty. The execution of the King, he wrote in his *Defence of the People of England* of 1651, was an act inspired not by factiousness, nor a desire to usurp the rights of others, nor mere quarrelsomeness, nor perverse desires, nor fury or madness, but by love of country in the sense of *patriae caritas*, as he writes in the Latin version; that is, a love of country which is the sum of 'love of your liberty and your religion, of justice and honor'.[39] Men naturally feel their country's honourable achievements, Milton writes in 1654 in his *Second Defence of the People of England*, as their own; but the honour and the glory of our country comes from liberty as well as civil life and divine worship.[40] For Christian men love of country cannot be 'a blind and carnal love'; it must be a form of compassion, an affection for our fellows, for their and our liberty, their and our rights that has nothing in common with lust for power, wealth, and the false glory that comes from expansion.[41]

[38] In *The Complete English Poetry of John Milton*, ed. J. T. Shawcross (New York, 1963), 174.
[39] In *The Works of John Milton* (New York, 1932), vii. 455.
[40] *Works*, viii. 7.
[41] 'This virtue [love of country] should be sought by philosophers warily. For a blind and carnal love of country should not sweep us to deeds of rapine

Love of country, however, may fade, no matter how intense it has been. The country may become remote or alien; she leaves her former lover cold and indifferent. Milton speaks of his fading love of country in the last years of his life. Withdrawn from political life, living 'in strained and difficult circumstances' under the Restoration, he writes in a letter of 1666 that the very compassion for country (*Pietatem in Patriam*) that he had harboured for long in his heart has deserted him. He is, however, left with other virtues, and he is content with them: 'one's *Patria* is wherever it is well with him'.[42] The disappointed patriot has to look for consolation in Stoic wisdom. England under the Restoration was not the commonwealth that he had envisaged. His love of country faded away because he realized that the object of love was different from the ideal to which he was attached. As he had written, love of country is a moral and political love that condenses love of justice, liberty, and honour. By its nature, a moral and political love is not blind. It allows us to see the features of the object of our love; indeed, it requires us to look at it keenly. If he sees oppression and injustice, the patriot should not look elsewhere; compassion for his fellows should induce him to endure the horrors and yet find the strength to work for a better country, rather than looking elsewhere. The patriotism of liberty imposes severe burdens. Milton's letter records the dilemma of a genuine patriot; it is a powerful record of the agonies and pains of a moral and political love.

For later generations of Commonwealthmen Milton was the model patriot. What made his patriotism exemplary was the combination of a commitment to political, religious, and civil liberty and cultural openness. As John Toland stressed in his *Life of Milton*, Milton travelled abroad to enrich his culture and to know his own country better, since he believed that the best way to understand the merits and defects of his country was to study

and slaughter and hatred of neighboring nations in order that we may aggrandize our country by power, wealth, or glory; for so did the heathen act. Christians, however, ought to cultivate mutual peace and not covet other men's goods.' *Commonplace Book*, in *Works* (New York, 1938), xviii. 164–5.

[42] Letter to Peter Heimbach, 15 Aug. 1666 in *Works* (New York, 1936), xiii. 112–15.

other peoples' institutions and customs.[43] He returned to his country when the cause of common liberty needed his support. The same love of country that drove him to look at his own country from a distance—taking as moral and political standards other peoples' institutions—brought him back. Like the *patriae caritas* described by his Latin mentors, his love of country was a passion that pushed him to embrace and enlarge his affection for other peoples beyond the sphere of family and to extend respect and understanding to peoples beyond the boundaries of his own country.

For Toland, patriotism demands cultural openmindedness. The same qualities he praised in Milton were, he believed, instilled through education in the young Romans. They were taught

to understand the Customs, Laws, and Religion of their Country. The knowledge of Mankind (a mighty art) they communicated to 'em by comparing ancient History with the daily observations they made on strangers, their own acquaintance, and fellow-citizens. By reading the customs and constitutions of other places, they show'd 'em what in their own was blameable or praiseworthy, what requir'd to be amended, added, or abolisht.

The goal of education was to inspire love of country, but country to them meant liberty. The love that they were encouraged to cultivate did not make them blind; on the contrary, it empowered them to see well the distinction between good and bad government.

They inspir'd them with an ardent passion for Liberty, with an equal abhorrence of Tyranny and Anarchy: persuading 'em to prefer death to slavery, and readily to expose their lives and estates in defence (not of any form indifferently) but of a Government which protected their persons, preserved their property, encourag'd industry, rewarded merit, and left their sentiment free. Such a government it was that they call'd their Country, and for this they thought honorable to dy.[44]

[43] (London), 1699, 15; See also Toland's description of James Harrington as a model patriot in *The Oceana and other Works of James Harrington Esq. Collected, Methodiz'd and Review'd, with An Exact Account of his Life Prefix'd By John Toland* (London, 1747), p. vii.

[44] *A Letter concerning the Roman Education*, in *A Collection of Several Pieces of Mr. John Toland* (London, 1726), ii. 6–7.

'One's *Patria* is wherever it is well with him', Milton had said, playing with the words of the Latin motto *ubi patria ibi bene*; 'wherever they enjoy'd liberty, there they thought themselves at home', says Toland, speaking of the Romans. He meant to say, like Milton, that our home does not necessarily coincide with the place where we are born, but with the place in which we live well; and this place can only be one in which we live in freedom; that is, a commonwealth or republic. Liberty can be enjoyed in different places; one can be attached to but one soil. One can be a citizen of the world as well as a citizen of this or that country, but one can hardly be as attached to the soil of the world or any other country as to one's native soil. As long as the fundamental value that inspires love of country is liberty, one can find his country elsewhere. To be fond of any spot on earth because we were born there is, he writes, 'not only a false notion of our country, but, in my opinion, as childish a prejudice as that of some old Men, who order their dead bodies to be carry'd many hundreds of miles to be laid with deceast Progenitors, their Wives, or other Relations'.[45]

Toland intended to separate love of country from cultural rootedness; he wanted to turn it into a pure political love that grows wherever there is political liberty. He did not recognize, however, that liberty found in another country cannot have the same flavour as the liberty that one enjoys in his or her own country. A pure love of country is surely more rational than one contaminated by 'childish prejudices'; but it is a different love. One may wonder whether a purely political love can still be called 'love of country'.

In seventeenth-century England republican patriotism was contrasted by another version of patriotism based not on love of liberty, but on loyalty to the king. An eloquent example of monarchical patriotism can be found in Robert Filmer's *Patriarca*, published in 1680. A true patriot, he claims, must be a royalist: 'Many an ignorant subject hath been fooled into this faith, that a man may become a martir for his country by being a traitor to his Prince; whereas the new coined distinction onto Royalist

[45] Ibid. 6–7.

and Patriots is most unnatural, since the relation between King and people is so great that their well-being is reciprocal.'[46] In Filmer's interpretation, *Patria* does not mean republic, but the community founded on the power of the fathers; it is literally the *res patrum*, thing of the fathers. The power of the prince over his subjects derives from the power of the father over his children; hence the king legitimately holds the title of *Pater Patriae*,[47] and as *Pater Patriae* he can command absolute fidelity from his subjects; disobedience, as Filmer remarks, means treason and impiety.

Royalist patriotism based on fidelity to the crown did not weaken the intellectual and ideological presence of the language of republican patriotism in eighteenth-century England. The most significant effort to preserve the tenets of patriotism is perhaps Shaftesbury's reflections in his *Characteristics of Men, Manners, Opinions, Times*, published in 1711, in which he denounces the confusion between love of the republic and love of place and notes the English language's inability to express the distinction clearly.

I must confess, I have been apt sometimes to be very angry with our language for having denied us the use of the word Patria, and afforded us no other name to express our native community than that of country, which already bore two different significations abstracted from mankind or society [*rus* and *regio*, in French *campagne* and *pays*]. Reigning words are many times of such force as to influence us considerably in our apprehension of things. Whether it be from any such cause as this, I know not, but certain it is, that in the idea of a civil state or nation we Englishmen are apt to mix somewhat more than ordinary gross and earthy.[48]

Patriotism is the affection that a people feel for their country understood not as native soil, but as a community of free men living together for the common good:

A multitude held together by force, though under one and the same head, is not properly united. Nor does such a body make a people. 'Tis the social league, confederacy, and mutual consent, founded in some

---

[46] ed. P. Laslett (Oxford, 1959), 55.   [47] Ibid. 61.
[48] (Gloucester, Mass., 1963), p. 248.

common good ore interest, which joyns the members of a community
and makes a people one. Absolute power annuls the public. And where
there is no public or constitution there is in reality no mother country
or nation.[49]

True love of country is love of the 'constitution and polity by
which they are free and independent'.[50] It is, as Shaftesbury nicely
puts it, a 'generous passion' because its object is the most noble
goal in human life—that is, that very civil life which is the foundation of man's happiness—and because it concerns a common
and public good.

Love is necessarily particular: it is always love of particular
persons, objects, or places. It may be more or less general: it
may be an exclusive attachment to something that belongs to us
exclusively or to something that we share with very few, with
few, or with many other persons. Patriotism in Shaftesbury's
account is an inclusive love. Its primary aim is not to reinforce
the differences between Britons and other peoples, or their
uniqueness, but rather to unite them in the defence of common
liberty, which is a shared good whose value does not depend on
its being an exclusive good that only one particular people enjoys. The liberty of other peoples has never made patriots
unhappy.

The difference between true patriots and the 'patriots of the
soil' does not lie in the intensity but in the nature of the attachment. It is one thing to love our country because we believe that
it is ours alone and that the possession of it makes us better than
all the others; it is another to love something that we have in
common with other individuals regardless of its being only ours.
The former type of love of country sustains 'as overweening an
opinion of ourselves as if we had a claim to be original and earth
born', and encourages an inclination to contract our views within
the narrowest compass, and to despise all knowledge, learning,
or manners which are not of a home growth'; the latter encourages openness toward other people's culture and naturally encompasses duties toward humanity, hospitality, and benignity
regardless of difference of race. Patriotism understood as a

---

[49] Ibid. 244 n. 4.   [50] Ibid. 245.

desire for liberty works as an inclusive, uniting force; it brings together, it does not push away or exclude.

The patriot's love for his fellow-citizens is a 'moral and social' relation. It needs a sense of similarity, since no love or friendship can grow among individuals who have nothing in common. But it needs only the similarity of members of the same civil society. It does not need other types of cultural or racial similarity. For this reason the patriot can also be benign and kind towards men who are not his fellow-citizens, and who come from remote countries and belong to a different race. The fact of belonging to the same race is neither a reason to feel love or friendship toward one's fellow-citizens nor a reason to hate and exclude. What seems to matter so much to patriots of the soil leaves the patriot of liberty cold, no matter whether he is dealing with compatriots or with foreigners.

This does not make patriotism an impersonal attachment. It rather defines it as a self-confident love. It is remarkable, writes Shaftesbury, that

in that truly ancient, wise, and witty people, [the Greeks] that as fine territories and noble countries as they possessed, as indisputable masters and superiors as they were in all science, wit, politeness, and manners, they were yet so far from a conceited, selfish, and ridiculous contempt of others, that they were even, in a contrary extreme, 'admirers of whatever was in the least degree ingenious or curious in foreign nations.'[51]

Englishmen, who have changed masters and mixed race several times display on the contrary a 'ridiculous contempt of others'.[52] Fear and insecurity about ethnic and historic roots seem to generate the exclusive attachment to one's own soil and the tendency to extol one's own cultural uniqueness and superiority. Patriotism of liberty is immune from anxieties and fears concerning a people's ethnic background and history.

Shaftesbury portrays patriotism as a noble passion contemptuous of lower, ignoble, and restricted attachment to the soil. He restates the core of republican political patriotism but he makes the gap between the patriotism of the soil and political patriotism too wide and he offers no indication as to how to

[51] Ibid. 250.   [52] Ibid.

incorporate natural attachment to a place into a moral and general political patriotism. The secret of the alchemic transformation of patriotism of the soil into moral patriotism could be, we may suppose, the reduction or removal of fear. Attachment to one's own soil, with all its cultural and existential implications, needs not to be too severely censored; it may well live together with commitment to common liberty; it may even turn into a powerful support of commitment to liberty, if we speak not of liberty in general, but of the common liberty of a people living generation after generation over the same territory.

In eighteenth-century England, the title 'patriot' was one that all parties were eager to claim for themselves. As Quentin Skinner has remarked, both the Whigs and the Tories used the concept of patriotism to mean 'the ideal of acting in such a way as to defend and preserve the political liberties which their fellow-countrymen enjoyed under, and owed to, the constitution'.[53] Even the works on patriotism of the arch-enemy of Walpole, Lord Bolingbroke, are replete with republican idioms. To serve our country, he remarks in *The Spirit of Patriotism*, is a 'moral duty' that each man should discharge 'in proportion to the means and the opportunities he has of performing it' as long as the country needs it. And to serve the country means, for him, to support good government and to guard 'public liberty'. To be prevented from serving the common good is not at all relief, but a descent into a life of sloth and idleness.[54]

Political involvement, however, is not just a duty, but a highly gratifying activity. Not even the intellectual pleasures of Montaigne, Descartes, or Newton, writes Bolingbroke, can be compared to that of a real patriot 'who bends all the force of his understanding and directs all his thoughts and actions, to the good of his country'.[55] In addition to being necessary to protect liberty, political activity is also rewarding in itself. The philosopher's pleasure ends with speculation; that of the political man

[53] 'The Principles and Practice of Opposition: The Case of Bolingbroke versus Walpole', in N. McKendrick (ed.), *Historical Perspectives* (London, 1974), 93–128.
[54] In *The Works of Lord Bolingbroke* (London, 1967), xi. 358–9.
[55] Ibid. 360.

continues while he endeavours to enact his political schemes. He has to deal with treacherous friends and malicious enemies, but he also has the chance to discover the fidelity and docility of others. He sees both the best and the worst of men. Unlike the philosopher who has made himself immune to patriotic commitment, his mind is agitated by fear and hope, but the agitation is pleasant. If the great event that he is pursuing is successfully decided, his pleasure is comparable to that which 'is attributed to the Supreme Being'; if he is defeated, his conscience will console him.[56]

For Bolingbroke, the fundamental requirement of a patriot is commitment to a free constitution and the common good of the people.[57] It follows that to be a patriot one need not be a citizen of a free republic, but can also be a subject of a monarch, and indeed the monarch himself. In fact, a king has the chance the accomplish the most glorious patriotic deed, namely to re-establish a free constitution and redeem a people from corruption.[58] However, he admits, a 'Patriot King [is] the most uncommon of all phenomena in the physical or moral world'.[59]

Bolingbroke supports his ideal of a patriot king with the authority of Machiavelli, an author, he says, 'who should have great authority with persons likely to oppose me'.[60] He takes from the *Discourses* the argument that it is in the best interest of a prince to be a good prince and to accept limits to his power rather than ruling, like a tyrant, without any rule of law'.[61] He also uses Machiavelli's remark that a corrupt people can be corrected only by a 'kingly power' to mount an argument for the superiority of monarchy over republican government.[62] Whereas a republic has no remedy against widespread corruption, a 'free monarchical government' can easily 'renew the spirit of liberty'.[63] A patriot king, as he puts it, is therefore 'the most powerful of all reformers'. Under him the people will not only cease to do

---

[56] Ibid.
[57] 'The obligation, therefore, to defend and maintain the freedom of such constitutions will appear most sacred to a Patriot King': *The Idea of a Patriot King*, in *Works*, xi. 391.
[58] Ibid. 388.   [59] Ibid. 357.   [60] Ibid. 389.   [61] Ibid.
[62] Ibid. 395.   [63] Ibid. 396.

evil, but learn to do well: a new patriot king creates a new people.

As the century progressed, however, the language of patriotism assumed more pronounced radical connotations.[64] An example of the ideological shift is Samuel Johnson's *Dictionary*. In the 1755 edition he defines the patriot as 'one whose ruling passion is the love of his country'; in 1773 he adds the following lines: 'ironically for a factious disturber of the government'; in 1775 he crafted one of the most-quoted definitions in the English language: patriotism is 'the last refuge of a scoundrel', and he was referring to the Radicals.[65]

---

[64] H. Cunningham, 'The Language of Patriotism, 1750–1914', *History Workshop*, 12 (1981), 8–33.
[65] Ibid. 12.

3

Patriotism and the Politics of the Ancients

In the eighteenth century the language of patriotism also flourished in continental Europe within the context of the renaissance of republican political thought. As has been emphasized, eighteenth-century republicanism was sometimes a throw-back to classical ideas, but more often the result of concrete experiences of political and military resistance against absolutism. Although they dominated the political and military scene in Europe, great monarchies did not succeed in their repeated efforts to eliminate the republics of Genoa, Lucca, Venice, Holland, and Switzerland, not forgetting San Marino, and the survival of a handful of republics no doubt contributed to the persistent liveliness of republican patriotism.[1]

The language of republican patriotism was a powerful medium through which to re-emphasize, against the politics of the moderns (that is, the politics of states, princes, and kings) the politics of the ancients (that is, the politics of the republic). *Patria* was again taken to mean *respublica*—a self-governing community of individuals living together in justice under the rule of law—not just any state, and patriotism was therefore understood as a generous love for the republic and common liberty, a love that could not exist under despotic and tyrannical regimes nor flourish in monarchies. Republican patriotism meant politics: the politics of the ancients as opposed to the politics of the moderns; politics understood as good government and self-government as opposed to politics as bad government and government from above.

[1] F. Venturi, *Utopia and Reform in the Enlightenment* (Cambridge, 1971), 21.

An example of the connection between republican patriotism and politics as good government and self-government can be found not only in the classic works of Montesquieu and Rousseau, but also in other, minor, and now almost-forgotten texts. An example is *La vita civile* by Paolo Mattia Doria, published in 1729, which criticizes *raison d'état* in favour of the old ideal of politics as civil philosophy and is also a refined advocacy of patriotism. The duty of the political man, he writes, is to shape a new civil life sustained by religion and love of country (*amore della patria*) which he defines as a rational bond that can be strengthened through good government.[2]

Love of country, explains Doria, is grounded in the awareness that our happines rests upon the security of our country. People should feel attached to their country like plants to the soil in which they are rooted because if the country is dissolved, they can no longer enjoy their properties, their personal security, and all the goods of life.[3] They should therefore love their country out of the awareness that it is in their best interest to do so. However, stresses Doria, people form their judgements out of direct experience rather than rational evaluation: they will love their country if they experience that it is pleasant and safe to live there, and this can be done through justice, concord, and good customs.

Doria interprets patriotism as a virtuous passion which results from the political transformation of pernicious passions. 'The good political man', he writes, 'uses men's passions in the interest of the country'.[4] Through justice and a wise distribution of public honours (*buona politica*), he can convert people's selfish inclinations into a passion useful to the country. If the country is well

---

[2] (Naples, 1729), II. i. 2.

[3] 'L'amor della patria riguarda solo l'umana felicità. Nella sicurezza della patria, il libero esercizio della religione, la sicurezza della vita e della propria casa e de' figliuoli sta appoggiata. La qual patria devono amare i popoli in quella guisa, che le piante (per cosí dire) amano il terreno, nel quale stanno fisse le loro radici. E in somma . . . devono preferir l'amor di lei a quello della vita, considerando sempre, che lei distrutta non son stabili gli averi, non è sicura la vita, ed ogni altra cosa si perde.' Ibid.

[4] 'Il buon politico si serve delle passioni de' popoli in utilità della patria.' Ibid. 147.

governed, good men will understand that their own good rests on their country's safety and will therefore love it wholeheartedly.

To be able to transform self-love and ambition into love of country, good government must be accompanied by public rituals and glorified by the outstanding virtue of the prince and the magistrates. Public festivities, remarks Doria, distract people from entertaining the desire to change their polity. They should be neither too frequent as to encourage laziness (*'l'ozio è pernicioso alle repubbliche'*) nor too rare because people need opportunities to rest. Public ceremonies should convey to the people the sense of the majesty of the republic or the prince. Along with majesty and greatness, public festivals and feasts must instil courage. Although civil men cannot devote themselves to the art of war, they should not altogether lack the valour that is necessary to defend their country: if enemies defeat the army and invade the country, they must find a people ready to resist servitude with all their vigour.[5]

The *Vita civile* goes much deeper than previous works on patriotism in studying the ways in which self-love and ambition can be transformed into a noble love of country. The decisive element that makes possible the metamorphosis of self-love into love of country is, he writes, the people's esteem of their prince and their magistrates.[6] Men never love individuals whom they despise; they may find them interesting, but they do not love them. Even the most debased men can love only virtue and true good. If princes, magistrates, and senators want to gain the people's friendship, they must first merit their admiration and their respect. Since men, remarks Doria, love mystery and esteem highly those virtues that they associate with God's perfection, princes, magistrates, and senators must appear in people's eyes as semi-divine beings. They can do that only if they possess outstanding virtue; they must be grave and yet kind, severe yet compassionate. They must behave, in sum, in a way that persuades people of their superiority.

According to Doria, patriotism is not only a transformation

---

[5] Ibid. 148.

[6] 'l'amore deriva dalla stima: e la grandezza e la generosità sono efficacissime a cagionar questa stima, dalla quale poi nasce l'amore.' Ibid.

of self-love, but also an antidote to love of great vices. The latter, like great virtues, command admiration since greatness, whatever its form, easily fascinates men's minds. A good prince must therefore impress the people with his outstanding virtue to prevent them from admiring great vices. People like Caesar and Alexander, remarks Doria, are regarded as heroes because they have been powerful and gave glory and greatness to their states, though never, or rarely, happiness. By their immoderate ambition they caused immense misery, and yet people regard them as heroes, love them, and love their country accordingly.[7] People love to belong to a glorious country; to share the light of their country's glory they are prepared to suffer the calamities of wars designed to satisfy their prince's ambition and to endure the burden of bad government.[8]

To find an antidote to love of country that comes from the admiration of false virtue, Doria resorts again to his theory of the conversion and remoulding of passions. Love of country generated by admiration of false virtue cannot be dissolved through rational argument but through a more powerful love, namely the love of true virtue that comes from gratitude for the security and the happiness that the people enjoy under good government. Love of true virtue is stronger and lasts longer than love of false virtue because it is based upon self-love, which never leaves men; love of false virtue is instead based on thirst for glory, a passion which never lasts for long.

In the volatile universe of passions, not only may love of false virtue be dissolved by the love of true virtue, but love of vice may turn into hatred. False politicians, remarks Doria, believe that they may keep their subjects docile and gain their love by encouraging their vices with their corrupt behaviour. They count on the fact that men, in the beginning, love vices and those who give them the opportunity to indulge themselves in a debased way of life. After a while, however, when they experience the

---

[7] Ibid. 152.
[8] 'E per consequenza amata ancor la patria: perchè i popoli amano sopra d'ogn' altra cosa l'esser figliuoli di una patria gloriosa; e perciò con lieto e forte animo sopportano i disagi che agli stati apporta il mal governo, cagionato dalla difformità delle virtù,' ibid.

bad effects of widespread vice, their love toward their corrupt rulers turns into hatred, not just of the bad rulers, but of the whole country.[9] Hatred, however, does not immediately generate rebellion against false politicians. A people accustomed to corruption lacks the spiritual strength to resist and rebel against false politicians who are responsible for their misery. Rebellion occurs when princes and magistrates are convinced that the people are so enervated that they can disregard even the simulation of virtue and freely unleash their vicious behaviour.[10]

In Doria's analysis, love of country is the central issue of politics, or, more precisely, of 'virtuous politics'. When he writes that patriotism, is the foundation of true politics (*il fondamento della vera politica*), he means that the goal of true politics is to generate and strengthen in the citizens' hearts the love of country that comes from love of true virtue. For him a true political man has to be a master of the art of transforming bad passions into good ones. Through his study of love of country, he rediscovered the subtlety and the greatness of true politics, that is the politics of the republic.

Doria's ideas reflected an important stream of eighteenth-century political thought soon to attain wider European circulation. Admiration for republican patriotism and the politics of the ancients, however, was not unanimous. A few years before the publication of Doria's *Vita civile*, Giambattista Vico published the *Scienza nuova*, which contains a radical critique of ancient patriotism designed to destroy modern men's fantasies and illusions. For Vico, the celebrated love of country of the ancients is the virtue of heroic societies which offends our sense of justice and humanity. It was in fact barbarism; that is, a combination of ignorance, superstition, fierceness, selfishness, avarice, and cruelty. When Roman authors speak of liberty, says Vico, they mean the liberty of the patricians, that is the liberty of the masters; when they speak of *patria* they do not mean a free community of citizens, as philosophers wrongly believe, but the property or the interest of the fathers.[11] Ancient patriotism

---

[9] Ibid. 155.   [10] Ibid. 157.

[11] 'Cosí sono state finora guardate le azioni degli antichi eroi dagli uomini di menti spiegate, che vennero appresso dopo i filosofi; quelle, che in lor ragione

was not a generous love of common good but an ignoble attachment to particular interests and to power.

The Spartans, the most celebrated example of ancient virtue, took a solemn oath to be eternal enemies of the plebeians; the legendary Roman heroes were equally selfish and insensitive to the suffering of the latter. Not one of the celebrated republican heroes ever did anything for them. They only increased their burdens by war in order to sink them deeper in the sea of usury, and to bury them to a greater depth in the private prisons of the nobles, where they were beaten with rods on their bare backs like abject slaves. And if anyone in this period of Roman virtue (*nel tempo di essa Romana Virtù*) attempted to relieve the lot of the plebeians with some sort of agrarian or grain law, he was accused of treason and sent to his death.[12]

Roman 'patriotism' deeply offends modern ideas of virtue which are based upon justice and benevolence to all mankind:

> For certainly Roman history will puzzle any intelligent reader who tries to find in it any evidence of Roman virtue where there was so much arrogance [*superbia*], or of moderation in the midst of such avarice [*avarizia*] or of justice or mercy where so much inequality and cruelty [*fierezza*] prevailed.[13]

The famous Roman education that republican philosophers have always praised was not for Vico a school of citizenship and liberty, but a stern, cruel, and rough affirmation of paternal power. And the Spartan education was simply cruelty: 'in order to teach their sons to fear neither pain or death, [the fathers] would beat them within an inch of their lives in the temple of Diana, so that they often fell dead in agonies of pain beneath their blows'.[14] They were ferocious in war and extremely inhospitable to foreigners. Their virtue was the only one appropriate to their times;

non si facevano dagli eroi degli antichi tempi che per troppo affetto particolare che avevano alle proprie sovranità, conservate loro sopra le loro famiglie dalla loro *patria*, che perciò fu così appellata, sottintesovi *Res*, cioè *interesse di Padri*, come poi negli Stati popolari fu detta *Respublica*, quasi ESPOPULICA, *interesse di tutto il popolo*.' *Principi di una scienza nuova* (1725), II. 22, ed. G. Ferrari (Naples, 1859), 52.

[12] Giambattista Vico, *Seconda scienza nuova* (1744), ed. G. Ferrari (Naples, 1859), 213; Eng. trans. *The New Science of Giambattista Vico*, ed. Th. G. Bergin and M. H. Fisch (Ithaca, NY, 1968), 254.

[13] Ibid. 214.   [14] Ibid.

it is not appropriate to Vico's times since the distance from contemporary ideas of benevolence and charity is too great. Ancient patriotism and ancient politics must simply be forgotten.

Vico's words are a powerful critique of a patriotism which had degenerated so that it was neither committed to liberty nor based upon compassion and respect. His rebuttal of ancient virtue, however, had no significant intellectual impact. On the contrary, the ideal of ancient patriotism gained a central place in eighteenth-century political language through the mediation of Montesquieu's *Spirit of the Laws*. The historical significance of Montesquieu's recovery of ancient patriotism was, however, double-edged: he rescued it from oblivion but at the same time he presented it as a virtue suitable, in its genuine form, only for ancient citizens of ancient republics.

Love of country is for Montesquieu a duty and a virtue.[15] It is an attachment to a particular good: human beings love their own country, the country that has for them a particular meaning. Love of country is similar in this sense to the friendship or the generosity that one feels toward particular persons but not towards humanity in general nor towards just anybody. To remain a virtue, however, it can never contradict the principles of justice, which Montesquieu defines as a general or impersonal relationship.[16] When it violates the principles of justice, patriotism is the source of the worst crimes; rectified and tempered by justice, it becomes the source of the most splendid actions that honour a whole nation.[17]

Although they cannot be expected to imitate the patriotism of the ancients, modern men are capable of a patriotism of their own which consists of the desire to live in a well-ordered

[15] 'Quoiqu'on doive aimer sa patrie, il est aussi ridicule d'en parler avec prévention que de sa femme, de sa naissance ou de son bien,' *Mes pensées*, in *Œuvres complètes*, ed. R. Caillois, i (Paris, 1949), 1287; 'Je n'aime que ma patrie; je ne crains que les Dieux; je n'espère que la vertu', ibid. 1003.

[16] 'Presque toutes les vertus sont un rapport particulier d'un certain homme à un autre; par exemple: l'amitié, l'amour de la Patrie, la pitié, sont des rapports particulières. Mais la justice est un rapport général. Or, toutes les vertus qui détruisent ce rapport général ne sont pas des vertus': ibid. 1304.

[17] 'Mais, s'il est vrai que l'amour de la Patrie ait été, de tout temps, la source des plus grands crimes, parce que l'on a sacrifié à cette vertu particulière des vertus plus générales, il n'est pas moins vrai que, lorsqu'elle est une fois bien rectifiée, elle est capable d'honorer toute une nation': ibid. 1143.

community where they can enjoy public tranquillity, the correct administration of justice and share the blessings of the rule of law and the general stability of the monarchy or the republic. The 'spirit of citizenship' that one can demand of the moderns is a love of the laws and the common good, even when it conflicts with particular interests. Though different from the political participation of the ancients, modern men also exercise a sort of sovereign power in their daily activity, out their family, and in the administration of their property.

This interpretation of patriotism also informs *The Spirit of the Laws*, in which he recovered the original meaning of the concept, but also added important specifications. As he remarks in the 'Avertisment', the term *vertu* that appears throughout the first four books does not mean Christian or moral virtue, but political virtue (*vertu politique*), which is love of country (*amour de la patrie*); that is, love of equality (*amour de l'égalité*).[18] Like Machiavelli, he describes the love of country as love of the laws and institutions that protect the common liberty. Love of equality is the love of civil equality, equality as citizens, that is to say equal political rights and equality before the law. In the state of nature, explains Montesquieu, men are born equal but in society they lose their natural liberty. They become equal again through the law, through citizenship. The true spirit of equality consists 'neither in making everyone command nor in placing no one in command, but in obeying and commanding one's equals'.[19] The love of equality that sustained the political virtue of the Romans, explains Montesquieu, was a 'jalousie du pouvoir du sénat et des prérogatives des grandes', always tempered, however, by respect. It was vigilance that prevented the senate or powerful citizens from oppressing the common liberty.[20] For this reason the true sense of equality emerges only in well-constituted democracies where one is 'equal only as citizens', whereas in a corrupt democracy citizens want to be equal in all respects.[21]

[18] *L'Esprit des lois*, 'Avertisment', in *Œuvres complètes*, ii (Paris, 1951).
[19] Ibid. VIII. 3.
[20] *Considérations sur les causes de la grandeur des Romains et de leur décadence ch. IX* in *Œuvres complètes*, ii.
[21] *Esprit des lois*, VIII. 3.

Where there is no longer virtue there is not only no place for liberty, but also no mores, no love of order, and no civility.[22] Political virtue demands self-restraint and therefore goes perfectly well with the respect for laws and the magistrates and nourishes orderliness and decorum in private life. Love of country and of equality makes men capable of putting the common interest above excessive private and factional interests. For this reason political virtue is for Montesquieu, as it was for Machiavelli, the foundation of liberty: the natural place of virtue, he writes, 'is with liberty'. On the contrary, when ambition and avarice—the mortal enemies of political virtue—become the dominant passions of the citizens, they are no longer capable of living freely.

Montesquieu also stressed, however, that in its most intense or heroic form political virtue is a virtue of the ancients. Modern men know of it only by hearsay. Because of their attachment to private interest, they cannot love their homeland nor display the same degree of self-sacrifice of which the ancients were said to be capable. The patriotism of the ancients was in part a necessity; when a city was conquered, he explains in his *Pensées*, the inhabitants were killed or enslaved. They were so strongly attached to their country because their life and their individual liberty were one and the same with the life and liberty of the city.[23] The love of country of the Greeks, he remarks, was the outcome of their *fureur de la liberté* and coupled with their heroic courage and their hatred of kings, gave them the strength to accomplish their memorable deeds.[24] And when he points out that political virtue is at the heart of republican[25] or democratic or popular[26] government, he actually means the republics or the democracies of the ancients; that is, forms of government in which the people as a body had not only sovereign power but also 'see to the execution of the laws'.

---

[22] Ibid. 3 and 2.

[23] 'Les Anciens devoient avoir un plus grand attachement pour leur patrie que nous: car ils étoient ensevelis avec leur patrie. Leur ville étoit-elle prise? Ils étoient faits esclaves ou tués. Nous, nous ne faisons que changer de prince,' *Mes pensées*, 1353.

[24] Ibid. 1364.   [25] *Esprit des lois*, II. 2.   [26] Ibid. III. 3.

According to Montesquieu, political liberty is both necessary for republican governments and extremely difficult to instil and preserve. It is necessary because in a republic the citizens who pass the laws and watch over the magistrates in charge of their implementation are also subject to laws; if out of ambition or avarice they do not love the republic and its laws, the laws become ineffective and the republic dissolves. Political virtue is extremely difficult to instil, remarks Montesquieu, because 'it is a renunciation of oneself'; it demands the citizens to curb their desire to attain exclusive goods.[27] To be virtuous, the citizens of a republic have to be educated to direct their passions and their attachments toward common goals. The more they are deprived of the possibility of pursuing their self-interest and indulging in the pleasures of private life, the more they love the republican order. Like the monks who love their order because 'their rule deprives them of everything upon which ordinary passions rest', citizens must follow an austere way of life: the more the republic succeeds in curbing particular attachments and private passions, the stronger it becomes.[28]

For Montesquieu, the love of equality that forms the core of patriotism is not only love of civic equality but also love of frugality. In addition to the desire to be equal before the law and enjoy equal political rights, the citizens should have 'the same happiness, the same advantages, and the same expectations'. Democratic equality may be attained only through a frugal life that limits 'the desire to possess' to the minimum which is necessary for oneself and one's family.

The more people are content with the satisfaction of their basic needs, the more they are likely to long for the glory of their country.[29] Grand passions, and above all the desire of glory, demand the moderation of the attachment to particular goods. Deprived of the possibility of satisfying particular interests, they naturally divert their love to their country and have to look for

[27] Ibid. IV. 5.   [28] Ibid. V. 2.
[29] 'Il faut que, dans les républiques, il y ait toujours un esprit général qui domine. A mésure que le luxe s'y établit, l'esprit de particularisme s'y établit aussi. A des gens à qui il ne faut rien que le nécessaire, il ne reste à désirer que la gloire de la Patrie et la sienne propre,' *Mes pensées*, 1434.

the happiness that comes from serving one's country. Paraphrasing, Cicero's classic words from the *De officiis*, Montesquieu stresses that each citizen contracts at birth a debt with his homeland that can never be fully repaid. For this reason each citizen must serve the common good to the best of his abilities. One can reasonably expect civic virtue from citizens of a democracy because they have no means of pursuing exclusive pleasures; that is, pleasures that are available to some but not to all. Since they have very few private or particular interests, it is not too great a sacrifice for them to be virtuous.

Montesquieu sees a threat to political virtue not only in avarice and ambition, but also in individual interest. In order to prevent the growth of particular interests, republics must strive to keep their territory small. In large republics 'interests become particularized' and the common good 'is sacrificed to a thousand considerations'.[30] In small republics, on the other hand, the common good is better felt, better understood, and lies closer to each citizen. The proper soil for political virtue is then to be found in small, austere, and frugal republics.

In his discussion on the spirit of democracy Montesquieu introduces a disjunction between political virtue and individual interest that one does not find in the analyses of Machiavelli and earlier republican writers. The more remote in time the republic becomes, the more it appears pure and unattainable. For Machiavelli, as we have seen, the citizens love the republic and are capable of virtuous deeds because they realize that the republic is the foundation of their liberty, security, and prosperity. They love their country and its laws because they feel the republic to be their own cause and because they perceive that it is in their interest to live in that republic. When they are discharging their civic duties, they are not sacrificing their interests, as Montesquieu maintained, but securing them. When the citizens are corrupt and do not discharge their civic duties they behave in the most imprudent way; they fail to act in their own self-interest.

Classical and early modern theorists had stressed that love of country is a broad spirit of benevolence that embraces parents,

[30] *Esprit des lois*, VIII. 16.

relatives, friends, and citizens. Montesquieu remarks instead that love of country requires renunciation and sacrifice; when the citizens extend their love to their country, they must cease to love other things, or at least they must love other things—themselves, their families, their friends—less intensely. For him love does not expand; it shifts. Modern men have a limited amount of it: they can invest it either on their private life or on their country. Because their love has to be divided between their country and their private life, they cannot equal the legendary patriotism of the ancients who channelled, so the story goes, all their love toward their country.

From this analysis of the dynamics of love of country, however, Montesquieu does not conclude that modern men cannot be virtuous but only that their political virtue cannot be as intense as that of the ancients. The spirit of commerce itself, which permeates the modern world and reinforces the attachment to private interest, is not a fatal threat to patriotism. Like Machiavelli, he stresses that republics must keep the citizens poor and frugal to preserve the love of equality that nurtures political virtue. By 'poverty' he means a middle level between luxury and indigence. A poor citizen is one who 'needs to work in order to preserve and to acquire'.[31] The spirit of commerce is hence perfectly compatible and indeed sustains this sort of poverty and frugality. It may well happen that commerce makes some citizens so wealthy that they do not need to work any more. This would not only spoil republican social equality, but also the *spirit* of commerce. In fact, idle citizens living in luxury lose the habits of moderation, frugality, economy, wisdom, work, tranquillity, order, and discipline that constitute the spirit of commerce.[32]

Montesquieu distinguishes between poverty which is part of a people's servitude and poverty which is part of a people's liberty. The former is imposed upon a people by the harshness of government; the latter is a poverty that the people have selected either because they disdain, or because they do not know, the comfort of life. The two kinds of poverty have very different effects on civic virtue. Whereas peoples whose poverty is the

---

[31] Ibid. v. 6.   [32] Ibid. xx. 1.

consequence of their servitude 'are capable of no virtue', people whose poverty is part of their liberty 'can do great things'.[33] Against Cicero, who maintained that the same people cannot be both the rulers and the clerks of the universe, Montesquieu stresses that great projects and bold hearts are not incompatible with small projects and ordinary concerns. Far from being incompatible with republican equality, commerce indeed finds in republics the most favourable soil. In republics citizens gladly devote themselves to commerce, even to grand commercial enterprises, because they feel secure that they will not be deprived of the profits of their activity. The spirit of commerce, in turn, has beneficial effects on republics because it encourages the frugality and the poverty that keep the mores incorruptible, and nurtures civility and orderliness in both private and public life. It also encourages the love of country and political virtue, particularly if the laws maintain a suitable social equality.[34] A tradesman can perfectly easily love the country that protects its trade and allows him to prosper. The feeling of security that Montesquieu calls 'political liberty' is for modern men a powerful source of attachment to one's country and its laws.

Montesquieu presents two interpretations of patriotism. In his reflections on democracy based upon classical sources, he rediscovered the patriotism of the ancients based upon social unity and described it as a noble but unrealistic ideal for modern men living in commercial societies; in his reflections on the spirit of commerce, he argues for a patriotism based upon a love of liberty that is within the reach of the moderns. Whereas the former is threatened by private interests, the latter is compatible with them. Montesquieu indicates two ways to achieve patriotism: one through unity and sacrifice, another through liberty and self-interest. The first leads to a pure but impossible patriotism; the second to an impure but more viable and appealing one.

Montesquieu's ideas on political virtue became part of the patriotism of the Enlightenment. The article 'Patrie' in the *Encyclopédie* repeats Montesquieu's definition almost verbatim and presents political virtue as a noble ideal that requires,

---

[33] Ibid. 3.   [34] Ibid. xx. 4.

however, too great a moral strength for modern men. Political virtue, reads the article, is 'love of the fatherland [*amour de la patrie*]', love of the laws, love of the welfare of the state, and is particularly strong in democracies. It is, as Montesquieu had said, a renunciation of one's self, a preference for the public over the particular interest. Since it is a passion and not a philosophical reasoning, all men can attain it;[35] it is a vigour of the soul that empowers even the weakest men and makes them capable of doing 'great things for the public good [*de grandes choses pour le bien public*]'.[36] However, when modern men read of the stories of the heroes of ancient patriotism, they consider them not as moral exemplars, but as illustrious fools.

The article of the *Encyclopédie* is not only important to illustrate the ambivalent character of the rebirth of the language of patriotism paved by *The Spirit of the Laws*, but also to grasp the meaning of the eighteenth-century definitions of political virtue as *amour de la patrie*. *Patrie*, we read, does not mean the place in which we are born, as the vulgar conception believes. It means instead the 'free state' [*état libre*] of which we are members and whose laws protect 'our liberty and our happiness [*nos libertés et notre bonheur*]'.[37] The term *patrie* is synonymous with 'republic' and 'liberty'.[38] Under the yoke of despotism there is no *patrie*.[39] Following once again in Montesquieu's footsteps, the authors remarks that

Those who live under the oriental despotism, where no other law is known than the whims of the sovereign, no other maxim than the adoration of his caprices, no other principles of government than terror, where no fortune and no one are safe, those people have no *patrie* at all and do not even know its name, which is the true expression of happiness.[40]

---

[35] *Encyclopédie* (Neuchatel, 1765), xii. 178.
[36] Ibid. 179.   [37] Ibid. 178.
[38] As Cicero's definition reads, *respublica* means *respopuli*; that is, a congregation of individuals living together for the common good under the laws to which they have consented. In a true republic sovereign power belongs to the people and this is the best guarantee of common liberty. Cicero, *De republica*, I. 25. 39, and 31. 47.
[39] *Encyclopédie*, 178.
[40] 'ceux qui vivent sous le despotisme oriental, où l'on ne connoit d'autre loi

Correctly understood, *patrie* means a country that all the inhabitants have an interest in preserving (*sont intéréssés à conserver*) and that is hospitable to foreigners. It is their common mother who loves all her children equally; she honours the citizens who have distinguished themselves for their virtue, but does not discriminate or admit unfair preferences. She accepts that some citizens are richer than others, but demands that the pathway to public honours and offices be open to all; and above all else she cannot tolerate the oppression of even a single citizen. She smiles when she can benefit her citizens and punishes only with the deepest sorrow.

Voltaire, too, in his *Dictionnaire philosophique* assimilates the *patrie* with the *polis* or republic. The *patrie*, he writes, is a unity of several families. Individuals are attached to their *patrie* by the same self-love that unites them to their family, unless they have an interest contrary to the common good. In the *patrie*, particular interests of the citizens naturally translate into the general interest: 'on fait des vœux pour la république, quand on n'en fait que pour soi même'.[41] Thus the word *patrie* applies to republics or to the rule of a good king, but never to tyranny:

What then is the *patrie*? Would it not be, perchance, a good field in which its owner, comfortably lodged in a well-kept house, could say: this field which I cultivate, this house which I have built, is mine. I live there under the protection of laws which no tyrant can infringe. Whenever those who own, like myself, assemble in their common interests, I have my voice in this assembly; I am a part of the whole, a part of the community, a part of the sovereignty; this is my *patrie*.[42]

que la volonté du souverain, d'autre maximes que l'adoration de ses caprices, d'autres principes de gouvernement que la terreur, où aucune fortune, aucune tête n'est en sureté; ceux là, n'ont point de *patrie*, et n'en connoissent pas même le mot, qui est la véritable expression du bonheur': ibid. 180.

[41] In *Œuvres complètes* (Paris, 1826), lvii. 289.

[42] 'Qu'est-ce donc que la patrie? ne serait-ce pas par hasard un bon champ, dont le possesseur, logé commodément dans une maison bien tenue, pourrait dire: Ce champ que je cultive, cette maison que j'ai bâtie, sont à moi; j'y vis sous la protection des lois, qu'aucun tyran ne peut enfreindre. Quand ceux qui possèdent, comme moi, des champs et des maisons, s'assemblent pour leur intérêts communs, j'ai ma voix dans cette assemblée; je suis une partie du tout, une partie de la communauté, une partie de la souveraineté: voilà ma patrie.' Ibid. 285–6.

For Voltaire and the 'cosmopolitan' philosophers of the Enlightenment, *patrie* has no essential reference to a particular culture, or language, or ethnicity; what constitutes a *patrie* is the rule of law, liberty, and self-government. For him the *patrie* is the republic reduced to its essential political and legal structure; the place does not matter, and history matters even less: one can find his or her *patrie* wherever civil and political liberties are guaranteed. A *patrie*, so conceived, can command from her citizens an attachment that comes from self-love and self-interest. For Voltaire citizens feel for their *patrie* the same love that they feel for their family; by 'love', however, he does not mean benevolent love, but self-love. He solves the contrast between self-love and love of country posited by Montesquieu by reducing the *patrie* to the purely legal and political structure of the republic and then interpreting love of country as enlightened self-love. His account of love of country as self-love is perfectly consistent with his view of the *patrie*: if the *patrie* is simply a legal and political structure that protects the citizens' rights, it can only demand from them an attachment that comes from self-love. They will love their *patrie* as long as they find it convenient to be citizens of that republic; if they believe that this is no longer the case, they will probably leave, if they can. Their patriotism is a rational love in the fullest sense; a love that fits rational individuals who know how to calculate their interest. No trace of the patriotism of the ancients is left: no compassion, no *pietas*, no thirst for glory. It is a patriotism well within the reach of modern men, a patriotism perfect for citizens of the world who can enjoy a good or even a great life anywhere, as long as others—perhaps less rational, who love their countries not just because they find it convenient to live there, who rely on their countries to keep them alive and who work to make them good republics—do not live.

Although he despised the *philosophes'* cosmopolitanism as a mask for their egotism, the 'nationalist' Rousseau also uses the term *patrie* as equivalent of 'republic' and accepts the conventional conception of political virtue as love of the fatherland. As with Montesquieu, Rousseau's political virtue is neither a state of innocence nor a Christian virtue, but a precious legacy of the ancients that the politics of the moderns relentlessly endeavours to destroy. Paraphrasing Montesquieu, he wrote that 'ancient politicians spoke incessantly about mores and virtue; ours speak only of commerce and money'.[43] For him, virtue is the *conformité de la volonté particulière à la générale* and the love of one's country is the most effective means to encourage virtue: 'Do we want people to be virtuous? Let us then begin by making them love their country.'[44]

Although Rousseau adopts Montesquieu's vocabulary and uses some of his arguments on the decline of political virtue among modern peoples, he parts company with the author of the *Spirit of the Laws* on the evaluation of virtue versus civility. Whereas Montesquieu had celebrated both the political virtue of the ancients and the civility of the moderns, Rousseau began his career as the zealous champion of the virtue of the ancients and the enemy of the corrupt civility of the moderns. The virtue of the ancients becomes in his hands an ideological weapon against the corruption of the moderns. Virtue, he writes in the *Discours sur les sciences et les arts*, is *la force et la vigueur de l'âme* that shines against the 'suspicions, offenses, fears, coldness, hatred, betrayal' that hide under 'that uniform and deceitful veil of politeness, under that much vaunted urbanity that we owe to the enlightenment of our century'.[45] Against polite but corrupt modern European man, Rousseau opposes his exemplars of virtue: the rustic peasant, and, above all, the citizens of Sparta, 'a republic of demi-gods', and Republican Rome, the 'temple of virtue'. His concept of virtue is reminiscent of Machiavelli's *virtù*. The princes and the nobility of Italy, he writes in a passage that recalls *The Prince*, 'had a good time becoming ingenious and learned more than they exerted themselves trying to become vigorous and

---

[43] 'Les anciens politiques parloient sans cesse de mœurs et de vertue; les nôtres ne parlent que de commerce et d'argent.' *Discours sur les sciences et les arts*, in *Œuvres complètes* (Paris, 1964), iii. 19; Eng. trans. in J. Rousseau, *The Basic Political Writings*, ed. D. A. Cress (Indianapolis, 1987)), 12.

[44] 'Voulons-nous que les peuples soient vertueux? commençons donc par leur faire aimer la patrie.' *Économie politique*, in *Œuvres complètes*, iii. 255; Eng. trans. *Basic Political Writings*, 122.

[45] *Discours, sur les sciences*, 8–9; Eng. trans. *Basic Political Writings*, 4–5.

warlike'.[46] Indeed, in his praise of military virtue he goes as far as to glorify Rome's conquests as a way to impose virtue in the world: 'The only talent worthy of Rome is that of conquering the world and making virtue reign in it.'[47]

Although he does not use the term 'political virtue' and speaks simply of *vertu*, Rousseau means civic virtue; that is, the moral strength of the citizen who is capable of fighting against corruption and oppression. It is a strength that comes from a moral indignation that sets his soul afire and encourages his will to resist and fight. Civic virtue is not a rational evaluation, but a passion; it is an alteration of the soul and the body rather than a state of mind. The opposite of a virtuous citizen is the citizen who remains cold and inactive before corruption, even if he condemns it.

Patriotism may go together with mildness and love of humanity, but it may also require severity and even cruelty. Brutus, writes Rousseau, was not at all a mellow man, but it cannot be said that he was not virtuous. When they hold office, citizens may well be compelled to be severe in order to be virtuous: Brutus sentenced to death his own sons because they had conspired against the Republic, and presided over their execution.[48] The eighteenth century, wrote Rousseau in a response to a critic of the *Discours sur les sciences et les arts*, judges his conduct cruel; Brutus deserves, on the contrary, our deepest admiration for his commitment to the Republic and the strength with which he discharged his duties as a magistrate.[49] Had he granted pardon to his sons, the other conspirators would have been let off altogether, with the obvious consequence of weakening the newly founded republic. Even if the Republic had survived, an act of clemency toward his sons would have undermined the rule of law: if citizens guilty of high treason are granted pardon, how can ordinary criminals then be punished? Brutus, argued

[46] 'S'amusoient plus à se rendre ingénieux et savans, qu'ils ne s'exerçoient à devenir vigoureux et guerriers,' ibid. 22 (Eng. trans. 15).
[47] 'Le seul talent digne de Rome est celui de conquerir le monde et d'y faire regner la vertu,' ibid. 15 (Eng. trans. 9).
[48] *Dernière réponse de J.-J. Rousseau de Genève*, in *Œuvres complètes*, iii. 72.
[49] Ibid. 88.

Rousseau's critics, should have resigned from his magistracy and let someone else sentence the conspirators to death. If a magistrate abandons his post in a moment of extreme danger for the republic, responds Rousseau, he acts like a betrayer and would deserve to be put to death. The *Discours sur les sciences et les arts* ends with a celebration of virtue as 'the sublime science of a simple soul', as the voice of conscience that can be heard 'in the silence of passions'.[50] However, the virtue that he exalts throughout the entire essay is the *virtù* which is not the voice of conscience speaking in the silence of passions, but a passion itself, a strength and a vigour of the soul, inspired by the love of one's country.

As has already been remarked, Rousseau defines civic virtue as the conformity of the particular with the general will, but what makes this identification or unity of the particular with the universal will possible is the love for our fellow-citizens. 'We willingly love what is wanted by the people we love.'[51] The love of the country that sustains civic virtue is not the love of an impersonal or abstract entity, but the attachment to particular people, people whom we know because we see them, we live with them, we have interests and memories in common. One cannot love strangers, or unknown or anonymous individuals.[52] The love of country, writes Rousseau, is 'a hundred times more ardent and delightful than that of a mistress'.[53] It inspires a 'fiery and sublime ardour' which cannot be found in pure moral virtue (*pure vertue*); that is, the virtue of the philosopher. The philosopher's virtue teaches us the pathway to our personal happiness; civic virtue commands us to look for a happiness that we share with our fellow-citizens. Between Socrates who teaches the truth and Cato who stood against the tyrant to defend the republic, the laws, and the common liberty, we should have no hesitation in choosing Cato.

---

[50] *Discours, sur les sciences*, 30 (Eng. trans. 21).

[51] *Économie politique*, 254 (Eng. trans. 121).

[52] *Considérations sur le gouvernement de Pologne*, in *Œuvres complètes*, iii. 970; (Eng. trans. *The Government of Poland*, ed. W. Kendall (Indianapolis, 1985), 25).

[53] *Économie politique*, 255 (Eng. trans. 121).

If we want to understand the meaning of Rousseau's concept of (political) virtue, we must remember that for him, too, *patrie* means above all else the common liberty. The love of country which sustains political virtue is thus the love of the common liberty, our own liberty and that of our fellow-citizens. Without liberty and without citizens, there is a *pays*, but not a *patrie*.[54] The connection between *patrie* and liberty is reiterated using the same words in the *Considérations sur le gouvernement de Pologne:* 'the love of one's country; that is, love of the laws and liberty'; in another version of the work the order is reversed: 'the love of the liberty; that is, love of one's country and the laws'.[55] For Rousseau what constitutes a *patrie* is primarily the relationship between the state and the citizens and the way of life that the laws and the political institutions foster. A letter that Rousseau wrote on 1 March 1764 to Lieutenant Charles Pictet in Geneva is particularly illuminating in this respect. On 12 May 1763 as a response to the decision of the Small Council of the Republic of Geneva to prohibit the publication of his *Lettre à Cristophe de Beaumont,* following similar measures taken against the *Contrat social* and *Émile,* Rousseau formally renounced his rights as a citizen (*bourgeois*) of Geneva. It was, he wrote, a painful decision, a definitive break. He was aware that he would not be able to see his country anymore. And yet he said that the pain seemed attenuated: he felt no love, no bond. All that it left was a cold sense of duty and indifference. What had caused a love once so intense to fade?

The answer lies in Rousseau's patriotism as described in his earlier texts, particularly the Dedication of the *Discours sur l'origine de l'inégalité* where he had solemnly reaffirmed his attachment to the Republic of Geneva. He was already a *bourgeois* of Geneva by birth; he wanted to be so by choice. He had left

---

[54] 'La patrie ne peut subsister sans la liberté, ni la liberté sans la vertu, ni la vertu sans les citoyens', ibid. 259 (Eng. trans. 124). On the difference between *patrie* and *pays*, see *Émile,* in *Œuvres complètes,* iv. 858, where Rousseau writes: 'qui n'a pas une patrie a du moins un pays'. Another important passage in the *La Nouvelle Héloïse,* in *Œuvres complètes,* ii. 657: 'Plus je contemple ce petit Etat, plus je trouve qu'il est beau d'avoir une patrie, et Dieu garde de mal tous ceux qui pensent en avoir une, et n'ont pourtant qu'un pays!'
[55] pp. 966 and 1754 (b) (Eng. trans. 19).

his native city when he was a young boy. Geneva had also forced his father to leave and the very laws of the Republic prevented Jean-Jacques from going back. Yet, he declares that he would choose Geneva as his *patria*.

He loves the Republic and loves Geneva because it is his republic, a good republic, at least in his imagination. He would love, he says, to live in a republic where 'the delectable habit of meeting and knowing one another made love of country [*amour de la Patrie*] a love for fellow-citizens rather than a love for the land [*amour des Citoyens plutôt que celui de la terre*]'[56] and where the sovereign and the citizens 'could have only a single and identical interest' so that sovereign deliberations tended to promote the common happiness. He would have wished, in other words, to live in a well-ordered democratic government. His love belongs to a republic in which the rule of law protects each citizens' liberty; to 'a happy and peaceful republic of which the origins are lost in the darkness of times; one which had endured only such hostile attacks as might serve to bring forth and fortify the courage and the patriotism [*amour de la Patrie*]'; a republic whose citizens 'being long accustomed to a wise independence not only are but deserve to be free'; a free city with no desire for conquest and protected by a favourable location from fear of being invaded by powerful neighbours.[57]

Patrie means for Rousseau a peaceful community in which one can live in 'sweet society' with one's fellow-citizens, exhibiting toward them humanity and friendship; a community in which one can hope to be remembered 'as a good man and an upright, virtuous patriot [*d'un homme de bien, et d'un honnête et vertueux Patriote*]'.[58] The thought of ending his life far from his *patrie* evokes feelings of regret, tenderness, longing:

If, less fortunate or wise too late, I were to find myself reduced to ending an infirm and languishing sojourn on earth in other climes,

---

[56] *Discours sur l'origine de l'inégalité*, in *Œuvres complètes*, iii. 112.

[57] 'J'aurois voulu vivre et mourir libre, c'est-à-dire tellement soumis aux loix que ni moi ni personne n'en pût secouer l'honorable joug; Ce joug salutaire et doux, que les têtes les plus fiéres portent d'autant plus docilement qu'elles sont faites pour n'en porter aucun autre,' ibid.

[58] Ibid. 115.

vainly regretting that repose and peace of which a misspent youth had robbed me, I would at least have kept alive in my soul the feelings that I was unable to express in my own country (*pais*)...[59]

No one can understand the value of *patrie* better than he who has lost it, as Rousseau did. And for a true patriot (*un vrai Patriote*) the value of the *patrie* consists above all else in the constitution designed to protect liberty and in the way of life and the customs that it sustains. The same true patriot, acting as a patriot, decided nine years later to give up his citizenship because he realized that the *patrie* to which he was attached no longer existed. Geneva was still there, with its people, its history, its language, institutions, and laws. What was no longer there was the republic and liberty. Even though everything else was still in place, the corruption of the political relationship between the state and the citizen was sufficient to extinguish the *patrie*.[60] His decision, he says in a letter to Picted, was the outcome of disillusionment: after what she did to him, he could no longer continue to believe that he too had a *patrie* and that his *patrie* was the Republic of Geneva. Disillusion, as he explains in his letter, leaves no anger or resentment, just indifference and detachment. Community and meaning have to be sought elsewhere.

For Rousseau patriotism is primarily a political love; a love that is the product of good government and stems from gratitude for the liberty and the welfare that good government assures to all citizens. To command the love of its citizens the *patrie* must love each and every one equally. Her love too is political and expresses itself through a caring protection of the liberty and political rights of all citizens. By protecting their liberty the country (*patrie*) makes the citizens feel secure; by recognizing their political rights, it makes them perceive their country to be something that belongs to them:

---

[59] Ibid.

[60] 'Ce ne sont ni les murs, ni les hommes qui font la patrie; ce sont les loix, les mœurs, les coutumes, le Gouvernement, la constitution, la manière d'être qui resulte de tout cela. La patrie est dans les rélations de l'Etat à ses membres; quand ces rélations changent ou s'aneantissent, la patrie s'évanoüit,' Rousseau to lieut.-col. Charles Pictet, in *Correspondance complète de Jean-Jacques Rousseau*, ed. R. A. Leigh (Voltaire Foundation, Oxford 1965), xix. 190.

Let the homeland, therefore, show itself as the common mother of all citizens. Let the advantages they enjoy in their homeland endear it to them. Let the government leave them a large enough part of the public administration so that they can feel that they are at home. And let the laws be in their sight merely the guarantees of the common liberty.[61]

A good political constitution and a good government are sufficient conditions for patriotism, whereas a bad constitution and bad government induce citizens to disregard their civic duties. As Rousseau explains in the chapter of the *Contrat social* on deputies or representatives, 'dans une cité bien conduite chacun vole aux assemblées; sous un mauvais Gouvernement nul n'aime à faire un pas pour s'y rendre'.[62] The citizens gladly go to public meetings if they believe that there is a good chance that the common interest, and therefore their individual interest, will be carried out. In this case commitment is rewarding: each citizen collects a valuable portion of the common happiness that good public deliberations bring about. If they know that the meeting will ratify the particular interests of a faction, they would rather stay at home to pursue happiness in private life. Their love of country cools off; and what has cooled it off is bad government.[63]

For Rousseau, however, love of country is not just a political love; it is not just love of the laws and the constitution. It is also love of a way of life, of a culture, of a language, of a place; but it remains above all a political love: language, culture, religion cannot keep alive the *amour de la patrie* if there is no political and civil liberty, if there is no republic. The contention, that for Rousseau and for classical republicans patriotic feeling and political participation 'rested and could only rest on social, religious and cultural unity' and 'were the political expression of a homogeneous people',[64] is therefore only partially correct. The

---

[61] 'Que la patrie se montre donc la mere commune des citoyens, que les avantages dont ils jouissent dans leurs pays le leur rend cher, que le gouvernement leur laisse assez de part à l'administration publique pour sentir qu'ils sont chez eux et que les lois ne soient a leurs yeux que les garants de la commune liberté,' *Économie politique*, 258 (Eng. trans. 123–4).

[62] *Contrat social*, III. 15, in *Œuvres complètes*, iii.

[63] Ibid.

[64] M. Walzer, 'Civility and Civic Virtue in Contemporary America', in *Radical Principles* (New York, 1980), 64.

cultural, religious, and social unity of a people encourages civic virtue but the essential prerequisite is political: that is, good government. A people may be totally homogeneous from a cultural, religious, and social point of view and yet, if they are under a despotic regime or a tyranny, love of country will never grow among them. Homogeneity and good government together are the best soil for civic virtue, but homogeneity and despotism produce docility and corruption. Cultural, religious, and social homogeneity are helpful supports to, but not necessary conditions for the flourishing of civic virtue. Good government joined with diversity (social or religious) can still produce civic virtue in its most genuine sense; that is, love of liberty.[65] If the people are politically corrupted, however, they cannot recover liberty and restore good government, no matter how homogeneous they are.[66]

Mère commune, liberté commune: the adjective 'common' is the recurrent element in the metaphors that Rousseau uses to characterize the *patrie*. The commonality that Rousseau evokes indicates the commitment of the state to protect the liberty of each and every citizen, thereby making liberty and security a common good. This commitment is a consequence of the principle that the liberty of a single citizen is as important as the liberty of the whole *patrie*.

In Rousseau's theory of the legitimate political constitution, commonality implies the obligation to treat all citizens justly. The liberty of each member must be protected by the common force of all the members. This means, in the ideal model, that an injustice perpetrated against a citizen affects not only the relationship between the state and that particular citizen but also the relationship between the state and the whole citizenry; it dissolves the citizens' political obligation to the state. The social contract establishes that the liberty of each citizen is part of the common liberty. If a citizen or some citizens are treated unjustly, it is not only their liberty which is infringed, but the

---

[65] Ibid. 69.

[66] *Contrat social*, II. 8; Rousseau follows here Machiavelli, *Discourses*, I. 17 ('Uno popolo corrotto, venuto in libertà si può con difficultà grandissima mantenere libero').

common liberty. Powerful citizens or corrupt magistrates are the enemies of the unfortunate citizens who are the victims of their ambition, and are also the enemies of the whole republic and for this reason they must be punished by the republic as a whole.

As I have stressed, Rousseau's point that the liberty of each citizen is part of the common liberty and must therefore be a concern of all, is a *normative* principle which is part of the theory of the republic. In practice, the violation of the liberty of one or some citizens may and indeed does leave perfectly untouched the liberty—again understood as personal or negative liberty—of all the others. But if the republic were a true republic, it would not tolerate the infringement of the liberty of any of them; and if the citizens were true citizens, they would consider the violation of the liberty of one of them as an attack against the liberty of them all. The point of Rousseau's argument is to provide a political justification for the citizens' resistance against the government when it commits injustice or does not do what is in its power to protect the citizens' liberty. If the state claims to be a republic, the citizens are entitled, and have the duty, to resist and fight against the magistrates or the powerful citizens who infringe the common liberty.

The implication of the theory of the republic that Rousseau develops in the *Économie politique* and the *Contrat social* is that political virtue is the product of political conditions; it is a love that depends on the fulfilment, on the part of the republic, of the political obligations that it has toward the citizens. When the country denies the political love that it owes to each citizen, it engenders in turn, and deserves, the political hatred or the scorn of the citizens: the word *patrie* becomes *odieux ou ridicule*.[67]

While Montesquieu had defined political virtue as the spirit of democracy, Rousseau stresses that it must be the principle of any well-constituted state, thereby emancipating civic virtue from an exclusive connection with a form of government that he considers to be too perfect for men and above all for modern men. As is well known, by democracy Rousseau means the

---

[67] *Économie politique*, 256.

democracy of the ancients; that is, a form of government in which the citizens are both members of the sovereign body and rulers: they pass and execute the laws. The concentration of both powers in the same hands offers numerous opportunities for corruption. For a democratic executive not to become corrupt, the citizen must possess a truly exceptional degree of virtue: 'so perfect a government is not suited to men'.[68]

Rousseau repeats in various instances that the political virtue of the ancients cannot be an example for modern citizens but also admits, at least in the *Lettres écrites de la montagne*, the possibility of a more sober sort of political virtue within the reach of modern men. Ancient peoples, he writes, 'are no longer a model for the moderns'.[69] He was as aware as his critic Benjamin Constant that modern men are neither willing nor able to cultivate the 'liberty of the ancients'. They (referring to the citizens of Geneva) are tradesmen and craftsmen concerned with their particular interest, their work, their profit; they cannot and do not want to devote most of their time to politics. They are reluctant to involve themselves in public affairs because they find their activity and their family life more interesting and rewarding than participation in government, and because they know that politics is often dangerous and prejudicial to private interests. They cannot and do not want to be virtuous in the same way that was said of the Spartans, the Athenians, and the Romans, but they can be, and often are, civilized, peaceful, industrious, and law-abiding citizens. They know what their rights are and are prepared to discharge their duties toward their community. They possess, at least in the best cases, the appropriate qualities for civil life: modesty, decency, and gravity. They love the laws of their country and respect civic equality because they know that the laws and civic equality are the foundation of their personal security and prosperity. Liberty is for them 'un moyen d'acquérir sans obstacle et de posseder en sureté'.[70]

Having acknowleged that the virtue of the ancients cannot be expected from modern citizens, Rousseau also remarks that a

---

[68] *Du contrat social*, III. 4; Eng. trans. *Basic Political Writings*, 180.
[69] In *Œuvres complètes*, iii. 881.
[70] Ibid.

complete lack of commitment to the common liberty necessarily brings about the loss of that individual liberty to which they are so deeply attached. For modern citizens to serve the common good is onerous, but disregard for their civic duties brings about servitude: 'ceux qui ne peuvent supporter le travail n'ont qu'à chercher le repos dans la servitude'.[71]

The cause of the loss of liberty is not just a reluctance to participate in the legislative process or in government, but the habit of remaining silent and passive before the abuses perpetrated by the government or by powerful citizens. If the citizens do not speak up and resist when the government imposes unfair taxes, manipulates electoral procedures, violates property rights, or denies fair trial, they put at stake their personal and political liberty. As soon as an injustice is perpetrated, no matter against whom, they must raise their voice and react promptly. If they do not realize that the public interest is also their personal interest, and do not defend the common liberty when there is still time, they will not be able to stop tyranny from destroying the republic.[72] Tyranny affirms itself in an oblique manner. It does not attack the public good directly, but erodes and weakens the citizens' belief that the republic is a good that they possess and enjoy in common. Not to resist the attacks on common liberty that take place when the liberty of a single citizen is oppressed is as sensible as the behaviour of the man who refused to get out of bed while his home was on fire because he was 'only a tenant'![73]

Rousseau situates patriotism between indifference and fanaticism; between complete disregard for the common good and total commitment to it. He condemns citizens who remain cold and passive before the injustices that affect other citizens, without expecting them to be martyrs. Patriotism is a passion, a strength of the soul that makes men able to act. But it is not the blind fury of the fanatic or the total devotion of the hero.[74] The

---

[71] Ibid.
[72] 'Persuadez à tous que l'intérêt public n'est celui de personne et par cela seul la servitude est établie; car quand chacun sera sous le joug où sera la liberté commune?' Ibid. 893.
[73] *Lettre à d'Alembert*, ed. L. Brunel (Paris, 1922), 65.
[74] Ibid. 48.

virtue of heroes is sublime: it is a total devotion to the happiness of others for the sake of glory. When it is joined with the desire for glory in the heroic soul, love of country degenerates into an ardour that does not hesitate to resort to the most hideous means (*moyens odieux*).[75] The world, Rousseau remarks, has had too many heroes; it has never had enough citizens.

The virtuous citizen is not eager to be a full-time legislator or ruler. He is simply prepared and able to stand up against domestic and foreign enemies of the common liberty, if need be; if not, he is happy to mind his own business and indulge himself in private life and even in transgression. He can be severe with the enemies of the republic, but he need not be too severe with himself. Patriotism is incompatible with apathy and cowardice, but accommodates itself to situations with a merry spirit. Rousseau's descriptions of patriotism are often descriptions of feasts and dancings, celebrations of unity and concord. In the famous page of the *Lettre à d'Alembert* in which he describes one of the most intense moments of patriotic identification in his life, he recalls the admiration he felt for the order and the unity of the Regiment of Saint-Gervais; but those soldiers were not marching to war, they were dancing, and Jean-Jacques's excitement grew even higher when the soldiers broke ranks and mingled merrily with the citizens.[76]

On occasions, Rousseau advocated the priority of patriotism over the duties toward humanity and praises an exclusive patriotism. The Spartans, Rousseau writes, were ambitious, avaricious, and unfair to foreigners because to them they were 'just men'; that is, nothing. But the important thing, Rousseau remarks, is to be good to our fellow-citizens.[77] On other occasions he exhorts people always to obey the commands of conscience, the voice that speaks on behalf of humanity.[78] However, if a people is about to lose its liberty, or has lost its liberty, defence of national identity and national culture takes priority

---

[75] *Discours sur la vertu la plus nécessaire aux héros*, in *Œuvres complètes*, ii. 1271.

[76] *Lettre à d'Alembert*, 199–201.

[77] *Émile*, in *Œuvres complètes*, iv. 248–9.

[78] 'continuez de faire valoir, en toute occasion, les droits du Cœur et de la Nature au profit du devoir et de la vertu', *Discours sur l'inégalité*, 120.

over any other goal. The weaker the political institutions of a country, the more political liberty must rely upon the cultural, religious, or social unity of a people. If a country is surrounded by aggressive and despotic states, as was the case with Poland, the only way to defend its liberty or to hope to regain it, is to educate citizens who are patriots; that is, citizens who live only for their country and have the republic deeply rooted in their hearts. With poor political institutions, small population, and no military discipline, Poland can count only upon the virtue and the patriotism of its citizens. If they want to remain free, or to be free again one day, the Polish must become so deeply Polish as to resist any cultural contamination from their powerful Russian neighbours. Their cultural unity, their common memories have to provide them with the *force national* that they need to resist external threat. The most urgent goal for them is thus to become patriots *par inclination, par passion, par necessité.*

A divided or politically unfree people must above all else love and be proud of its own national culture.[79] They must be themselves, to be able one day to be free. In the *Government of Poland*, he writes:

I repeat: *national* institutions. That is what gives form to the genius, the character, the tastes, and the customs of a people; what causes it to be itself rather than some other people; what arouses in it that ardent love of the fatherland that is founded upon habits of mind impossible to uproot; what makes unbearably tedious for its citizens every moment spent away from home—even when they find themselves surrounded by delights that are denied them in their own country.[80]

Students of nationalism have stressed that this text is emblematic of the shifting from republican patriotism centred around the political concepts of the republic to nationalist language focusing

---

[79] 'Mais soit que vous adoptiez ou non ce régime, commençez toujours par donner aux Polonois une grande opinion d'eux-mêmes et de leur patrie'; *Considérations*, 961.

[80] 'Ce sont les institutions nationales qui forment le génie, le caractère, les gouts et les moeurs d'un peuple, qui le font etre lui et non pas un autre, qui lui inspirent cet ardent amour de la patrie fondé sur des habitudes impossibles à déraciner, qui le font mourir d'ennui chez les autres peuples, au sein des délices dont il est privé dans le sien.' Ibid. 960 (Eng. trans. 11).

on the concept of nation as a particular cultural or spiritual unity.[81] It seems to me that Rousseau's *Government of Poland* should be interpreted not as a dismissal of the value of the republic in favour of the value of the cultural or spiritual unity of a people, but as an exhortation to the Polish to keep alive in their hearts the republic that he believed was about to disappear as a political entity. Since they cannot be politically free, they must try to remain at least spiritually free; that is, to remain Polish. If they remain spiritually free, if they resist cultural assimilation, they may in the future regain their political liberty; but if they also lose their national identity, they are doomed to remain slaves for ever.

You cannot possibly keep them [the Russians] from swallowing you; see to it, at least, that they shall not be able to digest you. Whatever you do, your enemies will crush you a hundred times before you have given Poland what it needs in order to be capable of resisting them. There is one rampart, however, that they will always be readied for its defense, and that no army can possibly breach; and that is the virtue of its citizens, their patriotic zeal, in the distinctive cast that national institutions are capable of impressing upon their soul. See to it that every Pole is incapable of becoming a Russian, and I answer for it that that Russia will never subjugate Poland.[82]

The central exhortation of Rousseau's *Government of Poland* is that people must have a strong national character; but he also

---

[81] Cf. F. Chabod, *L'idea di nazione* (Bari, 1962), 128; see also R. Derathé, 'Patriotisme et nationalisme au XVIIIᵉ siècle', *Annales de philosophie politique*, 8 (1969), 78.

[82] 'Vous ne sauriez empêcher qu'ils [the Russians] ne vous engloutissent, faites au moins qu'ils ne puissent vous digerer. De quelque façon qu'on s'y prenne, avant qu'on ait donné à la Pologne tout ce qui lui manque pour être en état de resister à ses ennemis, elle en sera cent fois accablée. La vertu de ses Citoyens, leur zéle patriotique, la forme particulière que des institutions nationales peuvent donner à leur ames, voilà le seul rempart toujours prêt à la défendre, et qu'aucune armée ne sauroit forcer. Si vous faites en sorte qu'un Polonois ne puisse jamais devenir un Russe, je vous réponds que la Russie ne subjuguera pas la Pologne.' *Considérations*, 959–60 (Eng. trans. 11); see also Rousseau's defence of national customs: 'Il faut maintenir, rétablir ces anciens usages, et en introduire de convenables qui soient propres aux Polonois. Ces usages, fussent-ils indiférens, fussent-ils mauvais même a certains égards, pourvû qu'ils ne le soient pas essentiellement, auront toujours l'avantage d'affectionner les Polonois a leur pays et de leur donner une répugnance naturelle à se mêler avec l'étranger;' ibid. 962.

knows that national character by itself can only make a people one, not free. To be really free a people needs a nation and a republic; it needs a particular culture based upon shared memories, ceremonies, language, customs, but it also needs political liberty. To be good citizens they have to be Polish, but if they are just Polish, they are not yet free, and liberty, rather than national identity is for Rousseau the necessary precondition for living as human beings.

National cultures are a value to be preserved against the tendency to absorb them in a uniformly European or cosmopolitan way of life:

Say what you like, there is no such thing nowadays as Frenchmen, Germans, Spaniards, or even Englishmen—only Europeans. All have the same tastes, the same passions, the same customs, and for good reason: Not one of them has ever been formed *nationally*, by distinctive legislation.[83]

We surely must be and remain attached to our country: be and remain French, German, Spanish, English; but if we are just French, German, Spanish, English without being citizens, we are nothing.[84] He urges us to choose to be citizens of a particular country, not citizens of the world, and to be a citizen of a particular country implies having a national culture, but it is more than that.

There is a subtle and yet important intellectual distance that separates Rousseau from later nationalist thinkers. For them, as we shall see, what really matters for human fulfilment is not just to be Polish, or German, or French. For Rousseau one can live as a human being in the fullest sense only as a citizen of a free republic. For the founders of nationalism the distinctive feature

[83] 'Il n'y a plus aujourd'hui de François, d'Allemands, d'Espagnols, d'Anglois même, quoiqu'on en dise; il n'y a que des Européens. Tous on les mêmes gouts, les mêmes passions, les mêmes mœurs, parce que aucun n'a reçu de forme nationale par une institution particulière.' Ibid. 960 (Eng. trans. 11).

[84] 'Celui qui dans l'ordre civil veut conserver la primauté des sentimens de la nature, ne sait ce qu'il veut. Toujours en contradiction avec lui-même, toujours flotant entre ses penchans et ses devoirs il ne sera jamais ni homme ni citoyen; il ne sera bon ni pour lui ni pour les autres. Ce sera un de ces hommes de nos jours; un François, un Anglois, un Bourgeois; ce ne sera rien.' *Émile*, 249–50.

of the fatherland is the spiritual unity based on language; for Rousseau only a republic is a true *patrie*. The birth of the language of nationalism involved a change in the meaning of the concept of fatherland, which gradually became a non-political concept no longer centred on political and civil liberty, but on the cultural and spiritual unity of a people. Rousseau understood the crucial importance of the cultural and spiritual unity of a people, but he continued to speak of *patrie* as an old republican, not as a nationalist.

4

The Birth of the Language of Nationalism

BY the end of the eighteenth century, after the French Revolution, the language of republican patriotism had established itself as a language of liberty and as a major intellectual tradition. "Twere an abuse of words to call him a *patriot*', wrote John Cartwright in 1782, 'who held not sacred as the life of his parents, those rights of his country *without which it cannot be free.*'[1]

The words of Cartwright reveal that eighteenth-century language of patriotism was still deeply indebted to the teaching of the ancients. Love of country was understood as a benevolent love for the common liberty of our own people: we want to see them living in freedom, and to live in freedom with them, because we hold them dear. Theorists of patriotism, however, did not limit themselves to merely restating the classical doctrine. Rather, they integrated the tradition of republican patriotism with the principle of the modern theory of natural law. The combination did not alter the genuine sense of republican patriotism: since love of country is, as the Latin authors had explained, *caritas civium* or *pietas reipublicae* (charity towards our fellow-citizen or respect for the republic) it must respect the principles of justice set by right reason. In fact, the addition of the principles of natural law enriched the moral value of the language of patriotism since it defined the boundaries that justice imposes on compassion and on commitment to the common liberty.

[1] *Give us our Rights! Or, A Letter to the present electors of Middlesex and the Metropolis* (London, n.d. [1782]), 9.

An important example of a theory of love of country within the limits of natural law is Richard Price's *Discourse on the Love of Our Country* delivered on 4 November 1789 to the Society for Commemorating the Revolution in Great Britain. Love of our country, says Price, 'is certainly a noble passion'. It can, however, be mistaken and misled by prejudices. It is therefore necessary to clarify what is meant by 'country', and what sort of love the love of our country is.

By our country is meant, in this case, not the soil, or the spot of earth on which we happen to be born; not the forests and fields, but that community of which we are members; or that body of companions and friends and kindred who are associated with us under the same constitution of government, protected by the same laws, and bound together by the same civil polity.[2]

A political community composed of equal citizens united by bonds of friendship and companionship demands a love based upon justice, not a love sustained by beliefs in the superiority of our country or animated by partiality in our methods of of judging and evaluating. We are disposed to overvalue 'our friends, our country, and in short, every thing related to us'. But patriotism does not require that. The patriot can and must remain a wise man who

will study to think of all things as they are, and not to suffer any partial affections to blind his understanding. In other families there may be as much worth as in our own. In other circles of friends there may be as much wisdom; and in other countries as much of all that deserves esteem; but notwithstanding this, our obligation to love our own families, friends and country, and to seek, in the first place, their good, will remain the same.[3]

Love of country is neither an attachment to a good that we are not entitled to scrutinize in all its parts because if we did so we would find it unworthy, nor is it an attachment to a good that we value more than any other of the same sort because it belongs to us exclusively. It simply asks us to set aside comparisons between our country and others and to remain sensitive to

---

[2] (London, 1790), 6–7.   [3] Ibid. 8.

both the good aspects of other countries and the faults of our own.

To remain a noble virtue, love of our country must remain immune not only to false beliefs, but also to the passions of ambition and 'spirit of rivalship' that are responsible for the degeneration of love of country into love of domination.

> What has the love of their country hitherto been among mankind? What has it been but a love of domination; a desire of conquest, and a thirst for grandeur and glory, by extending territory, and enslaving surrounding countries? What has it been but a blind and narrow principle, producing in every country a contempt of other countries, and forming men into combinations and factions against their common rights and liberties?[4]

Price equates degenerate patriotism with selfishness. The same inclination that compels individuals to encroach on one another's rights and to pursue one's own advancement to the degradation of others compels countries to violate other countries' rights and to dominate them. The celebrated patriotism of the ancients was in fact a love of country corrupted by pride, partiality, and a desire for domination:

> What was the love of their country among the Jews, but a wretched partiality to themselves, and a proud contempt of all other nations? What was the love of their country among the old Romans? We have heard much of it; but I cannot hesitate in saying that, however great it appeared in some of its exertions, it was, in general, no better than a principle holding together a band of robbers in their attempts to crush all liberty but their own.[5]

Love of country is a blend of passions, and different combinations seem to be possible. It can be made up of love of liberty, respect for common rights, benevolence toward humanity, and courage; it can also turn into a combination of pride, ambition, self-centredness, and partiality. Only reason can 'correct and purify this passion [of love of our country]' and make it a just and rational principle of action'; but reason cannot be expected to carry purification of love of country as far as absorbing and

---

[4] Ibid. 8–9.   [5] Ibid. 9.

transforming it into love of humanity. Reason must impose boundaries on passions, but must in turn respect the boundaries that nature and God's wisdom impose on her:

I must desire you to recollect that we are so constituted that our affections are more drawn to some among mankind than to others, in proportion to their degrees of nearness to us, and our power of being useful to them. It is obvious, that this is a circumstance in the constitution of our natures which proves the wisdom and goodness of our Maker; for had our affections been determined alike to all our fellow-creatures, human life would have been a scene of embarrassment and distraction.[6]

A purified love of country is no less ardent than a love contaminated by ambition, selfishness, and pride: it is simply not exclusive. What changes is the type of love, not the intensity. Purified, love of country remains a powerful passion which allows us to devote our best energies to the common good and at the same time to 'consider ourselves as citizens of the world, and take care to maintain a just regard to the rights of other countries'. Because of its composite nature patriotism is open to alchemy. One possible product of the alchemy might be an intense love of country joined with a profound benevolence toward humanity: this would indeed be a rare and beautiful product. It certainly requires a lot of work on the part of reason; but the enterprise is surely a worthy one.

Love of country means not only to give ourselves to her, but also to give her the best that human life can offer; that is, truth, virtue, and liberty. If we really love our country and our fellow-citizens, we must want them to be able to live as free human beings. For this to be possible, they must know true and just ideas on civil government; they must know that the purpose of government is to protect them from injury and to defend their rights. By telling our fellow-citizens the truth we give them a powerful weapon to resist tyranny. The distinctive marks of a patriot are not hatred, intolerance, persecution, and ignorance, but commitment to truth.

The inseparable companion of truth and knowledge must be virtue since virtue without knowledge makes blind enthusiasts,

---

[6] Ibid. 12.

and knowledge without virtue makes devils.[7] The patriot must cultivate truth and virtue and make liberty the primary object of his zeal. Commitment to liberty means that he has the duty to be vigilant against the government's tendency to despotism; whenever vigilance is withdrawn, remarks Price, restating the classical republican argument, the people are in danger 'of being enslaved, and their *servants* will soon become their *masters*';[8] in acting like good patriots we are therefore promoting 'in the best manner our own private interest, as well as the interest of our country'.[9] It also means that the patriot must be ready to go to war to defend his country against external aggression. Only defensive wars are, however, 'just wars'; offensive wars are on the contrary 'wicked and detestable'. Love of country may require the patriot to give his life to defend his country's liberty, but never to give his life to conquer or dominate other countries.

In his *Discourse* Price spoke like a republican; but he also spoke as a Christian. He readily acknowledges that Christ taught love of God, and next, love of all mankind, not love of country. By his own example, however, Christ showed that love of country can be included among our duties. From the Gospels, it appears that Christ possessed a tender and 'particular' affection for his country, even though his country was a very wicked one. In one of his last journeys to Jerusalem, reads Luke 19: 42, Christ wept over Jerusalem and said: 'Oh! that thou hadst known (even thou, at least in this thy day) the things that belong to thy peace.' Jerusalem rejected his love, and yet Christ responded with a lamentation, not with an invective. He uttered words of sorrow, not of hatred. The evil that Jerusalem did to him and the prophets did not extinguish his compassion. 'Jerusalem, Jerusalem, thou that killest the prophets, and stonest them who are sent to thee, how often would I have gathered thy children together, as a hen gathereth her brood under her wings, but ye would not' (Luke 13: 34).[10]

Fear easily makes love of country blind. When external aggression and invasion seem imminent, there is little room for distinctions nor to maintain a critical distance. And yet in 1803–4

---

[7] Ibid. 17.   [8] Ibid. 26.   [9] Ibid. 39.   [10] Ibid. 38.

in England, while fear of Napoleon's invasion pervaded the country, patriots did not abandon the language of patriotism of liberty. They called on their fellows to volunteer to defend their country, but also reminded them that patriotism is in the first place commitment to political and civil liberty protected by equal laws, to freedom of opinion, to an impartial administration of justice, and to a decent standard of living.

A text which better expounds the meaning of patriotism as commitment to the ideal of commonwealth is William Frend's essay *Patriotism; or the Love of our Country*, issued in 1804 in the aftermath of Napoleon's threatened invasion of Britain. Patriotism, he stresses, is a passion of generous and dignified souls induced by nature and sustained by habits of liberty. He then elaborates on Montesquieu and Rousseau's idea that a *patrie* cannot exist under despotic regimes by mentioning the example of the Hindus, who cannot regard the soil they inhabit—which belongs to their masters by right of conquest—as their country. Divided into a variety of castes, the Hindus have no common bonds, and therefore 'they have no country'. And without the sentiment of belonging to a country they cannot be expected to display the energies of patriotism.[11]

Unlike God's love, which proceeds from the whole to the parts, man's love proceeds from the parts to the whole.

> As the small pebble stirs the peaceful lake;
> The centre mov'd, a circle strait succeeds,
> Another still, and still another spreads;
> Friend, parent, neighbour, first it will embrace;
> His country next, and next all human race;
> Wide and more wide, the o'erflowings of the mind
> Take every creature in, of every kind,
> Earth smiles around, with boundless bounty blest,
> And heaven beholds its image in his breast.[12]

Love's expansive drive may, however, stop at any stage. If parents are cruel, cold, and partial, the child may be obedient, but he will not love them. The same holds true with love of country: to be beloved the country must be worthy of love. The lover

[11] (London, 1804), 110.   [12] Ibid. 116.

demands explanations, and his demands are meant to benefit the country itself and are more powerful than the requests for justification of an indifferent observer or a neutral enquirer.

We are all sensible of the injustice done by an individual to a community, and its power secures obedience to its laws by severity of punishment. The injustice of a community towards an individual will pass unnoticed: yet the duty is reciprocal, and though the community cannot be punished for its acts, nature does not suffer its laws to be broken with impunity: the moral character of each individual in the community suffers in the degree, in which he participates in its guilt; and, when the community is completely infected, the effects are seen in its decay and destruction.[13]

The country exists before the individual and shall exist after his death; she must embrace the individual with her love, if she wants the individual's love: 'the country must love the individual, or the individual will not love the country'.[14] She must be the well-spring of love. Love of country seems to work like the Christian *amor Dei*: the genitive case (love *of* God) does not indicate the object of love but the possessor of love. Love of God is the love that God generates in men's hearts through his love for them; through a love which, as Frend wrote, goes from the whole to the parts and generates a love that expands in the opposite direction from the parts to the whole. Likewise, the country can arouse the individual's love through her love. To have patriots is, for the country, a great blessing since her survival, unlike God's, depends on the citizens' patriotism. She must work to make it possible.

A country can generate patriotism through politics. If its laws, institutions, and customs are informed by the ideal of the republic, citizens will love their country. To act as a republic the country must first of all respect the principle of the equality of the law. Whatever their social status all citizens must be equal before the law. Preferential treatment and exceptions produce enmity and dissentions between citizens which weakens their commitment to the common welfare. The only privileges and distinctions that are beneficial to patriotism are, as republican

[13] Ibid. 117–18.   [14] Ibid. 128.

political thinkers have stressed for centuries, those that are founded on virtue.[15] In addition to being equal, laws must also be just: 'laws must be framed for the advantage of the people and suited to their situation'. Otherwise, no matter how equal they are, they create aversion and abhorrence toward the country. Equally important is protection of property, both 'personal and mental', and of the two, 'property of the mind is more important than that of the body':

If mental exertions are checked by goverment, if it declares war against every individual, who presumes to think on religious and political subjects differently from itself, it creates immediately a distinction between its subjects, which, according to the degree of persecution in the government, must alienate the minds of one party, without in the least increasing the patriotism of the other.[16]

In addition to good laws and good institutions, patriotism needs a community that rewards noble and generous minds and despises the luxury, sensuality, superstition, and selfishness that are normally to be found in wealthy men. The rich man refers everything to himself. He is incapable of extending his love beyond his self to encompass his fellows and his country, as patriotism requires. The greatest mistake that a country can make is to permit wealth to confer privileges. There is nothing wrong with being wealthy; but a country that honours and rewards wealth while treating poverty with scorn and contempt cannot expect to be loved: the wealthy do not love her because they are ignoble and selfish; the poor do not because they feel despised and neglected.[17]

For Frend, true patriotism may be found in the lower, rather than the higher, classes of society. The first duty of a country toward its lower classes is, in addition to treating them justly in courts, to be sure that they live decently. Patriotism demands the correction of social injustices caused by the avarice of the wealthy.

Many of the mansions of human beings in a great metropolis are filled with filth and stench: the light of heaven can scarcely penetrate into

[15] Ibid. 144–5.   [16] Ibid. 149–50.   [17] Ibid. 138–9.

their cells: objects of wretchedness and misery surround the infant from his birth. Is patriotism to be generated in spots like these?[18]

It also demands that people have a share in the government, beginning with elections, which ought to be more frequent and the number of voters enlarged. Popular participation increases turbulence, but it also sustains patriotism. Peace that comes from the exclusion of people from political rights is like the torpor of despotism; it cannot be preferred to the turbulence that comes from an active citizenship. Patriotism demands participation in public life, since individuals who have a share in the government of their country

are active, industrious, full of resources, and, unless peculiar circumstances have occurred to destroy the effects of their patriotism, invincible: where they have no share in the government, patriotism is unknown; a dull inert mass vegetates on the soil; the being is born and dies incapable of exercising the best energies of the mind, and the best feelings of his heart.[19]

Love of country, however, has its own boundaries as defined by our obligations to humanity and God. It may ask us to defend our country when attacked by an enemy; it cannot command us to join her in committing wrongs against 'the rest of mankind'. England's wars in India and slave-trading cannot be justified under the name of patriotism. There are always higher obligations to fulfil; if our country does not fulfil then, our love 'must cease'. One example is the story of the inhabitants of Canaan, the land that God had promised the Israelites. The right of the Israelites to occupy their country could not be disputed, as it was granted by 'him who divides the portion of the earth according to his own pleasure'; yet love of country roused them to resist the invader. They choose to ignore God's will and were therefore punished with total destruction. The same fate occurred to the Israelites. Vice and superstition had rendered the inhabitants of the kingdom of Judah odious to the sight of God and 'unfit to inhabit the land'. Their destruction was unavoidable and Jeremiah urged them to comply with God's will. In this

18 Ibid. 156.   19 Ibid. 159.

case the monarchs who incited the people to resist were impious, whereas Jeremiah 'was the true and only patriot'.[20] Had Jeremiah simply exhorted his people to obey God's will, he would have deserved to be called pious, but not a true patriot. He was a patriot, according to Frend, because he spoke to alleviate his people's distress and even more so because he accepted God's harsh but fair verdict: 'no love could be entertained for so odious and detestable a people'. Separation from our own people is painful as Jeremiah's elegies powerfully show; however, there are instances in which it must be done, not just for our sake but for our country's sake. To be loved, the country has to be worthy of love: imperialist England conquering for greed and the corrupt Israelites were not; they did not deserve the patriot's love.

Instead, when the individual has a country, and when the country is 'the object of esteem', no effort 'is to be left untried, no sacrifice is to be thought too great for the security or the deliverance of the country'.[21] True love of country does not go against Christ's teaching: 'When I hear him constantly inculcating the love of our neighbour, and extending that love to our enemies, I cannot persuade myself that one branch of the love of our neighbour was intended by him to be excluded, and that by becoming his disciple we were to throw off all regard for our country.'[22] Love of God compels us to restrain love of country, but it does not prohibit or disavow it. In its pure form, love of country is a branch of that love 'which is the noblest ornament of man' because it is a generous love of the commonwealth.[23] And commonwealth means constitution, equal rights, impartial justice, reward for honest industry, respect and protection for the poor. England must be loved, Frend stresses in his address to the volunteers, because liberty—the liberty that our forefathers fought for—makes her unique.

Yes! Volunteers of Britain! The soil which ye protect has claims upon your valour, which no other can boast. Where does the constitution lay down with a more equal hand the rights of every individual? Where is justice with fewer exceptions more impartially administered? Where are the efforts of honest industry more certain of their reward? Where is the poor man held in more respect, and the rich man less

[20] Ibid. 164.   [21] Ibid. 167.   [22] Ibid. 175.   [23] Ibid. 208.

induced to abuse his power, and to treat his inferiors with contempt? Liberty has been made the theme of the poets in various countries; but, in this, it has been practically enjoyed: here did our ancesters lay the basis of a true commonwealth.[24]

English radicals were not the only ones who used the language of republican patriotism to sustain their cause. Spanish patriots fighting against Napoleon's invasion also employed that language to forge a concept of *patria* based on the principles of liberty and good government. *Patria*—we read in an article of the period of the War of *Spanish* Independence, does not mean the place of birth of an individual or a group, as the conventional view holds, but the state of the society to which they belong and whose laws protect their liberty and assure their happiness, as the ancients rightly maintained. *Patria* comes from *pater*, and evokes family images of love, harmony, and happiness. The fundamental distinction is again between *patrie* and *pays*: a *pays* is any place or any community in which we are born or in which we live, *patria* is liberty and good government alone: 'where there were no laws oriented toward the interest of everyone, where there was no paternal government attentive to the common benefit . . . there there was without doubt a country [*pays*], a people, a group of men, but there was no *patrie*.'[25]

The idioms of republican patriotism were used to separate love of country from monarchical loyalty and heroic valour. True patriotism, we read in another article, is a greatness of soul, a moral strength that enables men to commit themselves to the pursuit of great things: 'You want to be taken for good patriots? Know how to be great! Do not shelter in your hearts any other ambition, any other preference than the desire to serve your country! Is not the joy of founding a *patrie* the highest reward upon which a generous heart can count?'[26] And *patrie* means again, in words typical of Rousseau, liberty and citizenship:

[24] Ibid. 216–17.

[25] 'où il n'y avait pas des lois tournées vers l'intérêt de tous, où il n'y avait pas de gouvernement paternel attentif au bénéfice commun . . . là il y avait sans doute un pays, des gens, un groupement d'hommes; mais il n'y avait pas de Patrie'. P. Vilar, 'Patrie et nation dans le vocabulaire de la guerre d'Indépendance espagnole', in *Annales historiques de la Révolution Française*, 43 (1971), 506.

[26] 'Vous voulez être tenus pour bons patriotes? Sachez etre grands! N'abritez

He would be grossly mistaken who, just by residing in his place of birth and among those things to which he addressed his first glances and his first utterings would think himself residing in his *patrie*... There is no *patrie*, according to the rigours of public law, where there are no citizens, and the latter exist solely where there is civil liberty. There can be no civil liberty without a political constitution, and where citizens do not intervene in the elaboration of laws and where they are not equal before these laws. *Patrie* is not that particular village, that province, or that state in which we were born; it is that society, that nation, where, sheltered under just, moderate and agreed-upon laws, we have enjoyed the pleasures of life, the fruit of our labour, the benefits of our industry, and the unalterable possession of our indeafisible rights.[27]

Understood in this way, patriotism is clearly separated from monarchical loyalty. As another perceptive patriot remarked in the same period, the word *patria* does not belong to the language of Spanish monarchs: they speak of 'my crown', 'my states', or 'my vassals'. The word *patria* regained currency and became meaningful when the Spanish people, confronted with the calamity of Napoleon's invasion, stood up and found the energy to commit themselves to a great cause: 'The word *patrie*, so magnificent and full of hope in this moment of calamity, this *patrie* which in political life was not just an idle word, we now see achieved in our own hearts.'[28]

Elsewhere in Europe, however, the language of patriotism

dans vos cœurs d'autre ambition, d'autre préférence que le désir de servire votre pays! La joie de fonder une Patrie n'est-elle pas la plus grande récompense sur laquelle puisse compter un cœur généreux?' Ibid. 507.

[27] 'Il se tromperait grossièrement celui qui, du seul fait de résider sur le lieu de sa naissance et parmi les objets auxquels il a adressé ses premiéres regards, ses premiers balbutiements, croirait résider dans sa *patrie*... Il n'y a pas de *patrie*, dans l'acception du droit public, là où il n'y a pas de citoyens, et ceux-ci n'existent que là où il y a liberté civile. Il ne peut y avoir liberté civile sans constitution politique, ni citoyens qui n'interviendraient pas dans la confection des lois et ne seraient pas égaux devant celles-ci... *Patrie*, ce n'est pas ce village précis, cette province, cet état qui nous ont vus naître; c'est cette société, cette nation, où à l'abri de lois justes, modérées et acceptées, nous avons joui des plaisirs de la vie, du fruit de nos sueurs, du bénéfice de notre industrie et de l'inaltérable possession de nos droits imprescriptibles.' Ibid. 508.

[28] 'Le mot *patrie* si magnifique et plein d'espérance en ce moment de calamités, cette patrie qui dans la vie politique n'était qu'un vain nom, voici que nous la voyons réalisée dans nos cœurs.' Ibid. 509.

derived from the republican tradition and the French Revolution proved inadequate as a means of helping peoples to find their way to liberty. The purely political ideal of *patrie* sounded too abstract; appeals to rebel for love of liberty left too many people cold or just lukewarm. A different idea of country had to be devised; a different love was needed.

The most illuminating example of the new line of criticism of republican patriotism is Vincenzo Cuoco's *Saggio storico sulla rivoluzione napoletana del 1799* (*Historical Essay on the Neapolitan Revolution of 1799*) and other texts of Neapolitan patriots. Though he shared and admired the patriots' commitment to liberty, Cuoco elegantly but firmly denounced their inadequate political wisdom due in part to their poor knowledge and poor understanding of the customs, history, and traditions of the Neapolitan people. The words 'republic' and *patria* sounded in their mouths unsincere.

Among our patriots (if we may use an expression that applies to all revolutionaries but does not offend the good ones) many had the republic on their lips, many had it on their minds, but few had it in their hearts. For many the revolution was a fashionable affair, and they were republicans only because the French were; some were republicans through want of purpose, other through irreligion, as if you needed a government patent to get rid of superstition; some confused liberty with licence, and believed that revolution could buy them the right to insult state activity with impunity; for many, finally, the revolution was a calculated undertaking.[29]

They spoke of liberty, but the people did not understand what they meant. And the patriots could not make themselves understood because they were culturally remote from the people. Overly abstract ideas of liberty destroy it. Liberty, remarks Cuoco,

is a good because it produces other good things, such as security, a comfortable existence, population, tax moderation, the growth of industry, and many tangible benefits; and the people, because they love such benefits, come then to love liberty. A man, who, without procuring such rewards, might come to command the love of liberty,

---

[29] *Saggio storico*, ed. Fausto Nicolini (Bari, 1929).

would resemble Alcibiades of Marmontel, who wanted to be loved 'for himself'.[30]

Neapolitans wished for fairer taxation, the end of quarrels and dissension among the nobility, and redistribution of the land belonging to the ecclesiastic orders and the king. During the revolution, wherever they had the chance to govern themselves without the intrusion of the 'patriots' or of the French, they passed laws designed to obtain these goals. And wherever they had won liberty for themselves, they defended it with the greatest heroism.[31]

The patriots' rhetoric and policy were inspired by ideals that were in fact dear only to a minority. 'You are free, at last!', they proclaimed to the people. But the people, remarks Cuoco, did not yet know what liberty was: it is a sentiment, not an idea; it must be experienced in practice, not demonstrated with words. ' "Your Claudius fled, Messalina trembles!" Should the Neapolitans have studied Roman history to understand their happiness? "Man regains all his rights!" Which rights? "You will have a free and just government grounded on the principles of equality; public offices shall no longer be the privilege of nobles and rich, but the reward for virtue!" ' These were powerful motives indeed for a people who were not concerned at all with virtue and talents but only wished to be well governed.

In Cuoco's analysis, liberty demands cultural unity. One of the main causes of the weakness of the Neapolitan revolution was the fact that the patriots' and the people's culture were different. They had, Cuoco remarks, different ideas, different customs, and even different languages. Patriots were, culturally, French or English; the people they called on to fight for the republic were culturally Neapolitans. The patriots' admiration for foreign culture was, in the earliest part of the republic, 'the greatest obstacle to the establishment of liberty' because the people could not understand their culture and despised them. Foreign culture caused division and delayed the civil and political education of the whole people. To serve the country well, one must love it; but love of country in the classical republican

---

[30] Ibid. 102–3.   [31] Ibid. 103.

sense of love of liberty must be sustained by a sense of self-respect: respect for one's own culture and history. That love of country which comes from public education and generates national pride (*orgoglio nazionale*) gave the French the strength to carry out their revolution successfully; the lack of cultural unity and national pride weakened the Neapolitans' love of liberty and doomed their revolution to failure.

Cuoco's *Essay* criticizes republican political patriotism for its cultural inadequacy which was in turn a major factor of political weakness. The patriot's commitment to political liberty had to be integrated with and completed by attachment to his own national culture. To be republican is not enough; one must be a Neapolitan republican. One can never be of service to the country (*giovare alla patria*) if one does not love it; 'and one can never love the country if one does not value the nation'; that is, the particular culture of a people.[32] For him *patria* and *nazione* indicate a republican political constitution and the culture of a people respectively. The patriots loved the *patria*, in the sense of republic, but held the nation—the culture, the way of life, and the customs of the Neapolitans—in contempt, or were at least distanced from it.[33] Their cultural distance made their love of the republic incomplete and politically ineffective.

The *patria* is an object of love; the nation an object of esteem and pride. However, to esteem one's own nation is, as Cuoco puts it, a necessary condition for loving one's country. He means that love of country must be political *and* cultural; that commitment to political liberty cannot be a commitment to impersonal political liberty, but to the political liberty of that particular people. It is not a mere pragmatic matter; what is at stake is not

[32] 'Le disgrazie de' popoli sono spesso le più evidenti dimostrazioni delle piú utili verità. Non si può mai giovare alla patria se non si ama, e non si può mai amare la patria se non si stima la nazione. Non può mai esser libero quel popolo in cui la parte che per la superioritá della sua ragione è destinata dalla natura a governarlo, sia coll'autorità sia cogli esempi, ha venduta la sua opinione ad una nazione straniera: tutta la nazione ha perduta allora la metà della sua indipendenza.' Ibid. 91.

[33] ' "Patriota". Che è mai un "patriota"? Questo nome dovrebbe indicare un uomo che ama la patria. Nel decennio scorso esso era sinonimo di "repubblicano"; ben inteso però che non tutti i repubblicani eran "patrioti",' ibid. 90 n. 1.

just the poor functioning of a political action sustained by a love of *patria* that is not corroborated by esteem of the nation's culture; it is a matter of the meaning and content of political liberty. The liberty that has to be sought and fought for has to be the liberty which that particular people loves and wants because it is close and congenial to its culture.

For Cuoco, *patria* (country) and *nazione* (nation) are distinct concepts. The former still means the republic, the latter the common culture of the people. They command different kinds of attachment: to the *patria* goes our love, while to the nation goes, or ought to go, our esteem and respect. Love is a passion of unity and sharing; we love the republic that we share with our fellow-citizens; we may become indifferent to it or even hate it, if she rejects our love. Esteem, respect, and pride are feelings based upon a comparison; we esteem and respect something or somebody if we value it or him or her at least as much as ourselves. Cuoco was in fact reproaching the patriots because they were looking at the culture of the Neapolitans as less valuable or worthy than French or English culture. The lesson he wanted his fellow Neapolitans and Italians to learn, was that the fight for the republic and liberty could not be led by patriots who were remote from the culture of the people they wanted to free from despotism.

The importance of connecting politics and culture, *patria* and nation, was stressed also by other Neapolitan patriots who had taken an active role in the Revolution of 1799. Francesco Lomonaco, for instance, remarked that to have a *patria* the Italians must have first a national spirit (*spirito di nazionalità*) and a political government.[34] Surely he was right, in the sense that the first step—the strengthening of the national spirit—cannot be avoided; but it is not certain that once we have made it we shall be able to make the others. Patriots' political commitment must rest upon and be at one with attachment to the culture of the people, but esteem and attachment to the culture of the

---

[34] 'Realizzandosi questa idea, gl'italiani, avendo nazione, acquisteranno spirito di nazionalitá; avendo governo, diverranno politici e guerrieri; avendo patria, godranno della libertà e di tutt'i beni che ne derivano.' F. Lomonaco 'Patriota Napoletano', *Rapporto al cittadino Carnot*; quoted ibid. 327.

nation does not necessarily evolve toward political liberty. The evolution has to be made to happen through political action and rhetoric, and the right political action and the right rhetoric have to be found for each individual case. No recipe is valid for all times and places.

More radical criticism of the language of republican patriotism came in the same period from Germany. Whereas Cuoco had criticized the patriots' exclusive attachment to the political values of liberty and their disregard for national culture, German theorists rejected the priority of those very values in favour of the value of the spiritual and cultural unity of the nation. They reacted against the language of the Enlightenment in general and the cosmopolitanism that had spread among eighteenth-century German intellectuals. As scholars have stressed, German intellectuals in the age of the Enlightenment were either cosmopolitan, or provincial patriots.[35] The language of patriotism, particularly republican patriotism, was for them of little use and appeal. Christoph Martin Wieland, to quote an obvious example, proudly presented himself in his *Kosmopolitische Addresse* as an insignificant isolated cosmopolitan (*Weltbürger*).[36] In a letter of 1758, Lessing powerfully expressed his coldness toward patriotism: 'Perhaps the patriot in me has not been smothered entirely, although the honour of being a zealous patriot is to me the last mode of thinking which I should covet; especially of a patriotism which would teach me to forget that I must be a citizen of the world.'[37] In another letter of the same year he described love of fatherland as a 'heroic weakness with which I gladly dispense'.[38] Goethe, a few years later, had spoken of the fatherland in a manner reminiscent of Voltaire's article in the

[35] R. R. Ergang, *Herder and the Foundations of German Nationalism* (New York, 1931), 30.

[36] 'Ich bin zwar nur ein einzelner unbedeutender Weltbürger, und spiele, Dank sein den Göttern'; *Kosmopolitische Addresse an die französische National-versammlung*, in *Gesammelte Schriften*, ed. W. Kurrelmeyer (Berlin, 1987), x. 316; see also *Ueber deutschen Patriotismus*, ibid. 586–95.

[37] Gottlob Ephraim Lessing to Gleim, 16 Dec. 1758, in *Sämmtliche Schriften*, ed. W. von Maltzahn (Leipzig, 1857), xii. 150.

[38] 'Ich habe überhaupt von der Liebe des Vaterlandes ... keinen Begriff, und sie scheint mir aufs höchte eine heroische Schwachheit, die ich recht gern entbehre.' Lessing to Gleim, 14 Feb. 1759, ibid. 152.

Dictionnaire philosophique: the fatherland is neither the republic nor the place where we are born, but, rather, any place in the world where we can live securely with our possessions, and find a field and a house that covers us.[39]

The few who declared themselves patriots meant by patriotism attachment to the German Empire over local loyalty. The name patriot, wrote Karl Möser, the most vociferous German patriot of his time, designates the 'good, honorable, law-conforming thinking German' and invokes the resurrection of 'the great common interest of freedom' and devotion to the common good against petty local despots who were responsible for the lamentable political conditions of Germany. By 'liberty' he meant the liberty of the Empire as a political body and by 'common good' the common good of subjects of the Emperor. His patriotism is immune from fascination with the liberty of the ancient republics or the liberal institutions of modern England. A German patriot, he says, must never forget that he is 'a German, and not a Greek, a Roman or a Briton'.[40] Greece, Rome, and England were the symbols of liberty; by saying that a German patriot must not forget that he is above all else a German, he meant that the cultural and ethnic identity as a German had priority over political and civil liberty.

A similar disjunction between patriotism and political liberty can also be found in Justus Möser. Patriotism means for him a vindication of German national character against French despotism (in the sense of cultural hegemony). He invokes liberty, but his liberty has nothing in common with the liberty of the republicans. His ideal polity is not the ancient republic, but medieval feudal society based upon rural serfdom, which he praises as a remarkable institution. French despotism, against which he directed his patriotic arrows, had imposed rational legal codes and bureaucratic regulations over local customs and privileges, and, more importantly, had championed civil and political equality, which he regards as a modern degeneration of the good old *Ständestaat*. The liberty of republicans and liberals was for him the liberty of the individual conceived as an abstract entity

---

[39] *Sämmtliche Werke*, xxxvi. 67; quoted by Ergang, *Herder*, 32.

[40] *Beherzigungen* (Frankfurt, 1761), 268; Eng. trans. in Ergang, *Herder*, 45–6.

separate from his membership in a particular guild or *Stände*; that is, as he puts it, an empty liberty without honour, dignity, or responsibility.[41] His patriotic liberty was instead the liberty to loyally discharge the duties that social and professional status impose; a liberty, he remarks, enriched by the sense of honour and responsibility that is absent from the liberty of the liberals. Patriotism meant for him German liberty, that is a liberty grounded upon German law against Roman law; the liberty of German medieval *Ständestaat* against civil and political equality. It was neither the liberty of man, nor the liberty of the citizen, but the liberty of the member of a *Stände*, particularly the liberty of the landowner and the peasant-proprietor. He justified serfdom with the argument that political community is not a commonwealth, but an association similar to a mercantile company in which each member holds a share. The fact that a serf was not a man without a share, but a share himself and therefore not a man, did not represent a problem for his patriotism because fatherland did not mean for him a community of individuals with equal political and civil rights, but a unity of corporate bodies hierarchically ordained.

The language of patriotism in late eighteenth-century Germany, was not only anti-egalitarian, but also apolitical or anti-political. Politics was equated with French *aritmétique politique*, a cold rational calculus insensitive to concrete historical culture and the spirit of the peoples, or associated with the dirty, mediocre, servile practice that flourished in the suffocating atmosphere of local courts and the exclusive circles of imperial burocracy. As Johann George Hamann, the spiritual mentor of Herder wrote, the state is a monster of reason that conscience, necessity, and prudence oblige us to venerate, but not to judge, even less to love. Whatever the form of government, the state remains an artificial creation, irremediably cut off from nature and spiritual life, which expresses itself in language. Thus we must direct our attention not to the state, but to the spiritual life of the nation in order to reconnect ourself with the divine arcane of life.

The clearest example of distrust for republican liberty and the anti-political orientation of German patriotism was, however,

---

[41] See C. Antoni, *La lotta contro la ragione* (Florence, 1942).

Johann Gottfried Herder. As he remarked in one of his earliest writings, *Do We Still Have a Public and a Fatherland of Yore?*, fatherland still means freedom, but no longer the freedom of the ancients.

Do we still have a fatherland whose sweet name is *freedom*? Yes, only we think differently than the ancients when we use the word *freedom*. For them *freedom* was untamed audacity, the daring to hold the wheel of the state in one's hand, the wilfulness not to suffer any other name above oneself.[42]

Modern patriotism does not require the spiritual strength that the ancients deemed necessary to repel the enemies of liberty. It is a more ordinary sense of duty and attachment to a more 'modest freedom' which a just emperor can assure better than a republic.

In our day, all states have settled into a system of balance; whoever cannot protect himself needs a patron, a father; our people no longer are characterized by the *brazen audacity* of the ancients; there prevails, instead, a finer, more modest *freedom*, the freedom of *conscience*, to be an honest man and a Christian, the *freedom* to enjoy in the shadow of the throne one's dwelling and vineyard in peace and quiet and to possess the fruit of one's labor; the *freedom* to be the shaper of one's happiness and confort, the friend of one's intimates and the father and guardian of one's children.[43]

For the young Herder patriotism is a love that gives the strength to accomplish great things for the common good of the country; however, he reserves this higher form of patriotism for emperors and monarchs. He points to Tsar Peter the Great as a 'true patriot', who became 'the father of his old, and the creator of a new fatherland'.[44] Patriotism gave him the inspiration to emancipate his subjects from serfdom against their will, and the

[42] *Haben wir noch jetz das Publikum und Vaterland der Alten?*, in *Frühe Schriften 1764–1772*, ed. U. Gaier (Frankfurt am Main, 1985), 50; Eng. trans. 'Do We Still Have a Public and a Fatherland of Yore?' in *Selected Early Works 1764–1767*, ed. E. A. Menze and K. Menges (Pennsylvania, 1992), 61.

[43] Ibid. (Eng. trans. 61).

[44] 'War *Peter der Grosse* nicht ein wahrer Patriot, da er, als der Name und das Wunder unsers Jahrunderts, der Vater seines alten, und der Schöpfer eines neues Vaterlandes wurde?'; ibid. 51 (Eng. trans. 62).

determination to stand up against adverse fortune. Without citizens, the fatherland can count on a father: the grand patriotism of the emperor and the common patriotism of the subject are sufficient to preserve the 'modest liberty' that modern men are longing for.

For him, patriotism is not a political virtue, as it had been for centuries, but an antidote to politics, which he identifies, like his mentor Hamann, with despotism, selfishness, blind obedience, and conflict. The essence of politics emerges in the works of Helvétius, 'who claims to find only selfish urges in man'; Mandeville, 'who transforms us into mere bees'; Hobbes; 'who inscribes hostility upon each man's forehead'; and Machiavelli, 'who creates that monster of a despot who sucks the blood through tax collectors, vampires, and ticks'. Such political monsters, Herder claims, deprive humanity of 'the gentle sentiment of patriotism' (*die sanfte Empfindung des Patriotismus*) and turn each man into the centre of the universe, instead of a part of the greater spiritual whole of the country.[45] Patriotism is therefore a sense of spiritual connectedness that sustains commitment to the common good. A monarch or an emperor without patriotism would be a Machiavellian despot; a non-patriotic magistrate would not be able to sacrifice private interest for the common good; non-patriotic subjects would not discharge their social duties.

Although modern men do not possess the intense political patriotism of the ancients, a patriot monarch can command from them the same degree of self-sacrifice that republics were said to be capable of exciting in their citizens. The words 'fatherland, monarch, empress', Herder writes, will sound for any man who is not a lifeless mercenary as 'the sound of victory impassioning his veins, stirring his heart, steadying his hands, and protecting his chest with iron armor'.[46] To die for the fatherland is sweet and honourable, no matter whether the fatherland is one where 'the Law and hundreds rule' or one where 'the Law and only one rule', as long as the ruler is the father or the mother of a happy people.

[45] Ibid. 51 (Eng. trans. 61).   [46] Ibid. 50 (Eng. trans. 60).

Herder's patriotism was substantially indebted, as he himself admitted, to the ideas of Thomas Abbt, who published in 1761 a successful pamphlet entitled *Death for the Fatherland*, to challenge the idea that love of fatherland can only flourish in republics. Abbt concedes the republican argument that the voice of the fatherland cannot be heard if there is no liberty; but he also remarks that monarchy assures to all a civil liberty protected by the rule of law.[47] The fatherland, he remarks, again in agreement with the republican view, does not mean the place where we are born, but a state based upon laws which do not simply restrict the liberty of the individual, but serve the good of the state as a whole.[48] A monarchy can then be a fatherland if all, including the monarch, are submitted to laws that sustain the common good. There is no difference between the subject of a monarchy and the citizen of the most free republic: they are both equally subject to the laws: no one is free, but everyone is free according to the spirit of the constitution of the state.[49] In a good monarchy all are citizens (*Bürger*), regardless of their different social rank, and their good is at one with the good of the fatherland.[50] A monarchy, concludes Abbt, may also be a fatherland that we can love; and if we can love it, we should do so (*'wir es lieben müssen'*).[51]

Although he fully endorses Abbt's ideas, Herder gives the concept of fatherland a decidedly greater cultural significance; the crucial issue is not whether the form of government is republican or monarchical, but whether a spiritual unity of the people exists. For the Greeks, he writes in *Yet Another Philosophy of History*, the name fatherland meant republic; that is, obedience

---

[47] *Vom Tode für dass Vaterland* (Berlin, 1770), 16.

[48] 'Was ist wohl das Vaterland? Man kann nicht immer den Geburtsort allein darunter verstehen. Aber wenn mich die Geburt oder meine friche Entschliesung mit einem Staate vereinigen, dessen heilsamen Gesetzen ich mich unterwerfe; Gesetzen, die mir nicht mehr von meiner Freiheit entziehen, als zum besten des ganzen Staats nothig ist: alsdann nenne ich diesen Staat mein Vaterland.' Ibid. 17.

[49] Ibid. 16.

[50] 'Sind wir nicht verbunden unsere Wohlfart zu beforden sie sicher zu gründen? Und diese Wohlfart ist so genau mit der Wohlfart des Vaterlandes, das heist, mit der Ausrechthaltung der Gesetze, deren Schuss ich geniesse, verbunden!' Ibid. 18.

[51] Ibid.

joined with liberty. But he also says, a few lines later, that the Greeks, although politically divided into different republics, peoples, and colonies, preserved a common spirit, the sentiment of belonging to a single nation, a single fatherland. They had a common fatherland because they had a common culture that transcended political divisions. When he claims that modern men, on the contrary, 'no longer have a fatherland or any kinship feeling', he does not mean that they are unfree, but that they have lost their national character to become 'philanthropic citizens of the world [*Menschenfreunde und Weltbürger*]'.[52] A fatherland can be a republic, but it need not be; it can be any form of government, as long as there is a spiritual unity grounded in common language.

The concept of the common good occupies a central place in Herder's patriotism. On occasions, he sustains devotion to the common good by using conventional republican themes:

Love your fatherland, he exhorts, for to it you are indebted for your life, education, parents and friends, in it you have enjoyed the happiest years of your childhood and youth. Be an asset to it and worthy of it; concern yourself about its laws. Be not however its judge but its supporter. He who contributes to the common good is a worthy child of his fatherland.[53]

The word fatherland excites the sense of belonging to a greater unity that prompts one to do one's share, be it little or great, for the common good. Attachment to the common good is nurtured by a sense of unity which is cultural and spiritual rather than political.[54] Understood as culture, fatherland no longer

---

[52] *Auch eine Philosophie der Geschichte zur buildung der Menschheit*, in *Sämmtliche Werke*, ed. B. Suphan (Berlin, 1891), v. 551; Eng. trans. in *J. G. Herder on Social and Political Culture*, ed. F. M. Barnard (Cambridge, 1969), 209.

[53] 'Liebe dein Vaterland: denn ihm hast du dein Leben, deine Erziehung, deine Altern und Freunde zu danken; in ihm hast du die fröhlichen Jahre deiner Kindheit und Jugend genossen. Werde ihm also auch nützlich und seiner werth. . . . Wer zum gemeinen Besten beiträgt, der ist ein würdiges Kind seine Vaterlandes;' *Schulbücher* (1787–98), in *Sämmtliche Werke* (Berlin 1889), xxx. 391; Eng. trans. in Ergang, *Herder*, 114.

[54] On Herder's anti-political, but cultural, nationalism, see I. Berlin, 'Herder and the Enlightenment', in *Vico and Herder* (New York, 1976), 184.

distinguishes itself from the nation. In fact, Herder uses the two terms as synonyms. 'With us, thank God,' he writes sarcastically, 'national character [*Nationalcharakter*] is no more! We love each and every one, or rather, we can dispense with love; for we simply *get on* with one another, being all equally polite, well-mannered and even-tempered.' A few lines later, he restates the point substituting 'national character' with 'fatherland': 'To be sure, we no longer have a fatherland [*kein Vaterland*] or any kinship feelings; instead, we are all philanthropic citizens of the world.'[55] In Herder's language the concept of fatherland is absorbed within that of nation understood as the specific culture and sum of the spiritual life of each people in a given moment of its history: national soul 'is the mother of all culture upon the earth' and all culture is the expression of national soul.[56] A person without patriotic spirit, Herder remarks, 'has lost himself and the whole world about himself'.[57] He means that he has lost his own spiritual identity which comes from contact with national culture.

Nation means oneness. The cultural unity of a nation based on history, language, literature, religion, art, and science constitutes the people as an individual, as a single body with its own spiritual soul, faculties, and forces. Although each nation has a particular and 'inexpressible' (*unaussprechliche*) individuality, it can be said that each nation is in its own way, one.[58] Each nationality is 'one people having its own national culture as well as its language'.[59] It is a little world in itself which contains within itself the centre of happiness. Even though it changes over centuries, it preserves its own spiritual identity. The history of humanity can be told in terms of growing and declining national organisms interacting with each other. No two nations in the world have the same history, but each nation has its own finality

[55] *Auch eine Philosophie*, 551 (Eng. trans. 209).

[56] *Kritische Wälder*, in *Sämmtliche Werke* (Berlin, 1878), iii. 29.

[57] 'Ein Mensch, der sein vaterländisches Gemüt verlor, hat sich selbst und die Welt um sich verloren', *Briefe zu Beförderung der Humanität*, in *Sämmtliche Werke* (Berlin, 1883), xviii. 337.

[58] *Auch eine Philosophie*, v. 551 (Eng. trans. 181).

[59] *Idee zur Philosophie der Geschichte der Menschheit*, in *Sämmtliche Werke* (Berlin, 1887), xiii. 258; Eng. trans. in Ergang, *Herder*.

according to the peculiar talents and gifts with which God has endowed it. Not only does God not want the amalgamation of different nations, he also wants each nation to follow its own path, refusing to adopt artificial models which would damage its unity and the spiritual identity based on that unity.[60]

Herder rejects comparisons between nations and epochs; however, spiritual and social connectedness are for him more precious than civil or political liberty. He praises the 'strong, vital ties of the old republics' over 'the more delicate ties of our time,'[61] and he responds to the *philosophes'* mockery of feudal society with a eulogy of its social and spiritual connectedness and mocks in turn the Enlightenment's celebrations of the liberty of the moderns.

You mock the servitude of these [feudal] times, the simple country seats of the nobility, the numerous little social islands and subdivisions and all that depended on them. You praise nothing so much as the breaking of these ties and know of no greater good which ever happened to mankind than when Europe, and with it the world, became free. Became free? What wishful thinking! If only it were true! If only you could realize what these earlier circumstances (in the absence of which human ingenuity would have been stultified) did in fact achieve: Europe was populated and built up; generations and families, master and servant, king and subject, interacted more strongly and closely with one another.[62]

For Herder nationalism means spiritual centredness and rootedness in a particular national culture. He forges the term nationalism to mean exclusive attachment to one's own national culture, an attachment to be protected against cosmopolitanism and cultural assimilation:

If, in this development of particular national tendencies toward a particular form of national happiness, the distance between the nations grows too great, we find prejudice arising. The Egyptian detests the

---

[60] *Briefe zu Beförderung der Humanität* (Berlin, 1971). ii. 218.
[61] 'Die sinnlichen starken Bande der alten Republiken und zeitalter', *Auch eine Philosophie*, 579 (Eng. trans. 222).
[62] Ibid. 524–5 (Eng. trans. 192).

shepherd and the nomad and despises the frivolous Greek. Similarly prejudices, mob judgement and narrow nationalism [*Vorurteil! Pöbelei! eigenschränten Nationalismus*] arise when the dispositions and spheres of happiness of two nations collide. But prejudice is good, in its time and place, for happiness may spring from it. It urges nations to converge upon their centre, attaches them more firmly to their roots, causes them to flourish after their kind, and makes them more ardent and therefore happier in their inclinations and purposes.[63]

One may live a monotonous life in a small town where honour, esteem, desires, fears, hate, aversion, love, friendship, delight in learning, professional duties, and inclination become 'petty and restricted' and where the whole spirit is cramped and narrowed. And yet to leave it is a painful experience of uprootedness and moral disorientation, as Herder writes in his travel diary describing his departure from Riga in 1769.

Where is the solid land on which I stood so solidly, and the little pulpit, and the armchair, and the lecture desk at which I used to give myself airs? Where are the people of who I stood in awe, and whom I loved? O soul, how will it be with you when you leave this little world? The narrow, firm, restricted center of your sphere of activity is no more; you flutter in the wind or float on a sea—the world is vanishing from you—has vanished beneath you! What a changed perspective! But such a new mode of looking at things costs tears, remorse, the extrication of one's heart from old attachments, self condemnation![64]

Herder's language of nationalism is addressed against cultural contamination and impurity, never against political oppression. Asked by Carl Friedrich of Baden to draft a plan for a patriotic institute designed to foster 'a common spirit in Germany', Herder insists on the necessity of uniting the light of the spiritual forces of Germany 'so that it might become a common flame' and stresses that 'whoever lives in Germany should belong to Germany and should speak and write a pure German'. The foundations of the spiritual union of Germany are in fact the purity of language and national homogeneity:

---

[63] Ibid. 510 (Eng. trans. 186–7).
[64] *Journal meiner Reise im Jahr 1769*, in *Sämmtliche Werke* (Berlin, 1884), iv. 349; Eng. trans., *J. G. Herder on Social and Political Culture*, 66.

Our nationality can boast that since the most ancient times of which we know its language has remained unmixed with others, just as our people were not conquered by any other national group and in their wanderings carried their language into different parts of Europe. Hence it is just that this language not only be preserved as long as the nationality exists but that it also be clarified and strengthened just as the organisation of the national group is strengthened.[65]

The fatherland of republicans was a moral and political institution; Herder's nation is a natural creation. He regarded nationalities not as the product of men, but as the work of a living organic force that animates the universe. Republics originated from the outstanding virtue and wisdom of legendary founders; nations from God himself, just as the living force that fashions national organic units out of the chaos of homogeneous matter reflects God's eternal plans and will. When he stresses that nature has created nationalities but not states, he means that the former have a higher status than the latter: the loss of the republic was for republicans the greatest tragedy; for Herder what was more tragic was the loss of one's own nation: deprive men of their country (in the sense of nationality), he wrote, 'and you deprive them of everything'.[66]

Nation means life. Nature, explains Herder, has endowed each nation with a particular national language which 'is the bond of souls, the vehicle of education, the medium of our best pleasures, nay of all social pastimes'.[67] National language is the mirror of a nation's history, deeds, joys, and sorrows, and the means for 'transmitting human ideas, inclinations and deeds, bequeathing the treasures of former times to later generations'. Through their national language, members of the nation interact with one another to a greater or lesser degree and share a common spiritual character. 'Without a common native tongue', remarks Herder, 'in which all classes are raised like branches of one tree there can be no true mutual understanding, no common

[65] *Idee zum ersten Patriotischen Institut für den Allgemeingeist Deutschlands*, in *Sämmtliche Werke* (Berlin, 1887), xvi. 600; Eng. trans. in Ergang, *Herder*, 130.

[66] *Idee zur Philosophie*, 261–2 (Eng. trans. 90).

[67] *Kleine Schriften 1791–1796*, 384 (Eng. trans. 149).

patriotic development, no intimate common sympathy, no patriotic public'.[68]

The nation is given and is entitled to men's love, a deep attachment as strong as a plant's attachment to the soil and the air from which it takes its vital energies. The lifeless state and mechanical politics is given and is entitled only to passive obedience and the cold discipline of the modern army:

Look at the armies; this archetype of human society! How free and comfortable they must feel in their motley apparel, being but lightly fed and lightly clad! They think in unison and their actions are most nobly inspired! What splendid tools they possess! In each of their daily tasks they add to their stock of virtue—in short, the very image of a perfect human mind and a world of government.[69]

Love of our national culture is attachment to a good that is distinctively our own and allows us to be distinctively ourselves. 'Everyone', writes Herder, 'loves his country, his manners, his language, his wife, his children; not because they are the best in the world, but because they are absolutely his own, and loves himself and his labors in them'.[70] It is similar to the love of common liberty advocated by republican patriots in so far as it is love of a good that has for us a particular meaning: the common liberty of a particular people is nurtured by stories that they alone can understand; it is rendered concrete by a way of life that is only theirs. Love of nation is more opaque and impossible to share beyond the barriers of culture. The common liberty of the ancient Romans or that of the modern German free city, to cite an obvious example, were surely distinctively Roman and German respectively; but Machiavelli believed, rightly or wrongly, that he was able to understand what it meant for the Romans and the Germans, why they loved it so intensely, and why it should and could be imitated in different cultural and historical contexts. National culture, on the contrary is, as Herder puts it, 'inexpressible' and closed to foreign eyes. Based on

---

[68] *Briefe zur Beförderung der Humanität* (Berlin, 1971), i. 297; Eng. trans. in Ergang, *Herder*, 150.
[69] *Auch eine Philosophie*, 547 (Eng. trans. 207).
[70] *Idee zur Philosophie*, 26 (Eng. trans. 122).

language, it can be understood, or rather felt and lived, only by those who speak the mother tongue, which allows us to communicate feelings and modes of thoughts that we would never be able to convey, or convey with equal elegance, in another tongue.[71] It puts us in direct and inward connection with the deep spirit of the culture of our nation.[72]

Nature wants us to love our own culture. She has placed inclinations toward diversity in our heart, but has also placed all we need to satisfy them in our national culture and made us insensitive to what lies outside the horizon of our culture. We can assimilate or adopt what is similar to our nature and remain cold, blind, and even contemptuous of and hostile to anything which is alien and distant.[73] To comply with nature's plan we must therefore protect the purity and authenticity of our national culture, resisting both the arrogant inclination to conquer or dominate and the vain desire to imitate alien cultures. Herder's condemnation of conquest and imperialism is unequivocal and stems from the core of his nationalism.

The most natural state is *one* nationality with one national character. This it retains for ages, and this is most naturally formed when it is the object of its native princes; for a nationality is as much a plant of nature as a family, only with more branches. Nothing therefore appears so

[71] 'I may perhaps be able to ape haltingly the sounds of foreign nations', he writes in one of his earliest essays, 'without, however, penetrating to the core of their uniqueness. I may perhaps, with much effort, learn dead languages word by word, from their monuments, but their spirit has vanished for me.' *Ueber den Fleiss in mehreren gelehrten Sprache*, in *Frühe Schriften 1764–1772*, 23; Eng. trans. in *Selected Early Works*, 30.

[72] 'What better vehicle of expression is there than the mother tongue? Like the charm of the fatherland, her charm surpasses all other languages in the opinion of him who was the son of her heart, the infant of her breasts, to whom she is now the joy of his best years and should be the hope and the honor of his old age'; *Ueber die neure deutsche Litteratur* (1767), in *Sämmtliche Werke*, i. 400; Eng. trans. in Ergang, *Herder*, 150.

[73] 'She has put tendencies toward diversity in our heart; she has placed part of the diversity in a close circle around us; she has restricted man's view so that by force of habit the circle became a horizon, beyond which he could not see nor scarcely speculate. All that is akin to my nature, all that can be assimilated by it, I hanker and strive after, and adopt; beyond that kind nature has armed me with insensibility, coldness and blindness, which can even turn into contempt and disgust'; *Auch eine Philosophie*, 509–10 (Eng. trans. 186).

indirectly opposite to the end of government as the unnatural enlargement of states, the wild mixing of all kinds of people and nationalities under one scepter.[74]

Republican patriots presented love of country as a rational love, a love that reason urges us to cultivate and keeps within its proper boundaries. Reason recommends us to love liberty because liberty is man's greatest good: to love common liberty and become true patriots, we must learn to think in terms of public reason and impose the rule of reason over natural inclinations like love of self and love of family and relations. We must, in sum, undergo a moral training led by reason: one does not naturally become a civic-minded citizen. Love of our national culture in Herder is instead a natural inclination, a vital force that reason endeavours to corrupt. It requires cultural purification from alien elements and vigilant defence against intrusions: we must learn to hear the voice of nature within our heart and follow it. The progress of humanity, with its greatness and its misery, its splendour and its horrors, is not the product of reason, but the outcome of feelings and passions. The light of reason leads to uniformity and death; the warmth of natural and customary feelings reconnects us with life. By equating reason with the proud French *raison*, Herder changed the meaning of republican love of country and recommended another love, perhaps more intense and easier to cultivate, but surely different from the patriotic love of common liberty. He did not see that love of common liberty preached by republican patriots encompasses attachment to our own culture, that fondness for our own national culture encompassed within love of common liberty becomes an affection for the highest and best aspects of our culture and our tradition. Connected to love of liberty, attachment to national culture acquires nobility and dignity; disconnected from it, it corrodes into an ignoble and exclusive affection. Herder urged his fellows to see the beauty of the spiritual unity of the nation and to love it; but he did not teach them to look at it from the right angle and he did not teach them to love it in the best way.

[74] *Idee zur Philosophie*, 384–5 (Eng. trans. 243–4).

The tendency to disconnect patriotism and liberty emerges also in August W. Schlegel's *Vorlesungen über schöne Litteratur und Kunst* of 1803–4, which can be regarded as an exemplary compendium of Romantic nationalism. Schlegel advocates a 'European patriotism' which should harmonize patriotism and cosmopolitanism. Against national egoism, he entertains the vision of a spiritual renaissance of Europe led by the German people which alone, he stresses, embody the spirit of a cosmopolitan patriotism. As they did in the Middle Ages, when they re-created the political and spiritual unity of Europe through the Holy Roman Empire, the German people must carry out the mission of endowing Europe with a renewed unity based on common historical and cultural bonds and common religion.[75]

Unlike Herder, Schlegel does not support the right of each nation to pursue its own cultural destination, but envisages a cultural and religious unification of Europe. He sees patriotism as the opposite of humanitarianism, which he regards as a form of spiritual infirmity against which he extols religious war as an episode of intense spiritual significance; indeed, as a victory of liberty. Those who died for their faith died with joy and offered a grand example of the power of ideas and beliefs over natural inclination.[76]

For Schlegel, patriotism requires an interpretation of the past which he uses to find the basis of a common culture and the motivation to pursue a common historical mission. Like Herder and the other German patriots, he was looking in national history for spiritual well-springs for the regeneration of the nation. He believed he had found them in the Holy Roman empire, in the Crusades, and in the Wars of Religion. The starting-point of new history had to be found in the German Middle Ages. He was not interested in memories of liberty, but in memories of faith, unity, and religiosity.

Other nationalist thinkers, however, reconstructed different stories of the nation's past. Within the same national tradition,

---

[75] *Vorlesungen über schöne Litteratur und Kunst*, iii. *Geschichte der Romantischen Litteratur* (Stuttgart, 1883), 36; cf. X. Léon, *Fichte et son temps* (Paris, 1922–7), ii (2). 74.
[76] *Vorlesungen*, 95; cf. Léon, *Fichte*, 76.

other well-springs for spiritual renewal were waiting to be un-
covered to sustain different visions of the historic mission of the
German people. For German patriots the task of combining the
ideals of liberty with national history was not an easy one as
Athens did not belong to the German tradition and the Romans
were conquerors, and yet German history had much to offer to
a patriotism of liberty. A few years after Schlegel's *Vorlesungen*,
Fichte, in the *Addresses to the German Nation*, stressed that the
history of the German people encompassed also the strenuous
defence of liberty against the Romans, and that the Middle Ages
were not just *Ständestaat*, religion, and corporation, but also
free city-republics. Reconstructed from the angle of liberty, the
history of the German people offered a different picture, and the
new picture was no less German than the one sketched by
Romantic thinkers.

The historical foundation of German patriotism, Fichte remarks in the Eighth Address, is to be found in the victorious
war against Roman conquest. Ancient Germans resisted Roman
conquest on behalf of freedom: the freedom to be and to remain
Germans.

Freedom to them meant just this: remaining Germans and continuing
to settle their own affairs independently and in accordance with the
original spirit of their race, going on with their development in accordance with the same spirit, and propagating this independence in their
posterity.[77]

Roman domination might have brought ancient Germans
valuable advantages. But they would have had to become half-
Roman, and to become half-Roman meant for them slavery.
Their resolution to remain Germans gave them the strength to
fight and to avoid slavery. To them must go the gratitude of the
whole of humanity, and above all modern Germans, because it
is to them that they owe their nation.

It is they whom we must thank—we, the immediate heirs of their soil,
their language, and their way of thinking—for being Germans still, for

[77] *Reden an die deutsche Nation*, in *Schriften zur Gesellschaftsphilosophie*,
ed. H. Riel (Jena, 1928), 355; Eng. trans., *Addresses to the German Nation*, ed.
G. A. Kelly (New York, 1968), 123.

being still born along on the stream of original and independent life. It is them we must thank for everything that we have been as a nation since those days, and to them we shall be indebted for everything that we shall be in the future, unless things have come to an end with us now and the last drop of blood inherited from them has dried up in our veins.[78]

In addition to the victorious resistance against Roman conquerors, another powerful source of German patriotism is for Fichte the memory of medieval free cities. They were erected 'by men belonging to the people', and are to be regarded as a genuine product of German spirit. Their political constitution and their way of life offered an admirable picture of order and love of order. Through commerce they became prosperous and powerful; through their leagues they resisted the aggression of kings and emperors. Modernity, stresses Fichte, should bow to their memory 'and confess its own impotence'.[79] The German Middle Ages was more than this, but the rest may be forgotten. The rhetoric of patriotism must be selective. One must rescue from oblivion the memories that are apt to instil patriotic feelings in the audience or readers:

The history of Germany, of German might, German enterprise and inventions, of German monuments and the German spirit—the history of all these things during that period is nothing but the history of those cities; and everything else, for example the mortgaging of petty territories and their subsequent redemption and so on, is unworthy of mention.[80]

The history of the German people entails a momentous republican experience: 'The German nation is the only one among the neo-European nations that has shown in practice, by the example of its burgher class for centuries, that it is capable of enduring a republican constitution.'[81] In that history Fichte sees the mark of a particular German national spirit. Italy too had free republics in the later Middle Ages, but the difference is striking: in Italy, continual disorders, conflicts, war, revolutions; in Germany, peace, concord, and unity. The comparison demonstrates

[78] Ibid. 356 (Eng. trans. 123–4).   [79] Ibid. 312 (Eng. trans. 89).
[80] Ibid. 313 (Eng. trans. 89).   [81] Ibid. 314 (Eng. trans. 90).

the contrast between the spirit of the two nations. It uncovers the memory of a German spirit made up of respect, honour, modesty, sense of community, and devotion to the common good which should form the basis for the moral renewal of the nation.

Spiritual regeneration is the work of the prophet. Speaking of the nation's past, the prophet must move his compatriots to identify with the people and times that he is bringing again to life and offering to them like a 'ripened fruit', speaking in a language that every German can understand. He also needs a high degree of 'philosophical spirit', but should display just as much as is needed to convey to his fellows a faithful and loving disposition.[82] He need not invent or construct a national spirit; he has to remove the obstructions that prevent the original well from flowing. His work must be the fulfilment of the prophecy embodied in the nation's youth that came true in other nations but was forgotten in Germany.[83] He does not have to build a new road; he must bring the nation back to the right spiritual path.

Fichte's nationalism was anti-monarchical. He meant to revive the patriotism that flourished in the medieval free cities and was later suffocated 'by the avarice and tyranny of princes'. He believed that Germany's spiritual decline began with the end of republican freedom. German free republics, instead, had been the best source of German civilization and the chief guarantee of German national spirit. When free republics lost their independence, Germans became not only less free, but also less German. The best part of their spirit and culture died with the liberty of those cities. They went on to the wrong spiritual path. If Germany had been unified by a monarch, 'it would certainly have been a great disaster for the cause of German patriotism', a disaster second only to foreign domination which would have suffocated German national love even more.[84]

In Fichte's theory political liberty and national culture have to work together: political liberty allows the Germans to live

---

[82] Ibid. 315 (Eng. trans. 91).   [83] Ibid. (Eng. trans. 91).
[84] Ibid. 365 (Eng. trans. 131).

according to their genuine spirit and culture, according to what Fiche believed was their genuine spirit; national culture keeps alive the sense of common purpose that gives strength to the commitment to common liberty. To be free again, Germans must first of all learn to be German; that is, capable of exercising spiritual freedom and of emancipating themselves from ideas artificially imposed on national culture. Defeated and divided, they cannot live free; but they can cultivate spiritual freedom in their hearts. So long as they live spiritually as Germans, the prophecy of the German nation will never die.

Let us give [freedom] a place of refuge in our innermost thoughts, until there shall grow up around us the new world which has the power of manifesting our thoughts outwardly. In the sphere where no one can deprive us of the freedom to do as we think best—in our own minds let us make ourselves a pattern, a prophecy, and a guarantee of that which will become a reality when we are gone.[85]

To the Polish who were on the verge of being conquered, Rousseau had recommended that they at least preserved their own national culture within their hearts and minds, if they wanted to retain hopes of regaining political freedom. To his fellow Germans already partially conquered, Fichte issues a similar exhortation. In both cases the language of nationalism, with all its emphasis on the value of national culture, is used as a premiss or preparation for a call to struggle for political liberty. To be able to fight for Poland's liberty, the Poles must first believe that there is worth and dignity in being Polish; so must the Germans. In the case of politically unfree peoples, one must build national identity through defence and recovery of national language and history, then the proper political struggle for liberty may begin. In fact, political principles preside over, and direct the work of constructing and reconstructing national culture; they decide which moments of national history ought to be recorded, which ought to be forgotten; which aspects of common culture ought to be highlighted, and which set aside through literary or intellectual critique. Both the nationalist and the patriot have to define national identity, working on shared

[85] Ibid. 428 (Eng. trans. 177).

memories. The patriot, however, has an additional political task to accomplish. To simply educate Germans does not satisfy him: he wants German citizens. He knows that they can only be citizens as German citizens and for this reason he wants to instil the spirit of liberty in their very Germanness.

Fichte's nationalism is based on a commitment to spiritual liberty, which means to be capable of original, intentional acts of creation—intellectual, political, and historical acts of creation—that proceeds from the will and makes possible the endless progress of the human race. To be German means for him to be capable of spiritual freedom; the spiritual freedom which constitutes the German nation is itself a historical creation transmitted to modern Germans by their ancient forefathers who defeated Roman legions to remain Germans, transmitted by Luther and those who gave their blood to emancipate religious faith from all beliefs in external authority, by a political philosophy which has opposed to foreign statecraft a conception of politics as an education to citizenship modelled after the Greek ideal of the *polis*,[86] by a philosophy that has successfully resisted 'any foreign philosophy that believes in death' (*ausländischen todgläubigen Philosophie*) on behalf of freedom and infinite acts of creation.[87]

Spiritual freedom is the core of the German people's historical mission in the world: 'to you has fallen the greater destiny, to found the empire of the spirit and of reason, and completely annihilate the rule of brute physical force in the world'.[88] The voice of the forefathers who fought for freedom of conscience calls for the defence of what they achieved and the completion of their work. Not to answer their call would mean to make their sacrifice meaningless, thereby mutilating the German spirit.

'Save our honor too', they cry to you. 'To us it was not entirely clear what we fought for; besides the lawful resolve not to let ourselves be dictated by external force in matters of conscience, there was another and higher spirit driving us, which never fully revealed itself to us. To you it is revealed, this spirit, if you have the power of vision in the spiritual world; it beholds you with eyes clear and sublime. The varied

---

[86] Ibid. 325–6 (Eng. trans. 99).   [87] Ibid. 337 (Eng. trans. 108).
[88] Ibid. 409 (Eng. trans. 225).

and confused mixture of sensuous and spiritual motives that has hith-
erto ruled the world shall be displaced, and spirit alone, pure and freed
from all sensuous motives, shall take the helm of human affairs.'[89]

An equally powerful appeal to preserve national spirit comes
from future generations of Germans. They urge the need to
avoid repeating the tragic fate of many peoples of antiquity that
are now forgotten because their history has been written by
their conquerors.

Do not force us to be ashamed of our descent from you as from base
and slavish barbarians; do not compel us to conceal our origin, or to
fabricate a strange one and to take a strange name, lest we be at once
and without further examination rejected and trodden underfoot.[90]

For Fichte, the preservation of the German nation contributes
to the spiritual enhancement of humanity itself and foreign
nations too, at least those that understand their true interest.
A large part of humanity, Fichte remarks, descends from the
Germans; the other part owes the German people their religion
and civilization. Both 'appeal to us to preserve ourselves for
them too and for their sake, just as we are'.[91] Deprived of German
spirit the whole human race would be spiritually impoverished.
Obligations are multiple: to German forefathers, to future German generations, to the peoples of German descent, to humanity. They mutually reinforce each other; their call must then be
answered.

The true mark of German national spirit is not ethnicity or
language, but spiritual freedom. Those who live resigned to
accept their condition as an unalterable necessity and therefore
live in a derivative way as appendices to true spiritual life are to
be regarded as strangers and foreigners.

Whoever believes in spirituality and in the freedom of this spirituality
and who wills the eternal development of this spirituality by freedom,
wherever he may have been born and whatever language he speaks, is
of our blood; he is one of us, and will come over to our side. Whoever
believes in stagnation, retrogression . . . wherever he may have been

---

[89] Ibid. 490 (Eng. trans. 225).   [90] Ibid. 491–2 (Eng. trans. 226).
[91] Ibid. 492 (Eng. trans. 227).

born and whatever language he speaks, is non German and a stranger to us [*undeutsch und fremd für uns*].[92]

To believe in spiritual freedom is for Fichte the mark of true patriotism. Like republican thinkers, he identifies love of country with freedom. However, he gives freedom a different meaning; he defines it not just as the individuals' security protected by laws, but as a people's need for its continuance as an original, uncontaminated people.[93] He opposes freedom to slavery, but he means by it 'disregard for, and suppression of, the characteristic of an original people'.[94] An unfree people is not just a politically oppressed people, but a people that is no longer itself because it is spiritually corrupt and contaminated. True patriotism is not for Fichte 'the peaceful citizen's love for the constitution and the laws' that republicans had extolled as true patriotism, but 'the devouring flame of higher patriotism which embraces the nation as the vesture of the eternal'.[95] He believed that love of political liberty was not a sufficient motivation to mobilize his fellow Germans and endeavoured to reinforce it through an appeal to their fondness for their common culture. The language of republicanism seemed to him insufficient; political love had to be completed through the infusion of the desire to be true to one's own tradition, and this made it a different love.

Patriotism is for Fichte love of an eternity which can be attained on this earth only through the continuance of the people to which one belongs. As long as the people lives, the patriot who has lived as part of his people and loved his people never dies. He longs for eternity in this world and his longing makes him capable of true love of country.

Love that is truly love, and not mere transitory lust, never clings to what is transient; only in the eternal does it awaken and become kindled, and there alone does it rest. Man is not able to love even himself unless he conceives himself as eternal; apart from that he cannot even

---

[92] Ibid. 337 (Eng. trans. 108).   [93] Ibid. 350 (Eng. trans. 119).
[94] Ibid. 352 (Eng. trans. 120).
[95] 'Nicht der Geist der ruhigen bürgerlichen Liebe zu der Verfassung und den Gesetzen, sondern die verzehrende Flamme der höheren Vaterlandsliebe, die die Nation als Hülle des Ewigen umfasst'. Ibid. 352 (Eng. trans. 120).

respect, much less approve of, himself. Still less can he love anything outside himself without taking it up into the eternity of his faith and of his soul and binding it thereto. He who does not first regard himself as eternal has in him no love of any kind, and, moreover, cannot love a fatherland, a thing which for him does not exist.[96]

Patriotism inspires men to give their life for the fatherland because it promises eternity on earth. The Romans were capable of great sacrifices for their fatherland not because they loved liberty and laws but because they believed in Rome's eternity and confidently expected that with Rome they would continue to live eternally in the stream of time.[97] German Protestants did not give their blood for their own happiness; they fought for 'the bliss of their children and of their grandchildren as yet unborn and of all posterity as yet unborn'.[98] Their patriotism made them capable of original acts of creation; it gave them the strength to be spiritually free. Germans are capable of true patriotism because they are an original people and have a national character; a people who do not believe in spiritual freedom but only in the eternal recurrence of physical life are not, properly speaking, a people.[99]

Spiritual freedom, and the particular culture which sustains it, defines a clear moral and intellectual borderline between Germans and non-Germans, fellows and foreigners, peoples and non-peoples. Separation of the two camps must be complete and attained as soon as possible in the interest of humanity itself. If the Germans rediscover the patriotism that is only theirs and nobody elses, they can carry out their historical mission of spreading the light of spiritual freedom over the world. German patriotism is the precondition for effective cosmopolitanism. Action and life can only come from patriotism; severed from it, cosmopolitanism can at best be a pure, cold idea. A cosmopolitanism which would exist in the abstract and exclude patriotism is vain and useless and absurd:

'The individual, concrete thing is nothing', says the cosmopolite; 'I think of, am concerned about and live for the Whole; this shall be

---

[96] Ibid. 347 (Eng. trans. 117).   [97] Ibid. 348 (Eng. trans. 117).
[98] Ibid. 353 (Eng. trans. 121).   [99] Ibid. 346 (Eng. trans. 116).

improved and peace and order shall be spread over this.' Well and good; but tell me first how you propose to approach this Whole with the beneficent ideas and purposes which you harbor for it. Do you propose to benefit it in general and in wholesale fashion? Is the Whole anything different from the individual parts united in thought? Can the Whole in any way be improved if the individual parts are not improved? Take pains first of all to better yourself and then better your neighbor to the right and to the left.[100]

The most effective way of being a cosmopolitan, that is to commit oneself to the ideal of the moral progress of humanity, is to advance the cause of humanity in the nation of which one is a member. Of all nations, however, Germany has a special status, because the cause of humanity 'can only be furthered by philosophy' and Germany is the nation which has conceived philosophy and has the ability to understand it.

Only the German can therefore be a patriot. Only he can, in the interest of his nation, include all mankind. Since the instinct of Reason has become extinct and the era of Egotism has begun, every other nation's patriotism is selfish, narrow, hostile to the rest of mankind.[101]

The uniqueness of German patriotism rests on the particular combination of love of liberty, affection for one's own culture, and, above all, commitment to spiritual freedom. It is a patriotism that makes for a clear borderline between Germans and non-Germans, a borderline that can be crossed in only one direction as the light of spiritual freedom and reason can only spread from the German people to the others. The latter have no light of their own to offer in turn; incapable of original acts of creation, they can only receive spiritual light. The German patriot, in Fichte's account, has no fellows; beyond the boundaries of the nation he sees only spiritual death and darkness. The barrier constituted by its distinctive national spirit as a bearer of spiritual liberty cannot and must not be crossed by other peoples' ideas, values, and passions. They would contaminate

---

[100] *Philosophie der Mauerei (Briefe an Konstant)*, ed. W. Flitner (Leipzig, 1923); Eng. trans. in H. C. Engelbrecht, *Johann Gottlieb Fichte: A Study of his Political Writings with Special Reference to his Nationalism* (New York, 1933), 74–5.

[101] Ibid. (Eng. trans. 98).

the German people's originality and weaken its capacity to carry out the mission that history has entrusted to it. Their primary duty is to remain Germans, following the examples of their predecessors who defeated the Romans, and the disciples of Luther, the saint of freedom, who gave their lives for the eternity of the German nation.

By interpreting love of country as commitment to spiritual freedom rather than love of common political and civil liberty, Fichte introduced an important change in the language of patriotism: love of country is no longer *caritas* but fondness for one's own uniqueness as a people no longer understood as a community of free citizens, but as a community of individuals who share a culture and are capable of spiritual freedom. His patriotism was intended to make the Germans German, then to make them free as Germans, but also, one may add, solitary in their German freedom.

When they need to recover their liberty or redefine their spiritual identity, nations need the 'higher patriotism' that Fichte extolled above 'the peaceful citizen's love for the constitution and the laws'. This ordinary patriotism, however, in normal times provides the ethical support that the modern state needs and in exceptional times translates into a readiness for sacrifice and extraordinary actions. As Hegel put it in *The Philosophy of Right*, genuine patriotism is not a devouring flame but a 'political sentiment' (*politische Gesinnung*) based on a conviction and a volition which has become customary. It is a political sentiment because it is the product of the political constitution and the laws and it is based on the consciousness (*Bewußtsein*) that 'my interest, both substantive and particular, is contained and preserved in another's (i.e. the state's) interests and end, i.e. in the other's relation to me as an individual'.[102]

The 'secret of the patriotism of the citizen' (*das Geheimnis des Patriotismus der Bürger*), Hegel remarks, is the shared consciousness of a unity of interest between the individual and the political state that arises within the corporations of civil

---

[102] *Grundlinien der Philosophie des Rechts*, sect. 268, ed. Helmut Reichelt (Frankfurt, 1972), 225–6; Eng. trans., *Hegel's Philosophy of Right*, ed. T. M. Knox (Oxford, 1967), 163–4.

society. In the spirit of the corporation (*Korporationsgeist*), the citizens

know the state as their substance, because it is the state that maintains their particular spheres of interest together with the title, authority, and welfare of these. In the corporation mind the rooting of the particular in the universal is directly entailed, and for this reason it is in that mind that the depth and strength which the state possesses in sentiment is seated.[103]

The patriotism of modern citizens translates into law-abiding habits based on the belief that 'the community (*Gemeinwesen*) is [their] substantive groundwork and end'. Since they regard the community as the foundation and end of their individual lives, they regard their social duties as liberties, not as obligations imposed by an external authority: 'this very other is immediately not another in my eyes, and in being conscious of this fact, I am free'. Patriotism, properly understood, is then the source of that 'prodigious strength' and depth of the modern state which consists in the fact that it fully recognizes the right of individual and particular interests and allegiances, and yet succeeds in connecting them with the universality of the political state.

For Hegel the formation of modern civil society in which the individuals are free to pursue their private and particular interests has irremediably destroyed the complete identification of the citizen with the state that sustained the patriotism of the ancients. And yet, from within the same civil society a new patriotism may be generated. The *Philosophy of Right*, similar in this sense to *The Spirit of the Laws*, is a theoretical effort to redefine a political virtue or patriotism of the moderns no longer based on self-denial but on the individual self-interest as a member of a particular historical community.

Hegel's 'patriotism of the citizen' did not have a widespread influence upon the nineteenth-century language of patriotism. Champions of patriotism longed for a more intense love of country and for a stronger unity between the citizen and the state. They drew inspiration from Herder and Fichte rather than

[103] Ibid. 260 (Eng. trans. 189).

Hegel. The political city (*cité politique*), wrote Jules Michelet in 1846, presupposes the moral city (*cité morale*) which lives in man's soul. Man's soul, however, can only live in a particular place immersed in the spirit of a people. This implies that the political city needs a physically and spiritually defined space. If boundaries are dissolved or confused, the spirit of the people would die and both the moral and the political city must, as a consequence, perish. Men's moral and political flourishing need centredness and particularity: 'A mind fixed upon one point will go on fathoming itself. A mind floating in space, dissolves and fades away. Behold the man who shares his love with many: he dies without having known love; let him love but once, and long, and he finds in one passion the infinity of nature and all the progress of the world.'[104] The aim of politics cannot be just to establish a social order in which individuals can peacefully pursue their selfish interests. Its goal has to be to construct a *patrie*; that is, a 'grand social harmony' in which the advancement of each individual is sustained by the commitment of all. This goal can be attained only if citizens are educated from birth to death with the ideal of sacrifice. Patriotic politics is above all else a politics of moral education.[105]

Michelet makes ample use of classical patriotic metaphors and idioms. The *patrie*, he says, not only gives us life, she comprehends each of us in her and inspires toward her a love that in turn embraces all other loves. Love of country expands and ennobles the love that we feel and owe to parents and relatives. It is love in the sense of friendship which inspires a disinterested attachment. It is a passion that drives toward unity, closeness, solidarity. The right word for *patrie* is *amour des amours*, or, even better, *amitié*, following the language of ancient French communes:

It is a grand glory for our old *communes* of France to have been the first to have found the true name of our native land. In their simplicity, full of good sense and profound feeling, they called it *friendship*. Our

---

[104] *Le Peuple* (Paris, 1974, edn.) 219; Eng. trans., *The People*, ed. C. Cocks (London, 1846), 139.

[105] 'Quelle est la première partie de la politique? L'éducation. La seconde? L'éducation. Et la troisième? L'éducation.' Ibid. 244 (Eng. trans. 162).

country is, indeed, the great friendship which contains all the others. I love France, because she is France, and also because she is the country of those whom I love and have loved.[106]

The idea that advancement of civilization and the progress of humanity is better achieved through the defence of each nation's spiritual and cultural unity became a widespread belief in mid-nineteenth-century Europe. 'One's native land [*patrie*]', as Michelet put it, 'forms the necessary initiation to the country of all mankind [*patrie universelle*]'.[107] Human society (*la république du monde*) shall flourish through the strengthening and fullest development of each nation's spiritual particularity, not through cultural merging or assimilation. God, stressed Michelet echoing Herder, does not want us to lose ourselves in him, and what is true for individuals is even more so for nations. Each nation must be allowed to express its own original spirit. No voice can be suffocated in the concert of nationalities, and oppressed nations must be helped to redeem themselves.

To love one's *patrie*, one has to see it; one has to associate the word with inspiring, touching, tender, vivid images. As a skilled rhetorician, Michelet evokes the image of the father who takes his son to the public festival to instil in him love of country that Rousseau had made famous in the *Lettre à d'Alembert*:

He leads him from Notre Dame to the Louvre, the Tuileries, the triumphal arch. From some roof, or terrace, he shows him the people, the army passing, the bayonets clashing and glittering, and the tricoloured flag. In the moments of expectation especially, before the *fête*, by the fantastic reflections of the illumination, in that awful silence which suddenly takes place in the dark ocean of people, he stoops toward him and says, 'There, my son, look there is France, there is your *patrie*!' All this is like one man,—one soul, one heart.[108]

For Michelet the love that unites the citizens to one another and to the *patrie* is not a political love but a religious faith based upon the vision of the *patrie* as a 'living God'. God is unity and he reveals himself in the harmonic unity of the *patrie*, in the legends, the memories, and the heroes that constitute the living soul of the *patrie* and in the shared belief in a common national

---

[106] Ibid. 199 (Eng. trans. 121).   [107] Ibid. 140.
[108] Ibid. 240 (Eng. trans. 158).

destiny. The work to be done to keep the *patrie* alive (*vivante*) must then be a work of continual education, involvement, initiation, designed to protect France's cultural and spiritual unity. Like Herder and Fichte, he reserves his most vehement attacks for the intellectuals who contaminate national culture with alien ideas:

Poor imitators! so you think that is imitation? They take from a neighbouring people this or that which among them is a living thing; they appropriate it to themselves, ill or well, in spite of the repugnance of a frame that was not made for it: but is a foreign body that you are engrafting in your flesh; it is an inert lifeless thing; it is death that you are adopting.[109]

Michelet's patriotism is a blend of political ideals coming from the Revolution and claims for ethnic and spiritual unity and purity put forward by nationalist thinkers. France, he remarks, is a nation committed to the ideal of equality and is a nation ethnically and spiritually pure; but the emphasis is on unity and purity more than liberty and equality. Love of country is for him a unifying force that drives individuals and groups, particularly the comon people, to identify themselves with the larger body of the nation. The identification must be total; no distance is allowed; no conflicts or dissensions should trouble it. It is a unity based on devotion and sacrifice. For this unity to be attained, citizens cannot regard themselves just as citizens sharing the ideals of the *République*; they must feel themselves as equal in other respects; equal because they are of the same ethnicity, speak the same language, share the values of French Christianity. Michelet's *patrie* is more than just a republic of French citizens; it is a community of individuals united by bonds of love and friendship that stem from their being French. To generate true patriotism, the political ideal of the republic had to be absorbed within the spiritual unity of the nation; the love of country preached by republican thinkers had to be translated into a different love: love of one's own culture, one's own language, one's own religion. The old tradition of republican patriotism seemed to begin to exhaust its intellectual and political appeal.

[109] Ibid. 224 (Eng. trans. 143–4).

5

The Nationalization of Patriotism

In spite of criticisms and revisions coming from all sides, the language of patriotism continued to be used in early nineteenth-century Europe to sustain political reform and the extension of citizenship. In England, the supporters of the Catholic Emancipation Act of 1829 opposed a patriotism based on the principle of civil equality to the exclusive patriotism of Protestantism. The enemies of the Emancipation Act seemed to believe, as one Scottish MP put it, 'that the great principle of the constitution is the principle of exclusion; but I think, on the contrary, that the great principle of the British constitution is the diffusion to every class of the community of all those blessings which it is so well formed to bestow.'[1] A few years later, proponents of the Parliamentary Reform Bill also made extensive use of the language of patriotism. They called for a thorough reform of British electoral procedures and condemned the privileges and injustices that the old system allowed; however, they presented themselves as true Britons. As John Thelwall, a member of the London Corresponding Society, wrote in 1794: 'there must be something in the constitution of this country which a Briton will ever love and venerate'; that 'something' for the Radicals of the 1820s and 1830s was the idea of Britain as a nation committed to freedom. As one Radical ballad of the time put it:

> As for me, in all weathers, in peace or in war,
> My service my country commands;
> Her rights are at stake and the time is not far
> When her sons shall assert their demands:

[1] Quoted in Linda Colley, *Britons. Forging the Nation 1707–1837* (London, 1994), 328.

> Then, then, my brave Britons, we ne'er shall be slaves,
> Nor shall tyrants rule over this isle:
> See the goddes of freedom her banner high waves,
> And inspires her loved sons with her smile.[2]

By describing themselves as genuine Britons and by framing their claims on behalf of the nation or the people, the reformers attained a nationwide consensus and succeeded in portraying their opponents as an anti-national faction. They brilliantly performed a rhetorical masterstroke whereby self-styled patriots were recast as a privileged and corrupt clique and 'the voiceless millions' were promoted to the centre stage as 'the best of patriots'.[3]

In both the campaigns for the Catholic Emancipation Act and for the Reform Bill, the language of patriotism worked as a powerful language of unity, and specifically of political unity. It helped to unite individuals who differed on social, cultural, and religious grounds in the common struggle for emancipation and the extension of citizenship. It offered words and idioms that reshaped people's passions; old hatreds were placated and, perhaps, even translated into temporary solidarity. Protestant working- and middle-class patriots who regarded the Catholic Emancipation Act as a betrayal of the very idea of Britishness, probably marched with their former enemies in the campaign for the Parliamentary Reform Bill. A new idea of 'being British' superseded the old one; the ideals of equal citizenship, framed in terms of British patriotism, overcame, at least for a while, religious hostility.

Until the 1840s the language of patriotism in England was used not only to debate constitutional and parliamentary issues but also to address problems of social justice that 'arose directly from urbanisation and industrialisation', as Hugh Cunningham has remarked.[4] The new social conflict was described in terms of liberty versus despotism: industrial workers and the urban poor were the new slaves; the capitalists and landlords the new despots. The extension of the vocabulary of patriotism from

---

[2] Quoted ibid. 336–7.   [3] Ibid. 340.
[4] 'The Language of Patriotism, 1750–1915', *History Workshop*, 12 (1981), 16.

the political to the social sphere was an easy one. Poverty and exploitation were denounced as incompatible with the values of citizenship that patriotism had been sustaining for centuries.

With little amendment, the language of patriotism was available to fight new battles. All the parties and movements that dominated the nineteenth-century political and social scene resorted to it. William Cobbett, one of the leaders of the Chartist movement, hoped that many a father would 'be induced to spend his evenings at home instructing his children in the history of their misery, and in warming them into acts of patriotism'.[5] Richard Oastler, a Tory and churchman, was hoping that 'a strong army of patriots may yet arise in the plains of England resolved to assert their rights and tear the laurels from the brow of Capital'.[6] Old patriots fought to assert political and civil rights; the new patriots of the age of the Industrial Revolution, to assert social justice.

England proclaims itself to be a country of free men; if the poor are deprived of their rights and treated as slaves the 'British character is destroyed'; the very 'nature of the Englishmen will be changed', Oastler wrote in 1834 against the Poor Law. The patriot wants England to remain true to itself and loyal to the heritage of liberty that past generations have transmitted to the new.

In his *Letter on Yorkshire Slavery* of September 1830, Oastler begins his denunciation of the exploitation of child labour by quoting a statement of Revd. R. W. Hamilton on England's commitment to freedom: 'It is the pride of Britain that a slave cannot exist on her soil; and if I read the genius of her constitution right, I find that slavery is most abhorrent to it—that the air that Britons breathe is free—the ground on which they tread is sacred to liberty.' But slavery exists on the very soil of England: 'Thousands of our fellow-creatures and fellow-subjects both male and female, the miserable inhabitants of a *Yorkshire town* are this very moment existing in a state of slavery, *more horrid* than are the victims of that hellish system *"colonial slavery"*.'[7] Oastler called on the whole nation to protect the thousands of

---

[5] Ibid.

[6] C. Driver, *Tory Radical: The Life of Richard Oastler* (New York, 1946), 302.

[7] Ibid. 42.

little children, principally female, aged 7 to 14, who were compelled to work for twelve hours a day with only thirty minutes
allowed for eating and recreation. A nation devoted to liberty
must blush at an indictment that hits its very moral foundation;
every Briton must swear 'These innocents shall be free!'[8]

In 1833, in the midst of the campaign for the Ten-Hour Bill,
Oastler resorted again to the language of patriotism to rebut the
arguments of the Royal Commission in charge of investigating
factory conditions. He directed against the Commission seven-
teen indictments, all constructed around the idea that it is 'Un-
English' to treat children and workers like slaves. Oastler's
rhetoric is an example of the new language of patriotism:

Because it is 'Un-English' to rave against Slavery 5 or 6,000 miles off,
and to encourage a more abominable and more cowardly system of
Slavery at home, practised by those very individuals who are the most
noisy in their opposition to the accursed system of West India Slavery.
Because it is 'Un-English' to refuse the innocent and industrious Children of the poor of Britain the same legislative protection which is
already granted to the guilty Adult Felon and the unfortunate Adult
Black Slave.[9]

Love of country presses us to feel the oppression that some of
our fellows endure as an outrage. Oppression may take the form
of the denial of civil and political rights or exploitation, brutal-
ity, contempt for human dignity in workplaces and social life;
the victims may be adult, old or young, male or female; the
patriot reacts with particular passion to the sufferings of his
fellows: he feels not just compassion but indignation, and indignation gives him the motivation to change: 'he will be the
greatest patriot', wrote Oastler, 'who can produce the greatest
dissatisfaction'.[10] Indignation against and hatred of the oppressor drive the patriot to action and to call on others to join
the struggle. His commitment is a lasting one, since it is sustained
by love of country, by love of common liberty, which is a charitable love of particular people who are different in several respects but are all compatriots and victims of oppression.

If it is love of common liberty, patriotism can translate into

---

[8] Ibid.   [9] Ibid. 232.
[10] See Cunningham, 'Language of Patriotism', 17.

solidarity beyond national boundaries. All the oppressed are the patriot's fellows. Love of country strengthens his power of recognition; it allows him or her to recognize a foreigner as a fellow in the common struggle for liberty. 'We', reads the resolution of the London Corresponding Society, 'instead of natural enemies, at length discover in Frenchmen our fellow citizens of the world'.[11] The discovery is not the consequence of a moral principle, but the working of the passion of love of liberty.

There is, of course, no world of which to be citizens, but there have been examples of commitment to liberty that have crossed national boundaries. Against the despotism of rulers, patriots of all nations should, as the *Black Dwarf* wrote in 1823, 'melt down and amalgamate all national jealousies into harmony in the common cause'.[12] National jealousies are strong passions; it takes a lot of heat applied equally to each to be able to melt down and amalgamate them. Only the passion of love of liberty is sufficiently intense to do so, and acts with equal intensity against all jealousies. Once jealousies are melted down and amalgamated, patriotism has accomplished its job. It doesn't have to melt down and amalgamate all national identities. The cause of liberty against oppression does not need cosmopolitans; it simply needs patriots.

The ideal of a patriotism based on commitment to liberty beyond national barriers became the core of the nineteenth-century republican patriotism championed by Giuseppe Mazzini. He believed that to build a republic, it is not sufficient to appeal to the political values embodied in the classical ideal of *patria*; one must incorporate them into a larger discourse that encompasses also the cultural values of the nation. He took seriously the ideas of German nationalists with whose works he was familiar. He greatly admired Fichte for the *Addresses to the German Nation* and in an article of 1835 he mentions him as the philosopher who condensed the principles of the French Revolution.[13] In his review of the Italian translation of Schlegel's *Vorlesungen* issued in 1828, Mazzini praises Herder and Schlegel as the two

[11] Ibid. 19.   [12] Ibid.
[13] *Fede e avvenire*, in *Scritti politici*, ed. T. Grandi and A. Comba (Turin, 1972).

German thinkers who developed Vico's intuition and showed that 'peoples' intellectual life cannot be separated from their civil and political history'.[14] While Herder was an apostle of the moral regeneration of a people, Schlegel's history of ancient and modern literature ought to be read as a powerful exhortation to all 'human families' to learn that they all derive from the same tree.

While he praises the German nationalists' emphasis on national culture and on the spirit of the people, Mazzini found their patriotism unsatisfactory. They defended, and rightly so, the values of the nation, but they neglected the *patria*; that is, the republic. As a result their patriotism turned out to be too narrow and exclusive. It lacked the strength and impetus to cross national boundaries and be truly universal. Schlegel's works on literature, commented Mazzini, are negatively affected by an immoderate love of country (*intemperante affetto di patria*). Out of national pride, Schlegel reacts against the Enlightenment's superficial condemnation of the Middle Ages as an epoch of intellectual vacuousness between classical antiquity and the modern renaissance of letters and arts; he glorifies the Middle Ages in its entirety and proposes it as an ideal because he regards it as the birthplace of a German literary tradition inspired by the most noble values of chivalric spirit, unlimited faith, and a pure imagination. Patriotism allows him to recognize the value of national poetry and literature that serves a people's civil and political advancement; but his 'ignoble national vanity' which damages his patriotism and prevents him from seeing the different aspects of the Middle Ages and from appreciating the common trends of European intellectual and political life that pervade each nation's spiritual life.[15] Because of his patriotism, Schlegel deserves to be recognized as a voice of the new epoch which has at last recognized the value of national cultures; but his recognition is incomplete and too narrow. The Enlightenment was prejudiced against the Middle Ages, Schlegel against the Reformation and the modern world. For Mazzini the history of

[14] *Storia della letteratura antica e moderna di Federico Schlegel*, in *Scritti editi ed inediti di Giuseppe Mazzini* (Imola, 1906), i. 114.
[15] Ibid. 123–4.

European spiritual development is still waiting to be written. Sensitivity toward national culture is a necessary precondition of it, but national culture has to be studied in the broader context of European spiritual development toward liberty. To be able to understand one's own national culture and the national culture of other peoples, the historian must share a commitment to liberty and be immune from national vaingloriousness. It takes a patriot to accomplish the task, but not a patriot in Schlegel's sense.

Mazzini had outlined the essential features of his patriotism in his essay *On Dante's Love of Country*, composed a year or two before his review of Schlegel's *Vorlesungen*. Dante is for him the example of love of country well understood (*affetto patrio ben concepito*): his works and his life can be taken as a model for 'those who know what *patria* is and how she wants to be served'.[16] True love of country is an 'immense love' immune to prejudices and inspired by thoughts of unity and peace. It is a passion that animates and inflames generous souls who cannot stand their country's corruption and enslavement. While their fellows cry and suffer in silence, they speak up. They foresee their country's bleak future and share their fellows' needs, anxieties, and hopes. They do not share their vices and weaknesses. Like ancient prophets, they do not speak out of irrational fury or offended pride but out of indignation.[17] They say unpleasant things to their fellows; they denounce their faults and enumerate their responsibilities to call them to action. Reproach is not intended to humiliate, nor to emphasize the patriot's moral superiority, but to elevate the soul of his own people, with which he wants to work. He speaks to excite in his people the same passions that he feels, since he knows that working together against oppression and corruption requires a shared love of liberty. His voice is powerful and severe (*possente e severa*), never

---

[16] 'Ben diremo che siccom'egli siede, e siederà gran pezza primo fra i poeti, che durano eterni, cosí la sua vita può presentarsi con tutta fidanza a modello di coloro, che san cos'è, patria, e com'essa vuol esser servita'. *Dell'amor patrio di Dante*, in *Scritti editi e inediti di Giuseppe Mazzini* (Imola, 1906), vol. i, 20.

[17] 'Egli inveisce agramente contro le colpe, onde l'itala terra era lorda, ma non è scoppio di furore irragionevole, o d'offeso orgoglio; è suono d'alta mestizia, come d'uomo che scriva piangendo; è il genio della libertà patria che geme sulla sua statua rovesciata, e freme contro coloro, che la travolser nel fango.' Ibid. 14–15.

arrogant; his words express a noble sadness, like the words of man who writes while he is crying.

As Dante's example shows, true patriots often speak in vain. They rarely win glory and fame from their contemporaries; their reward is often exile. They must wander and carry their love of country with them; they cannot translate it into political action; they have to be content with words. Erudites and commentators will then analyse their works: each word will be isolated and studied, like the anatomist studies bones and nerves. Only a few generous souls who share their indignation and anger against corruption will be able to understand the spiritual life that animated their works. The first step to great accomplishments, stresses Mazzini, is to learn to understand and love great men of the past. Patriotism needs memories. They are a continuous source of inspiration and an invincible bastion: even the harshest oppression cannot deprive a people of its memories. The most precious memories are those of peoples who loved their country and their fellows with a noble love; not with national vaingloriousness or narrow parochialism. Italians must then study Dante not to vaunt the greatness of their national culture, but to find motivations to stand against their present misery and corruption. Parents must tell their children stories of patriotism not to nurture national pride but love of liberty.

Speak to them of their Country, of what it was, of what it ought to be ... tell them over again the great deeds of the common people in our ancient republics; teach them the names of the good men who loved Italy and her people, and endeavoured through suffering, calumny, and persecution to improve her destinies. Instil into their young hearts not hatred of the oppressor, but an energetic resolve to resist oppression. Let them learn from your lips and from the tranquil approval of their mother, how beautiful it is to follow the paths of virtue, how great to stand up as apostles of the truth, how holy to sacrifice oneself, if needs be, for one's brothers. Kindle in their tender minds, while planting the germs of rebellion against all *authority* usurped and sustained by force, reverence for the true, the only authority, the authority of Virtue crowned by Genius.[18]

---

[18] *Dei doveri dell'uomo*, in *Scritti politici*, 892; Eng. trans., 'Faith and the Future' (1835), in *The Duties of Men and Other Essays by Joseph Mazzini*, introd. T. Jones (London, 1936), 65–6.

For Mazzini *patria* is not an organism composed of different parts hierarchically ordained, as the nation was for Herder, but a democratic association of free and equal individuals.

A Country [*patria*] is a fellowship of free and equal men bound to-gether in a brotherly concord of labour towards a single end. . . . A Country is not an aggregation, it is an *association*. There is no true Country without a uniform right. There is no true country where the uniformity of that right is violated by the existence of caste, privilege and inequality.[19]

Mazzini gives the concept of *patria* a democratic meaning. He opposes the *patria* of the people to the *patria* of kings, and stresses that in a true *patria* all citizens must have equal political rights. A republic that excludes the poor, women, or Blacks from political rights is untrue to its principles.[20] He develops the concept of *patria* as a democratic republic which encompasses not only civil and political equality but also the right to educa-tion and labour. A true *patria* cannot have strangers within its borders. Whether it comes from denial of political rights or from social oppression, exclusion is incompatible with the principle of the republic. Since it has to be a community sustained by bonds of fellowship and love, the *patria* must assure everyone the dignity that comes from citizenship and the respect and self-respect that education and labour assure.

[19] Ibid. 884 (Eng. trans. 56–7).

[20] The struggle of 'brave and earnest British women' for the extension of the suffrage, he writes to Emilie Venturi on 2 May 1870, must be sustained by any logical, sensitive, and fearless man (*Mazzini's Letters*, ed. Bolton King (Westport, Conn., 1979), 201). Equally straighforward is his answer to an English corre-spondent who had asked his opinion on the question of the right of men of colour to vote in the USA: 'You have abolished slavery. This abolition is the crown of your glorious strife, the religious consequence of your battles, which otherwise would have only been a lamentable butchery. You have decreed that the sun of the Republic shall shine freely upon all; that as God is one, so on the blessed soil where liberty is not merely a chance fact, but a faith and a gospel, the stamp of Humanity shall be one. Can you mutilate this great prin-ciple? Can you curtail and reduce it to the proportions of the semi-liberty of the monarchies? Can you tolerate that any man amongst you should only be the half of himself? Can you proclaim the dogma of semi-responsibility? Can you constitute on the republican soil of America a class of political slaves like those of the Middle Ages? Does liberty exist without the vote?' Ibid. 196.

A Country is not a mere territory: the particular territory is only its foundation. The Country is the idea which rises upon that foundation; it is the sentiment of love, the sense of fellowship which binds together all the sons of that territory. So long as a single one of your brothers is not represented by his own vote in the development of the national life—so long as a single one vegetates uneducated among the educated—so long as a single one able and willing to work languishes in poverty for want of work-you have not got a Country such as it ought to be, the Country of all and for all.[21]

Only citizens can successfully demand social justice. The voice of the oppressed, the exploited, and the poor will not be heard unless they can speak as citizens, unless they can appeal to common membership of the same *patria*. The building of the republic must then be the concern of the working class too. It is their duty as much as anybody else's. The Venetians used to say of their republic 'Venice is our own: we have made her;' Italian workers must be able to say the same of Italy. If they can say 'this *patria* is ours' because they and their fathers have created, beautified, and consecrated it with their affection, joys, sorrows, and blood, they can rightfully demand to be recognized as equal citizens and to enjoy their share of the nation's wealth and prosperity. *Patria* is not only a *respublica*, but also a common workshop ('La patria è la nostra lavoreria'). The voice of the citizen-worker resounds more powerfully than any other voice: they can ask for their rights because they have accomplished their duties to the republic and done their share in the workshop.

Without Country you have neither name, token, voice, nor rights, no admission as brothers into the fellowship of the Peoples. You are the bastards of Humanity. Soldiers without a banner, Israelites among the nations, you will find neither faith, nor protection; none will be sureties for you. Do not beguile yourselves with the hope of emancipation from unjust social conditions if you do not first conquer a Country for yourselves; where there is no Country there is no common agreement to which you can appeal; the egoism of self-interest rules alone, and he who has the upper hand keeps it, since there is no common safeguard for the interests of all.[22]

[21] *Dei doveri dell'uomo*, 885 (Eng. trans. 58).
[22] Ibid. 881 (Eng. trans. 53–4).

For Mazzini *patria* is a common house in which we live with people whom we understand and love more than others because they are more similar and closer to us. It is also, however, a house among other houses of equal worth. When we stay in our house we have to fulfil our duties as citizens; if the circumstances of life bring us into other houses we have to fulfil our duties toward humanity. Defence of liberty is always our primary duty even if we live on foreign soil and the oppressed people is not our people: 'wherever you may be, into the midst of whatever people circumstances may have driven you, fight for the liberty of that people if the moment calls for it'.[23]

Our most fundamental moral obligations are to humanity. Before being citizens of a particular country we are human beings. National barriers cannot be invoked to justify moral deafness. Voices of peoples suffering oppression can be heard from any place; common political ideals make the translation possible.

That people whom you admire in victory and in defeat is a people foreign and perhaps almost unknown to you; speaking a different language, and with a manner of life which has no visible influence upon yours; what matters it to you whether it is dominated by the Sultan or the king of Bavaria, by the Russian Czar or by a government springing from the common will of the nation? But in your heart a voice cries, 'Those men . . . are your brothers: brothers not only by community of origin and nature, but community of work and purpose.'[24]

We may not be able to understand their suffering entirely; surely it cannot mean for us what it means for them. But we can understand enough to join their struggle. Love comes to assist the weakness of our understanding. The same love that sustains commitment to the common liberty of our people sustains commitment to human dignity:

If you do not embrace the whole human family in your love, if you do not confess your faith in its unity—consequent on the unity of God—and in the brotherhood of the Peoples who are appointed to reduce that unity to fact—if wherever one of your fellow-men groans, wherever the dignity of human nature is violated by falsehood or tyranny,

[23] Ibid. 882 (Eng. trans. 55).   [24] Ibid. 872 (Eng. trans. 44).

you are not prompt, being able, to succour that wretched one, or do not feel yourself called, being able to fight for the purpose of relieving the deceived or oppressed—you disobey your law of life, or not comprehend the religion which will bless the future.[25]

Even if we fight for another people's liberty on foreign soil, we must remain patriots. If we are Italians we have to fight as Italians. We do not need to give up our patriotism to support the cause of human dignity. On the contrary, the cause of humanity can be more effectively advanced by building our *patria*. As individuals we can do very little to help brothers who do not belong to our country. At best, Mazzini remarks, we can extend to them our charity or exchange with them occasional favours, like good neighbours; we cannot work with them in a common enterprise. We need a medium between us and humanity; and the correct mediums are nations and the free countries built upon them. They are the means by which God has elected to carry out the plan of the advancement of humanity. We must then begin by constructing our country, and we must never dream of serving humanity without serving our country first.

In labouring according to true principles for our Country we are labouring for Humanity; our Country is the fulcrum of the lever which we have to wield for the common good. If we give up this fulcrum we run the risk of becoming useless to our Country and to Humanity. Before *associating* ourselves with the Nations which compose humanity we must exist as a Nation.[26]

Liberty must be the guiding principle of each *patria*'s politics both at home and abroad. One cannot tolerate the political Jesuitism of those European countries that hold liberty sacred within but systematically violate it without. For Mazzini true patriotism demands full respect of sister-nations and the courage to stand bravely against those who proclaim themselves masters of the world, whoever they happen to be. Because you are ready to die for humanity, concludes Mazzini, 'the life of your Country will be immortal'.[27]

For Mazzini love of country, like other forms of political and

[25] Ibid. 878 (Eng. trans. 51).   [26] Ibid. 882 (Eng. trans. 55).
[27] Ibid. 886 (Eng. trans. 59).

moral love, proceeds from the universal to the particular. In a letter to German correspondents he writes: 'I am an Italian, but also a man and a European. I adore *my* Country, because I adore a *Country* in the abstract; I adore our *Liberty*, because I believe in abstract *Liberty*; *our* rights, because I believe in abstract *Right*.' Here he emphasizes duty, rather than love; the duty that each of us has to know and to fulfil God's Law. He uses in fact the verb 'to adore', which is perfectly appropriate to his religious sense of duty. As the context of the letter shows, however, Mazzini's point is that love of country has to be enlarged and ennobled by allegiance to universal principles. Our nation deserves our love as long as it remains an instrument for 'the good and the progress of all'. Geographical conditions, history, tradition, language, customs are not sufficient for a nation to be worthy of love. All that needs to be illuminated by a superior moral light that comes from a commitment to liberty and justice for all. If our country does evil, everything is spoiled; it no longer deserves our love; it deserves to disappear. 'If it does evil, if it resorts to oppression, if it becomes a missionary of injustice for temporary interests, it loses its rights of existence and digs its own grave. These are my inmost feelings about Nationality.'[28] He wanted to explain to his German friends that there is more than one way of being German. There is a Germany that oppresses and a Germany that stands for the power of the intellect; the Germany of Metternich and the Germany of Luther, and of the sixteenth-century peasants who proclaimed that *'the kingdom of Heaven ought to be reflected as far as possible here on earth'*. This latter Germany does not need expansion; it simply needs to rediscover and cultivate its own spiritual heritage; it does not need 'a mean nationalism'.[29] The same word 'nationalism' that Herder used to indicate a salutary antidote against cosmopolitanism and cultural hybridness signifies for Mazzini the degeneration of the principle of nationality.

Commitment to the nation degenerates into ignoble nationalism when it forgets or disregards the principle that 'the liberty of a people cannot be won and maintained except by the faith

---

[28] *Mazzini's Letters*, 175.   [29] Ibid. 168.

which declares the right of all to liberty'.[30] Separated from liberty, nationalism is for Mazzini just another way of masking illegitimate authority or unjust government. It is the opposite of the spirit of nationality that he believed animated nineteenth-century European revolutions. Nationality means the affirmation of right over force, the brotherhood of a people, and the commitment to transform the political map of Europe according to these principles. Born as a cultural concept, it becomes in Mazzini's analysis a political ideal for European patriots: the revolutionaries had loved their own nations—Italy, Germany, Poland—but in such a way that allowed them to recognize each other as fellows committed to the same ideal. The way in which each of them loved his country made them similar; their generous love of liberty transcended cultural barriers and, as love always does, made recognition and unity possible. Mazzini wanted to speak to them; he spoke out in order to encourage greater numbers of them. Only these kinds of patriots could work together; only the working together of these patriots could build the new humanity he was dreaming of.

Like that of Dante, Mazzini's voice sounded too severe to his fellow Italians, his call too high to be answered. When he spoke of Dante as a voice crying in the desert, he was speaking, without knowing it, of his own destiny. As he wrote in 1829, exile is man's worst fate;

Exile! He who first devised this punishment had neither father, mother, friend, nor lover. He sought to revenge himself on his fellow-men by saying to them:—*Be you accursed in exile, as I have been by nature! You shall be orphans, and die the death of the soul. I take from you father, mother, lover, and country, all but the breath of life; so that you may wander like Cain throughout the universe, and the iron of despair may enter your souls.*

The exiled must wander through foreign lands, always a stranger to other people's hopes and joy. In his heart there is a void that never leaves him. Only death may bring relief from pain, but death on a foreign soil evokes images of horror:

[30] Ibid.

The very tomb is doubly cold when a foreign soil covers the dead within, and death, who appears like an angel of glory on the battle-field, and often like an angel of consolation to those who expire in the arms of their kindred, glares like a hideous skeleton, darkening the pillow of him who expires in a foreign land.[31]

He was once again prophetic. He lived his entire life as an exile longing to return; he died in 1872 on Italian soil, but under a fictitious name. Had he lived in post-Risorgimento Italy, he would have experienced an even harsher exile; that is, a moral and political exile. Italy was not even remotely close to the ideal *patria* for which he had been fighting for all his life. He would have continued his struggle, but he would probably have felt the same sense of disillusionment and distance that Milton and Rousseau had described in their letters. The very nature of his patriotism made him prone to political and moral disillusion-ment. The *patria* he loved so intensely was a combination of political ideals, culture, memories, and places. It was not just the political ideal of the republic, it was other things in addition to that; but culture, memories, and places—without the republic—are not sufficient to make the patriot feel at home. In a letter of October 1848 to George Sand he decribes the sense of spiritual homelessnes that he felt while he was in Italy: 'The last emotion that I felt was on the Alps, in the midst of the snows of the St. Gothard; and that was not aroused by my Country. In Italy, in spite of the tokens of sympathy which accompanied my return, I never ceased for one moment to feel myself in exile.'[32] In April of the same year he had been welcomed in Milan like a hero; a few months later, disappointed by the failure of his plan for a revolutionary war against Austria, he says that he feels himself in exile in his own country. It is not just political resentment; it is cultural and spiritual estrangement: he felt he had no place between the masses who had noble instincts yet were so pro-foundly ignorant as 'to yield themselves to the first intriguing person who appears', and an élite who had *savoir-faire* without principles.

---

[31] *Life and Writings of Joseph Mazzini* (London, 1905), ii. 3.
[32] Letter to George Sand, 7 Oct. 1848, in *Mazzini's Letters*, 123.

Fifteen years later Italy was amost entirely unified and independent. Yet Mazzini did not recognize it as the *patria* for which he had been fighting for all his life: 'No; the Italy of to-day is not the Italy hoped for and foreseen by me thirty years ago, saluted in the germ in 1849, within the walls of Rome, by you and by the men who were then armed priests of the *Ideal*, and who are now the contented soldiers of a Power allied with despotism abroad and living by repression at home.'[33] He went as far as to say that 'Italy matters little to me, if she is not to accomplish great and noble things for the good of all'.[34] Places, memories, language, customs are not sufficient to make the country worthy of his love; they do not make up for the lack of moral and political belonging. When he was exiled in a foreign country, memories of places and peoples induced nostalgia and longing to be there; when he was in his own *patria*, they did not attenuate the sense of moral and political distance. Exit and exile were painful; but return also was hard, since he found only memories and places, but not the republic, to welcome him.

As Mazzini himself sadly acknowledged, the lessons and ideals of 1848 were lost and defeated in the Europe of the early 1860s. For 1848 patriots, the word 'nation' meant 'the organisation of the work of Humanity, of which the nations are the individuals'.[35] Accordingly, to fight on behalf of the nation meant to fight for the liberty of each people against despotism and foreign domination and to be clear that 'the liberty of a people cannot be won and maintained except by the faith which declares the right of all to liberty'.[36] As another great heretic of the Risorgimento, Carlo Pisacane, wrote in 1860 in the same vein, the principle of nationality that had excited the most generous souls in 1848 was an ideal of liberty. Nationality, he stresses, means the free expression of the collective will of a people; common interest; full and absolute liberty; no privileged classes, groups, or dynasties. Love of country can only grow on the soil of liberty and liberty alone can turn citizens into supporters of the republic. Under the yoke of princes and monarchs the

---

[33] Letter to Ernst Haug, Apr. 1863, ibid. 184.
[34] Letter to Daniel Stern, 24 Oct. 1864, ibid. 194.
[35] Ibid. 169.   [36] Ibid. 168.

generous passions of patriotism are bound to degenerate.[37] Mazzini and Pisacane were perceptive observers. In the Europe of monarchies, the 'principle of Nationality' was corrupted into 'a mean nationalism'; a politics of sheer force and interest replaced a politics of free and spontaneous development of nations. It was another victory of *raison d'état* against the politics of the republic and patriotism.[38]

The transition from patriotism to nationalism was not just an Italian intellectual trend. In England the demarcation between Radical and Conservative patriotism was becoming blurred under Palmerston's leadership. He frequently used the rhetoric of patriotism to stress the unity between the people and the government in the common cause of helping oppressed nations, thereby affirming England's historical mission as champion of liberty and rights in the world. The process of absorption of patriotism into Liberal and later Conservative patriotism continued under Gladstone, the champion of Italian independence, and even more forcefully under Disraeli, who explicitly proclaimed the Tory party as the national and patriotic party of England. The speeches that Disraeli gave in 1872 at Manchester offer an important example of a rhetoric designed to tranform working-class Radical patriotism into loyalty to the crown combined with pride for being subjects of a mighty empire. 'Working class people', he said, 'are English to the core. They repudiate cosmopolitan principles. They adhere to national principles. They are for maintaining the greatness of the kingdom and the empire, and they are proud of being subjects of our Sovereign and members of such an Empire.'[39] By the end of the 1870s the Conservatives had won the battle to be called the

---

[37] 'Per esservi nazionalità bisogna che non frappongasi ostacolo di sorta alla libera manifestazione della volontà collettiva, e che veruno interesse prevalga all'interesse universale, quindi non può scompagnarsi dalla piena e assoluta libertà, né ammettere classi privilegiate, o dinastie, o individui la cui volontà, attesi gli ordini sociali, debba assolutamente prevalere: è nazionalità quella che godesi sotto il giogo d'un assoluto sovrano?' *La rivoluzione*, in F. della Peruta, *Scrittori politici dell'Ottocento* (Milan, s.d.), i. 1181; see also ibid. 1184: 'Col dispotismo non v'è nazionalità, qualunque lingua parli il tiranno, qualunque sia il luogo dove ebbe i natali.'

[38] *Mazzini's Letters*, 169.

[39] See Cunningham, 'Language of Patriotism', 22.

party of patriotism; the connection between the unity of the nation and Conservatism became firmly recognized. Against the Conservatives' ideological initiative, Liberals and Radicals opposed the flag of internationalism and pacifism. The working class partly followed the allure of Conservative patriotism, and partly resisted by responding either with apathy, or by retrieving the language of Radical patriotism of the 1830s or 1840s, or by proclaiming hostility towards patriotism as such on behalf of socialist internationalism.[40]

In the age of imperialism, wrote Hugh Cunningham, 'it was impossible to demarcate a patriotism of the left; the language had passed to the right and those who employed it did so too'.[41] Perhaps historical circumstances were too unfavourable for the left to resist the Conservatives' ideological offensive on the battleground of patriotism. One might, however, question whether the left did all it could. Of the various possible modes of ideological resistance, the abandonment of the field of patriotism for the cause of cosmopolitanism or proletarian internationalism was the least effective. The old language of republican patriotism would probably have offered a more powerful rhetoric as it would have allowed them to oppose to the Conservatives' rhetoric another interpretation of 'being English' based upon a genuinely English intellectual and political tradition. When Disraeli proclaimed that the English working class 'are English to the core', the right answer, perhaps, was not 'no, we are cosmopolitans' or 'no, we are internationalist', but 'yes indeed, we are English to the core, because to be English means to be committed to the ideal of liberty and justice at home and abroad, as the founders of the English nation have taught by their example'. It would probably not have worked, but it would have been better than fleeing the field.

In France too, nation and republic parted company, and in spite of the legacy of the Revolution, the language of patriotism assumed nationalistic and monarchical tones. A century after Valmy, where revolutionary forces fought to the cry 'Vive la

---

[40] 'Thou shalt not be a patriot for a patriot is an international blackleg,' ibid. 27.

[41] Ibid.

Nation!', the right had gained the ideological monopoly of national and nationalistic issues. Nation and political right became synonyms. For Charles Maurras, to mention an extreme case, to be a French patriot one must fight the *république*, because republican spirit destroys national defence and favours religious ideas alien to traditional French Catholicism. The patriot's deep and uncompromising loyalty must go to the monarch, who is the true protector of the liberty, the honour, and the prosperity of the nation.[42] Nationalism, for the founder of the League d'action française, was a political commitment to protect the nation's cultural and religious integrity from the 'foreigner from within'; that is, from champions of ideas and values alien to the spiritual core of France. Patriotism, in this sense, has to work as a new religion since the nation alone can provide modern men with the spiritual centredness they need. The nation must therefore be restored to its purity, and for the nation to be restored one must first decapitate the wicked *République*.[43]

In Germany too, where republican patriotism was never a significant intellectual tradition, patriotism became synonymous with loyalty to the monarch and a commitment to protect Germany's spiritual uniqueness. As Bismarck remarked in his memoirs, German patriotism needs a prince, as a prince alone can offer the basis for a larger loyalty that transcends local allegiances. Historically and ethnically, Germans are divided. They need a monarch and a dynasty that ensures them unity and

---

[42] The appeal of the League d'action française reads: 'Français de naissance et de cœur, de raison et de volonté, je remplirai tous les devoirs d'un patriote conscient. Je m'engage à combattre tout régime républicain, la République en France et le règne de l'étranger. L'esprit républicain désorganise la défense nationale et favorise des influences religieuses directement hostiles au catholicisme traditionnel. Il faut rendre à la France un régime qui soit français. Notre unique avenir est donc la monarchie telle que la personnifie l'héritier des quarante rois qui, en mille ans, firent la France. Seule la monarchie assure le salut public et, répondant de l'ordre, prévient les maux publics que l'antisémitisme et le nationalisme dénoncent. Organe nécessaire de tout intérêt général, la monarchie relève l'autorité, les libertés, la prosperité et l'honneur.' J. Plumyène, *Les Nations romantiques* (Paris, 1979), 265–6.

[43] 'On ne saurait trop le redire, le premier bienfait de la monarchie ne sera pas de réaliser son programme réparateur, mais d'abord de détruire la République et ainsi d'arracher le pays à cette trahison permanente et profonde, à ce "mal" d'un gouvernement qui, au lieu de garder et de faire vivre, détruit.' Ibid. 270.

strength.[44] Once the political unity is achieved, the next step is the construction of cultural unity: the *Staatsnation* must find its completion in the *Kulturnation*. Politicians, assisted by artists, writers, and intellectuals, have to work to create a more spiritually centred and culturally pure Germany. Of the two key concepts that condense the intellectual project of late nineteenth-century German patriotism, *Kultur* and *Volk*, the former express the belief in the uniqueness of German spirit, while the latter suggests a magical or mystical identification with the original spirit of the German people and defines a cultural and ethnic borderline between Germans and non-Germans. The *Volk* celebrated by the *völkisch* ideology is original and uncontaminated by ethnic filth; it is an ideal of purity to be contemplated and dreamt of with nostalgia and resentment for the impure world.[45]

Even in the age of imperialism, however, the idea that the nation must be understood as a political community founded on the free consent of the citizens did not entirely disappear. In fact, it inspired the most influential late nineteenth-century interpretation of the meaning of nation, namely Ernest Renan's conference at the Sorbonne on 11 March 1882 on 'Qu'est-ce qu'une Nation?' As has been recognized by students of nationalism, the importance of Renan's conference consists in the fact that against the doctrines of nation as a community based on race, language, interests, religious affinity, and geography he opposes the idea that the nation is a spiritual principle based upon a people's 'clearly expressed desire to live a common life': a nation's existence, he said, is 'a daily plebiscite'.[46]

Equally important, though less remarked on, is that Renan connected his idea of the nation to the intellectual revolution of the eighteenth-century which restored the republican idea of *patrie*:

And then the eighteenth century had changed everything. Man had returned, after centuries of abasement, to the old spirit, to self-respect, to the idea of his rights. The words 'country' and 'citizen' had resumed their significance. Thus it was that the boldest operation ever attempted

---

[44] Ibid. 276.   [45] Ibid. 283–8.

[46] In *Œuvres complètes*, ed. H. Psichiari (Paris, 1947), i. 904; Eng. trans., 'What is a Nation?', in *The Poetry of the Celtic Races, and Other Studies by Ernest Renan* (Port Washington, 1970), 81.

in history was accomplished—an operation which might be compared to what in physiology would be the gift of life and its first identity, to a body from which head and heart had been removed.[47]

As Renan remarks, the idea of the nation as a combination of a political principle and a culture made of a people's memories of sacrifices and sufferings reflects eighteenth-century universalism. The doctrines that give priority to culture, race, or language over the political ideal of the republic are, on the contrary, to be regarded as an intellectual and moral degeneration:

When we thus exaggerate it [the importance of language and race], we imprison ourselves in a limited culture, held as being national; we are hemmed in, cooped up. We quit the great atmosphere that we breathe in the vast field of humanity, to shut ourselves up in conventicles of compatriots. Nothing can be worse for the mind, nothing more hurtful to civilisation.[48]

For Renan, the principle that the foundation of the nation lies in the people's will is a guarantee of cultural openness and a legitimate criterion to settle disputes over boundaries which will respect peoples' liberty. He meant to construct a work of intellectual clarification and make a political point. For this purpose he infused into the concept of nations a few fragments of the republican language of patriotism which had filtered through from eighteenth-century culture. In doing so, he was going in the opposite direction to the main ideological trend of late nineteenth-century Europe which was to dissolve the political values of the *patrie* within the spiritual unity of the nation. The ideal of a self-governing republic where equal citizens live freely in their own way, according to their particular culture, lost its appeal *vis-à-vis* the ideal of the nation as a community of culture, language, and ethnicity. What seemed to matter most was not to be an Italian, or an English, or a French citizen, but to be Italian, English, or French, even if that implied to be the subject of a monarch or an emperor. Separated from the republic, the ideal of nation no longer attracted democrats and radicals, while the *patrie*, confused with the nation, lost the connection with liberty which it had had for centuries.

[47] Ibid. 900 (Eng. trans. 69–70).   [48] Ibid. 894 (Eng. trans. 77).

Epilogue

Patriotism without Nationalism

THE ideological victory of the language of nationalism has relegated the language of patriotism to the margins of contemporary political thought. And yet, when peoples become engaged in struggles for liberty, when they have to face the task of rebuilding their nations after experiences of war and totalitarian regimes, theorists are able to recover elements of the old language of patriotism under the predominant rhetoric of nationalism. Their efforts are always historically and theoretically significant; in most cases they suggest the right intellectual path to be followed to reconstruct a language of patriotism without nationalism. But more work needs to be done; the search is unfinished.

One of the most important examples of rediscovery of the language of patriotism can be found in the writings of the Italian anti-Fascist martyr Carlo Rosselli. In his main work, *Socialismo liberale*, composed in exile in 1929, Rosselli remarked that the Italian socialists' attitude of 'ignoring the highest value of national life' was a serious political mistake. Even if they did so 'for the sake of combating ... primitive or degenerate, or selfish forms of devotion to country', their politics in fact helps the other parties 'that base their success on exploiting the national myth'.[1]

For Rosselli, the socialists failed to understand that national feeling (*sentimento di nazionalità*) is not an abstract theoretical

---

[1] 'Se i socialisti, pur di combattere queste forme primitive o degenerate o interessate di attaccamento al paese, si ostineranno a ignorare i valori più alti della vita nazionale, non faranno che facilitare il gioco delle altre correnti che nello sfruttamento del mito nazionale basano le loro fortune' (Turin, 1979), 135; trans., *Liberal Socialism*, ed. N. Urbinati (Princeton, 1994), 123.

construction, but a genuine human passion that is particularly strong in those countries like Italy and Germany which achieved their national independence later. Instead of trying to replace national sentiment with internationalism, socialists ought to purify it from all connection with state control, nationalism, imperialism, and all myths of national primacy and transform it into a constructive political force that works for the unity of Europe.[2]

Rosselli put a clear demarcation line between patriotism and nationalism. He identified the former with claims for liberty based on respect for the rights of other peoples; the second with politics of aggrandizement pursued by reactionary regimes.[3] Both ideologies addressed national sentiment, both commanded powerful passions. For this reason, Rosselli believed, they should be used against each other. Instead of rejecting it as prejudice, anti-Fascists should put patriotism at the centre of their programme: the anti-Fascist revolution, he said, is 'a patriotic duty'.[4]

To have their own patriotism, the anti-Fascists needed an idea of *patria* radically different from that used by Fascist demagogues. Our *patria*, he wrote, 'coincides with our moral world and with the *patria* of all free men';[5] it is a value that goes perfectly well with the other values of anti-Fascism: the dignity of men, liberty, justice, culture, and labour. Fascists exhalt the nation and Italy; anti-Fascists too must present themselves as the champions of the nation and exalt Italy and Italianness; but their nation has to be a free nation open toward Europe and the world, and their Italy and their Italianness has to incorporate the best of Italy: the Italy of Mazzini, Garibaldi, Pisacane; the Italy of the civilized Italians, of the peasants, of the workers, and of the intellectuals that have kept their integrity. To this Italy, and only to this belongs the anti-Fascists' loyalty: we can say loudly and with pride, wrote Rosselli, that we are traitors of the Fascist *patria* because we are loyal to another Italy.[6]

A few years later another anti-Fascist found the path to

---

[2] Id. 'La lezione della Sarre', in *Scritti dell' esilio* (Turin, 1992), ii. 96; and 'Discussione sul Risorgimento', ibid. 154–5.

[3] 'Irredentismo slavo', ibid. 46–9.   [4] 'Opposizione d'attacco', ibid. 233.

[5] 'Fronte verso l'Italia', ibid. 4.   [6] 'Realismo', ibid. 341.

rediscovering and reworking the content and the themes of the language of patriotism: in 1943 Simone Weil wrote *L'Enracinement* while she was in London working for Free France. Asked to write about the possibility of a regeneration of France, Simone Weil proposed a powerful reinterpretation of the patriotism of liberty and compassion which addresses the need for cultural and spiritual rootedness without turning love of country into blind identification or pride for the uniqueness of our own nation. Our obligation to our country, she writes, is grounded in the vital need of human beings for rootedness:

Just as there are certain culture beds for certain microscopic animals, certain types of soil for certain plants, so there is a certain part of the soul in everyone and certain ways of thought and action communicated from one person to another which can only exist in a national setting, and disappear when a country is destroyed.[7]

For Frenchmen, whom she was addressing, the vital medium is France. Each of them

knows that one part of his soul sticks so closely to France, that when France is taken away it remains stuck to her, as the skin does to some burning object, and is thus pulled off. There is something, then, to which a part of every Frenchman's soul sticks, and is the same for all, unique, real though impalpable, and real in the sense of something one is able to touch.[8]

And yet, great as their obligation is to their country—an obligation that may even require them to give everything to France —they are entitled to demand that France be faithful to the best of its history. They can demand of her not to hold an empire and—as patriots—they are not only entitled, but indeed compelled, to distinguish their patriotism from that of their fellow Frenchmen who speak with pride and joy about 'their' empire. They can and must fight against the patriotism modelled 'after the style of Richelieu, Louis XIV, or Maurras', for a patriotism inspired by the Christian ethic and the spirit of 1789.[9] In 1789

[7] S. Weil, *L'Enracinement: Prélude à une déclaration des devoirs envers l'être humain* (Paris, 1949), 138; Eng. trans., *The Need for Roots* (New York, 1952), 159.
[8] Ibid. 138 (Eng. trans. 159).   [9] Ibid. 145 (Eng. trans. 168).

France committed herself to liberty and justice not just for herself but for the world. If she becomes the owner of human flesh and blood, as she did during the Empire, she is no longer faithful to this commitment. To lose imperial France for Frenchmen would be to lose a degenerated part of their soul and to give all their strength to another and better part. Patriotism makes citizens demanding toward their country and themselves. It urges them to find in the history of their country inspiration and reasons to strengthen a commitment to liberty. France is not an exceptional case. In every people's history, one can find voices that have asked for liberty and justice whose echoes still live in the common memory. To retrieve them from oblivion is the task of the patriot of liberty and compassion.

Patriotism requires no exemptions. It allows us to keep both eyes clearly fixed on all the past, present, and future of our country while remaining, painfully at times, spiritually close to it. All that is the result of love of country in its purest form: a love that does not come from excitment and admiration for the greatness and glory of our country, but from the perception of its weakness and fragility. The choice is not between cosmopolitanism and patriotism, but between a patriotism of greatness and a patriotism of compassion. As Simone Weil explained, 'One can either love France for the glory which would seem to ensure for her prolonged existence in time and space; or else one can love her as something which, being earthly, can be destroyed, and is all the more precious on that account.'[10] She describes the two sorts of patriotism as 'two distinct ways of loving' which are probably incompatible with each other. And she also remarks that while admirers of the greatness and uniqueness of their own country have a wide range of rhetorical tools to use, patriots of compassion have no language of their own.

Compassion and charity describe a love that is not mere participation in the country's unhappiness:

Nor should it be supposed that the object of such love need necessarily be confined to an unhappy country. Happiness is as much an object for compassion as unhappiness, because it belongs to this earth, in other

---

[10] Ibid. 148–9 (Eng. trans. 172).

words is incomplete, frail, and fleeting. Moreover, there is, unfortunately, always a certain amount of unhappiness in the life of any country.[11]

The patriot of compassion needs not deny his or her country's greatness and glorious accomplishments. Recognition of good in the object of our compassion makes it 'all the more tender, all the more poignant': 'When a Christian represents to himself Christ on the Cross, his compassion is not diminished by the thought of the latter's perfection, nor the other way about'.[12] As Simone Weil puts it, patriotism of compassion 'is alone legitimate for a Christian, for it alone wears the Christian badge of humility'. Compassion is not only a Christian value, but also a distinctive character of republican patriotism. Christian or republican, the patriotism of compassion is righteous because it allows us to keep both eyes fixed on our country's greatness and miseries. It does not diminish when we confront our country's crimes, scandals, injustices, cruelties, mistakes, falsehoods; it simply suffers more. We feel ashamed to belong to our country and yet we do not run away; we do not give up our citizenship; we do not write Rousseau's letter to Pictet. 'Where compassion is concerned, crime itself provides a reason, not for withdrawing oneself, but for approaching, not with the object of sharing the guilt, but the shame'.[13]

Weil's patriotism of compassion is a powerful antidote to the nationalist's love of country that preaches the necessity of defending the country's culture and history as values to be retrieved and defended in their entirety, as goods to be cherished because of their distinctiveness and particularity, because they are ours. Like the patriot, the nationalist also looks at his country's history and feels attached to it. He sees, however, no fragility or reasons for shame: divinity and eternity is everywhere, in each single moment. His nation's culture appears to him as a wealth threatened by foreigners' cultural and political invasion or his fellows' weakness and corruption. The patriot sees a more variegated picture composed of transient greatness and glory; past or present crimes and scandals; past or present miseries and

---

[11] Ibid. 149 (Eng. trans. 172).   [12] Ibid. 149 (Eng. trans. 173).
[13] Ibid. 149 (Eng. trans. 173).

humiliations. It is all his; he does not flee, he does not want to forget. He accepts everything, but not everything has the same value or belongs to him in the same way. Some moments of the nation's history bring joy, others indignation, others shame—the most distinctive feeling, perhaps, of the patriot's love.

Simone Weil's pages are a poignant testimony to the surprising capacity of the language of patriotism to come to life again. Equally surprising, though intellectually much less refined, is the renaissance of patriotic language in Italy in 1943–5. What makes that renaissance particularly interesting is the fact that the language of patriotism in Italy had been totally transfigured by monarchical and Fascist rhetoric. An article published in 1943 in a Roman newspaper shows well the sense of the widespread distaste for patriotic rhetoric: 'Our famous Risorgimento never ends: we began in Eritrea, then Libya, then the world war; to obtain some nasty piece of land in the sun we went and got ourselves mixed up in Abyssinia, then we went and messed around in Spain, then we went to finish up in Russia. Where on earth will we go to end this situation!'[14] And yet, the same words that had been always been resoundingly false and hideous, suddenly sounded true and sweet. They no longer evoked images of pathetic colonial aggression and ignoble national pride; they inspired images of liberty and stimulated generous commitment. It was an intellectual and moral discovery, in the most genuine sense, as the testimony of Pietro Chiodi epitomizes:

I had never realized that the *Liceo* was so resplendent and full of light. I feel that it is a little part of my *patria*—the part in which I am asked to fulfil my duty towards it. For the first time I realize that I have a *patria* as something that belongs to me, something that is partly also entrusted to me, to my intelligence, to my courage, to my spirit of sacrifice.[15]

---

[14] 'Il nostro famoso Risorgimento non finisce mai: abbiamo cominciato dall'Eritrea, poi la Libia, poi la guerra mondiale, per ottenere un pezzaccio di terra al sole ci siamo andati a impelagare in Abissinia, poi ci siamo andati a battere la testa in Spagna, poi siamo andati a finire in Russia. Dove, dove mai andremo a finire di questo passo!' Quoted in C. Pavone, *Una guerra civile* (Turin, 1991), 181.

[15] 'Non mi ero mai accorto che il Liceo fosse cosí splendente e pieno di luce.

The rediscovery of the *patria* is remembered in the language of love: love of places that suddenly become meaningful, of peoples that are now felt close and dear. A love that changes life, as it makes those who feel it more generous, more capable of understanding and solidarity. Natalia Ginzburg condenses all this in a superb page:

The streets and the squares of the city, once the theatre of our adolescent boredom and the object of our greatest scorn, became the places that we had to defend. The words *patria* and 'Italy' which had nauseated us when they appeared on walls of our schools because they had been accompanied by the adjective 'Fascist', because they had been filled with emptiness, suddenly appeared to us without adjectives, and so transformed that it seemed to us that we heard them and thought of them for the first time. Suddenly they seemed real to our ears. We were there to defend the *patria* and the *patria* was those streets and those squares, our loved ones and our childhood, and all the people passing by. A truth so simple and so obvious seemed strange to us because we had grown up with the conviction that we did not have a *patria* and that we had been born, unluckily for us, at a point filled with emptiness. And even more strange to us was the fact that out of love for all those unknown people who were passing by, and out of love for a future unknown but which we could make out in the distance, in the midst of deprivation and devastation, solidity and radiance, every one of us was ready to lose himself and his own life.[16]

Sento che è una piccola parte della mia Patria. Quella parte in cui io sono chiamato a compiere il mio dovere verso di lei. E' la prima volta che mi accorgo di avere una Patria come qualcosa di mio, affidato, in parte, anche a me, alla mia intelligenza, al mio coraggio, al mio spirito di sacrificio.' Quoted ibid. 171.

[16] 'Le strade e le piazze delle città, teatro un tempo della nostra noia di adolescenti e oggetto del nostro altezzoso disprezzo, diventarono i luoghi che era necessario difendere. Le parole 'patria' e 'Italia', che ci avevano tanto nauseato fra le pareti della scuola perchè accompagnate dall'aggettivo 'fascista', perchè gonfie di vuoto, ci apparvero d'un tratto senza aggettivi e così trasformate che ci sembrò di averle udite e pensate per la prima volta. D'un tratto alle nostre orecchie risultarono vere. Eravamo là per difendere la patria e la patria erano quelle strade e quelle piazze, i nostri cari e la nostra infanzia, e tutta la gente che passava. Una verità cosí semplice e cosí ovvia ci parve strana perchè eravamo cresciuti con la convinzione che noi non avevamo patria e che eravamo venuti a nascere, per nostra disgrazia, in un punto gonfio di vuoto. E ancor più strano ci sembrava il fatto che, per amore di tutti quegli sconosciuti che passavano, e per amore di un futuro ignoto ma di cui scorgevamo in distanza, fra privazioni e devastazioni, la solidità e lo splendore, ognuno era pronto a perdere se stesso e la propria vita.' Quoted ibid. 172.

To lose oneself to find oneself richer; to give one's life for love of people who are not kin, who simply walk the same streets; to be willing to work with them for a vague, but brighter future; to discover a common good worth being defended that is visible in the streets and squares of the city: these are feelings of patriotism in its most genuine form; and they were widespread feelings during the Resistance and the reconstruction following the war. And yet, they did not translate into a common language of patriotism. Italian intellectuals did not or could not bring themselves to say what their own fellow Italians were feeling, namely that *patria* means common liberty, that love of country is a generous commitment that has nothing in common with nationalism. As Benedetto Croce lamented in 1943, after the fall of Mussolini's regime, Italians rediscovered the word liberty, but did not recover the word that had been in the past the natural companion of liberty; that is, *patria* and *amore della patria*. This happened, he explains, because patriotism was supplanted by so-called nationalism. Even though fascists had accused their political opponents of being anti-national, rather than of being anti-patriotic, their propaganda succeeded in confusing the two different concepts of nationalism and patriotism as well as the different feelings associated with them. As a result, the legitimate repugnance toward nationalism generated hesitation and a reluctance to speak of *patria* and *amor di patria*.[17]

Although the Italians' reluctance is understandable, remarks Croce, *amore della patria* must be used again against blind and stolid nationalism, as it is not similar to it but is in fact its opposite. *Amore della patria* and nationalism are as different as a 'gentle human love for another human being' and 'bestial lust, diseased luxury, and selfish whim'.[18] Love of country is a moral concept that helps to give our noblest ideals and most austere duties a particular form and content. It makes us feel our ideals and duties more acutely so that we can work for them and fulfil them more effectively. And by working for our *patria* we work effectively for the whole of humanity. As a moral ideal, Croce

[17] *Una parola desueta: L'amor di patria*, in *L'idea liberale: Contro le confusioni e gl'ibridismi* (Bari, 1944), 21.
[18] Ibid. 22.

remarks, *patria* is intimately connected with the idea of liberty. When we lament the loss of our dignity as citizens and of our liberty as men, we are in fact lamenting the hurt and the humiliations that Italy has suffered. If love of country were to be rekindled in the hearts of Italians, concluded Croce, the political parties on the verge of regrouping would find in it the basis for the sense of common commitment to a superior ideal which is necessary for a loyal and clean democratic conflict. The good of Italy will be the boundary beyond which political and social conflict cannot pass. Patriotism well understood is then the foundation of a healthy, dynamic, open, liberal society.

The distinction between patriotism and nationalism that Croce was urging emerges also in contemporary discussion. The language of patriotism is still used to sustain commitment to the ideal of the republic while the language of nationalism (or the variation of it which currently goes under the name of communitarianism) is employed to call for cultural, ethnic, or religious homogeneity. In spite of the malleability of language, intellectual traditions seem to have their own ways of setting boundaries that do not limit our language at all but make it richer and rhetorically more powerful.

An example of the continuing relevance of the language of political patriotism and of the distinction between patriotism and nationalism is Jürgen Habermas's analysis of national identity and citizenship. In European history, Habermas remarks, the nation state has constructed the ethnic and cultural homogeneity that has provided the necessary background for democratic and liberal institutions. Nation state and democracy are two twins generated under the shadows of nationalism. In Germany, however, nationalism affirmed itself against the republican spirit and later evolved into the racist aberrations that justified the Holocaust. From 1871 to 1945 the word 'nation' meant the unity and purification to be attained through the expulsion or confinement of the enemies of the people (*Volksfremde*): social democrats, Catholics, ethnic minorities, and then Jews, democratic radicals, the left, intellectuals, and so on. Against this conception of nationalism he proposes a 'patriotism of the Constitution' (*Verfassungspatriotismus*); that is, a patriotism based on loyalty to the universalistic political principles of liberty and democracy embodied in the constitution of the Federal Republic of Germany.[19]

Unlike nationalism, constitutional patriotism separates the political ideal of the nation of citizens from the conception of the people as a pre-political community of language and culture. This form of patriotism recognizes the full legitimacy and moral worth of different forms of life and is committed to the inclusion of different cultures within the framework of the republic. For this reason, stresses Habermas, constitutional patriotism is the only form of patriotism still available and possible for the German people after Auschwitz.

Habermas disconnects constitutional patriotism from the tradition of nationalism and connects it to the spirit of 1848, the last instance in German history in which national consciousness (*Nationalbewußtsein*) and republican spirit (*republikanische Gesinnung*) were intertwined.[20] However, he explicitly separates his own interpretation of *Verfassungspatriotismus* from republicanism, which he regards as an intellectual tradition derived from Aristotle (*auf Aristoteles zurückgreifenden republikanischen Tradition der Staatslehre*) that considers citizenship primarily as membership in a self-governing ethical and cultural community (*Zugehörigkeit zu einer sich selbst bestimmenden ethnisch-kulturellen Gemeinschaft*).[21] Identical in this respect with contemporary communitarianism, republicanism is for Habermas a doctrine that regards citizens as fully integrated parts of the community, to the point that each of them can develop his or her personal and social identity only within common political institutions and traditions. This theory of citizenship, Habermas logically concludes, cannot work in highly pluralistic societies and can offer no foundation for a patriotism fit for a nation of citizens (*Staatsbürgernation*).[22]

The interpretation of republicanism as an intellectual tradition

---

[19] *Die Nachholende Revolution* (Frankfurt, 1990), 151.
[20] Ibid. 158–9.
[21] Id. *Faktizität und Geltung* (Frankfurt, 1992), 640.
[22] *Die Nachholende Revolution*, 208.

derived from Aristotle is a gross historical error.[23] Modern republicanism, particularly republican theories of citizenship and patriotism, owe much more to Roman republican authors than Aristotle. If one were to study diligently the texts of Italian pre-humanist and humanist theorists of communal self-government, as well as the jurists who rebuilt the theory of citizenship, it would become very clear that their theories were almost entirely derived from Roman sources. And even after the translation of Aristotle's *Politics*, the core of humanist theories of citizenship and patriotism was Roman, as was the inspiration for Machiavelli's, and later republican theories of citizenship.[24] For them, citizenship did not mean membership in a self-governing ethical and cultural community, but the enjoyment and exercise of civil and political rights as a member of a *respublica*, or *civitas*, which is primarily a political community established to allow the individuals to live together in justice and liberty under the protection of the law. To love one's own country meant for republican writers, as I hope I have illustrated in previous chapters, to love the republic; that is, common liberty and the laws, and the civil and political equality that makes it possible.

Habermas's *Verfassungspatriotismus* does not break at all with republican tradition; it is instead a new version of it. It not only restates the tenet of republican patriotism that love of country

---

[23] The source of Habermas's mistake is probably Charles Taylor, who argued that one of the central themes of the civic humanist tradition concerns 'the conditions for a free society'; free, he explains, 'not in the modern sense of negative liberty, but more as the antonym to "despotic"'. He also remarks that the central good of the civic humanist tradition was 'participatory self-rule'; 'Cross-Purposes: The Liberal-Communitarian Debate', in N. L. Rosenblum (ed.), *Liberalism and the Moral Life* (Cambridge, Mass., 1989), 165 and 177. If one reads the canonic texts of classical and modern republicanism such as e.g. Livy, *Ab urbe condita*, II. 2, Machiavelli, *Discorsi sopra la prima deca di Tito Livio*, II. 2, and Rousseau, *Du contrat social*, I. 8, it is easy to see that in fact republican theorists place the highest value on liberty understood as 'negative' liberty under the shield of just laws.

[24] See Q. Skinner, 'Ambrogio Lorenzetti: The Artist as a Political Philosopher', *Proceedings of the British Academy*, 72 (1986), 1–56; id., 'Machiavelli's *Discorsi* and Pre-Humanist Origins of Republican Ideas', in G. Bock et al. (eds.), *Machiavelli and Republicanism* (Cambridge, 1993), 121–41; M. Viroli, *From Politics to Reason of State* (Cambridge, 1992), 11–70.

means above all love of the republic; it also recognizes, though with some conceptual vacillation, that the republic that is or should be the object of the citizens' love is their own particular republic; not just democratic institutions, but institutions that have been built in a particular historical context and are linked to a way of life—that is, a culture—of citizens of that particular republic. To live in the hearts and the minds of German citizens, remarks Habermas, constitutional patriotism must have a particular meaning. It cannot be presented as an attachment to the universal values of democracy, but as an attachment to the values of democracy as they are embodied in the political institutions and documents of the Federal Republic. For Germans, constitutional patriotism implies a particular pride at having been able to build democratic institutions that have outlasted Nazism and at having constructed upon them a liberal political culture. Democracy has for the Germans a unique meaning, since it is a democracy born out of the ashes of Auschwitz. Without a particular identity, universal political principles cannot live and survive.[25]

Habermas's theory of *Verfassungspatriotismus* has been criticized by, among others, Gian Enrico Rusconi in a book that has opened an important debate in Italy on the significance of national identity.[26] Habermas, remarks Rusconi, disconnects citizenship—which he defines in terms of universalistic political and legal principles—from the specific historical and cultural background of the nation. Though motivated by a laudable effort to contrast the nationalist interpretation of the concept of *Kulturnation*, Habermas's theory of *Verfassungspatriotismus* disregards the fact that the normal Western type of national identity is based on a 'synthesis of universalistic principles of citizenship and pre-political data or forms of life that are ethnic and cultural in kind'.[27]

'Constitutional citizenship' of modern democratic societies, Rusconi maintains, endures and flourishes not against, but

[25] 'Für diese Verwurzelung universaler Prinzipien braucht man immer eine *bestimmte* Identität', *Die Nachholende Revolution*, 152.
[26] *Se cessiamo di essere una nazione* (Bologna, 1993).
[27] Ibid. 127.

through or within ethnic and cultural elements. The nation is part of the *Lebenswelt* and therefore works as the historical and concrete context for the universalistic democratic discourse of modern citizens. If we do not take into account that the 'citizens' nation' lives neither opposed to nor outside but within national culture, it makes no sense to connect, as Habermas does, the formal-legal concept of constitution with words like 'fatherland' and 'patriotism' that are imbued with a pathos that comes from their connection with the *Lebenswelt*. A correct interpretation of the 'patriotism of the constitution' should therefore understand civic solidarity, Rusconi concludes, as the consequence of the recognition of belonging to a common culture and a common history, however onerous and in need of critical scrutiny.

Against Habermas's effort to disconnect citizenship and nation, Rusconi stresses that in all countries 'one becomes a citizen within and by means of a national history and a national culture. Instead of opposing nationality and citizenship, we should make the definition of citizenship concrete (in the sense of *lebensweltlich*). If we rely only on universalist reasons, as Habermas does, without resorting to arguments that refer to a 'common history and a common origin', we cannot understand or encourage civic solidarity. A political culture sustained by motivations for the common good can exist only if rooted in national tradition and identity.[28] The civic loyalty and solidarity that democracy needs to work does not simply stem from the universalistic principle of citizenship, but requires the identification with the concrete cultural and political community that we call 'nation'.[29] A democratic nation is therefore based on bonds of citizenship 'motivated by shared loyalties and memories' made up of ethnocultural roots, and good political reasons to live together; it is both *demos*—voluntary membership in a political community—and *ethnos*—attachment to shared historical and cultural roots.

The basic assumption of Rusconi's analysis—that democracy needs civic virtue on the part of the citizens (and above all on the part of the political élite)—is well taken and holds true for

---

[28] Ibid. 131.   [29] Ibid. 13.

any democratic polity.[30] He is also right when he claims, contrary to Habermas, that 'in the mind and the heart of the citizens' civic virtue is not sustained by universalistic political values but by identification with values that are part of the particular culture of a people.

While it is certainly true that democracy needs civic virtue on the part of the citizens (and even more on the part of the political élite), I do not think that it needs the sort of civic virtue that Rusconi advocates. As he says, civic virtues of loyalty and solidarity rest on both common ethnocultural roots and good political reasons to sustain democracy. But if we want, as Rusconi seems to want, a stronger democratic citizenship—that is, a greater inclination of the citizens to support common liberty and to do their share of social duties—a love of common liberty should be all that we need. We need, to put it simply, patriotism and we must at the same time help to reduce, rather than invoke, identification with ethnocultural values. We should not reinforce the Italianness of the Italians or strengthen their ethnic and cultural unity, but rather focus on the political values of democratic citizenship and present and defend them as values that are part of the culture of the people. The connection between being Italians and being good citizens does not work as a necessary correlation: one does not need to be genuinely or truly Italian—in the ethnocultural sense—to be a good citizen, while one can be the most genuine or true Italian—in the ethnocultural sense—and yet be the most corrupt citizen. Equally, but more subtly wrong, is to think of the distinction between being Italian and being a good citizen as a distinction between an ethnocultural identity on the one hand and a political identity on the other. The two identities are mixed: the ethnocultural identity has political significance, while the political identity is also cultural. The historical memory of the people, which is a fundamental component of its common culture, is multiple, controversial, and open to continuous interpretations and reinterpretations which are always politically oriented. At the same time, and perhaps more importantly, political values of

---

[30] See R. Putnam, *Making Democracy Work* (Princeton, 1993).

democratic citizenship that citizens share are not universalistic constructions of an impersonal reason, but are or are perceived and lived as cultural values. They are not attached to an abstract liberty or an abstract justice, but to a way of life informed by those principles. They are attached to a liberty and a justice that is part of their culture, that has for them a particular beauty, a particular warmth, a particular colour that is connected with particular memories and particular histories. Machiavelli, it is worth noticing, spoke of *vivere libero* and when he mentions examples of patriotic love of common liberty he meant love of the common liberty of that particular people. Ethnocultural identity and political values are neither connected by implication nor distinguished under the heading of particular culture versus universalistic principles. Cultural identity and political values do in fact overlap and many combinations are possible. There are many ways of being culturally Italians, one of which is to be an Italian *citizen* in a political and cultural sense.

To distance himself from German nationalism, Habermas wants to make citizenship as universal and as political as possible; to avoid the abstractness of Habermas's position, Rusconi wants to make citizenship as national as possible. Both go too far, though in opposite directions. Habermas's *Verfassungspatriotismus* risks not answering the concerns of his fellow—Germans for national identity; the very story of the unification seems to indicate that to be German meant something else beyond allegiance to political ideals. Rusconi, on the other hand, wants to make the Italians more Italian in order to be better citizens; the danger is that they simply become too Italian; that is, too eager to affirm and defend the unity of their ethnocultural identity: working so much on the Italianness, we may lose the citizen on the way. They both fail to indicate a language of patriotism that adequately connects the political love of the republic with the attachment to one's own cultural identity.

The ethnocultural unity may translate into civic solidarity, if a culture of citizenship is erected on it; or, better, if the sense of belonging based on common culture and common ethnic descent is translated into a culture of citizenship. Without a political culture of liberty, ethnocultural unity generates love of one's cultural uniqueness (if not superiority) and a desire to keep it pure from external contamination and intrusion. We would have the nation, but it would not be a nation of citizens. In today's world the temptation to be simply the member of a nation is far too strong; there is no need, it seems to me, to encourage the longing for ethnocultural oneness. Instead of polishing or retrieving the ethnocultural oneness, one should devise political changes able to educate democratic citizens. And the political means to be used are those suggested by republican patriots: good government and well-ordered participation in the many instances of civil society and in the political decision-making process. Democratic polities do not need ethnocultural unity; they need citizens committed to the way of life of the republic.

While Habermas and his critics have been discussing patriotism from a political perspective, other scholars have stressed that patriotism has to be understood as loyalty to shared moral values and the culture of a particular community. Since the community is the necessary background for the individual's moral significance, patriotism has to be considered a virtue even if it contradicts the universalist principles of moral impartiality. A good example of the metamorphosis of the language of patriotism is Alasdair MacIntyre's essay 'Is Patriotism a Virtue?', where he claims that patriotism is for him 'loyalty to a particular nation which only those possessing that particular nationality can exhibit'.[31] Not a 'mindless loyalty' to one's own particular nation, but a loyalty which involves a regard 'for the particular characteristics and merits and achievements of one's own nation'. The essential feature of patriotic loyalty is then particularity. The patriot, explains MacIntyre, values as merits and achievements particular characteristics of his or her country, but not 'just as merits and achievements, but as the merits and achievements of this particular nation'. Similar merits and achievements of other nations do not generate in the patriot's heart the same attachment. Though not blinkered with regard to his or her own nation, the patriot is not prepared to regard in the same manner similar achievements of other nations. It is a matter of

---

[31] Lindley Lecture, University of Kansas, 26 Mar. 1984, p. 4.

love and love is always love of particular individuals, people, and places. Unlike Habermas's *Verfassungspatriotismus*, which commands the approval of reason, MacIntyre's patriotism is a passion. It must face the charge of irrationality:

The morality of patriotism is one which precisely because it is framed in terms of the membership of some particular social community with some particular social, political and economic structure, must exempt at least some fundamental structures of that community's life from criticism. Because patriotism has to be a loyalty that is in some respects unconditional, so in just those respects rational criticism is ruled out. But if so the adherents of the morality of patriotism have condemned themselves to a fundamentally irrational attitude—since to refuse to examine some of one's fundamental beliefs and attitudes is to insist on accepting them, whether they are rationally justifiable or not, which is irrational—and have imprisoned themselves within that irrationality.[32]

To the charge of irrationality, the proponent of the morality of patriotism can reply that his morality offers a valid justification of bonds and loyalties that are essential for the moral life of the individual. Each of us, remarks MacIntyre, 'to some degree or other understands his or her life as an enacted narrative; and because of our relationships with others we have to understand ourselves as characters in the enacted narratives of other people's lives'.[33] To understand the story of our lives and be therefore able to live a meaningful moral life, we need a national community. What the patriot exempts from rational criticism is in fact, MacIntyre tells us, 'the nation conceived *as a project*, a project somehow or other born in the past and carried on so that a morally distinctive community was brought into being which embodied a claim to political autonomy in its various organized and institutionalised expressions'.[34] The patriot is then loyal above all else to the nation. Not just any nation, but the nation which acknowledges its true story and nurtures real communal bonds.[35]

In MacIntyre's interpretation patriotism turns out to be nationalism. Against the universalism of liberal morality he invokes the rights of particular loyalties and the value of

[32] Ibid. 12–13. [33] Ibid. 16. [34] Ibid. 13–14. [35] Ibid. 16.

membership in concrete national communities as the necessary environment for moral life. The only requirements that he asks to make patriotic loyalty rational is that national community is not one 'which systematically disowned its own true history or substituted a largely fictitious history for it' or one 'in which the bonds deriving from history were in no way the real bonds of the community' but one where these bonds have been replaced, for example, by 'the bonds of reciprocal self interest'.[36] The fundamental values to be preserved are then the authenticity of the nation's story and communal cultural bonds. To obtain the patriot's loyalty the country not only does not need to be particularly just—patriotism, he explains, is not primarily gratitude for received benefits—it also does not need to ensure the citizens' political and civil liberty. Provided it can keep alive its cultural and historical identity and communal bonds, it is rational, MacIntyre claims, to be loyal to our country.

Loyalty and love are demanding passions; they may require us to make serious sacrifices. We ought to be entitled to be demanding in turn as to whom we should love and be loyal to. Within the nation as a project that has brought about a morally distinctive community, selections must be made between what we love and what we despise. Even if selective and demanding, our loyalty remains particular. To demand that our country be committed to liberty and justice does not imply embracing a cold universalistic morality. Those who want to embrace a culturally distinctive community and be in turn embraced by it ought not to worry. We are still committed to our own country, even though we are committed to what constitutes the best of it.

While MacIntyre advocates the value of patriotism understood as loyalty to a particular culture, other theorists argue that the only patriotism possible and acceptable in multicultural societies is a patriotism based on the values of the republic. The concept of *patria*, writes Michael Walzer, 'has never captured the American imagination', probably because 'so many of us were fathered in other lands'. Nor is the nation a source of commitment and loyalty; American society lacks the cultural, ethnic, and religious

[36] Ibid.

unity that nationalist allegiance requires. The only kind of commitment that is compatible with the pluralism of American society is a commitment to the republic; it is a political allegiance.[37]

American patriotism should not only be political in content but can only be sustained through politics; that is, through political participation. To try to reinvigorate patriotism by reducing the cultural, moral, and religious plurality of American society would not only be impossible, but also frightening. 'Among people like ourselves', stresses Walzer, 'a community of patriots would have to be sustained by politics alone', by a politics that aims at sharing decision-making and reinforcing practices of citizenship without attacking private life and liberal values or dreaming of religious or cultural revival. Odd as it may sound, the road to patriotism in liberal societies passes through democratic socialist policies.

The idea that the only patriotism possible and desirable in America is a political patriotism has been sustained also by John H. Schaar. Like Walzer, he remarks that Americans do not have an attachment to the fatherland:

We do not and cannot love this land the way the Greeks and the Navaho loved theirs. The graves of some of our ancestors are here, to be sure, but most of us would be hard pressed to find them: name and locate the graves of your great-grandparents. The land was not granted to us in trust by a Great Spirit, nor are there in this land a thousand of places sacred to lesser deities. Having purged ourselves of pantheism, we do not dwell in a realm alive with sacred groves and fountains. We took the land from others whom we regarded as of no account.[38]

Nor is American patriotism a patriotism of the city, as 'cities have been from the beginnings products largely of the impulse of profit and hustle, owing little to the sacred and the traditional'.[39] American patriotism is not based on blood or religion, on tradition or territory, or on the walls of the city. It is 'a political idea' that was better articulated by Lincoln's words in City Hall, Philadelphia.

[37] *What it Means to be an American* (New York, 1993), 82.
[38] *Legitimacy in the Modern State* (New Brunswick, NJ, 1981), 288.
[39] Ibid. 290.

I am filled with deep emotion at finding myself standing here in the place where were collected together the wisdom, the patriotism, the devotion to principle, from which sprang the institutions under which we live . . . I have often inquired of myself, what great principle or idea it was that kept this confederacy so long together. It was . . . something in that Declaration giving liberty, not alone to the people of this country, but hope to the world for all future time. It was that which gave promise that in due time the weights should be lifted from the shoulders of all men, and that *all* should have an equal chance.[40]

And even more clearly in a speech delivered on the Fourth of July:

We have besides these men—descended by blood from our ancestors—among us perhaps half our people who are not descendants at all of these men, they are men who come from Europe—German, Irish, French and Scandinavian—men that have come hither and settled here, finding themselves our equals in all things. If they look back through this history to trace their connection with those days by blood, they find they have none, they cannot carry themselves back into that glorious epoch and make themselves feel that they are parts of us, but when they look through that old Declaration of Independence they find that those old men say that 'We hold these truths to be self-evident, that all men are created equal', and then they feel that that moral sentiment taught in that day evidences their relation to those men, that it is the father of all moral principle in them, and that they have a right to claim it as though they were blood of the blood, and flesh of the flesh of the men who wrote that Declaration, and so they are. That is the electric cord in that Declaration that links the hearts of patriotic and liberty-loving men together, that will link those patriotic hearts as long as the love of freedom exists in the minds of men throughout the world.[41]

Lincoln's texts, remarks Schaar, propose a 'strictly political definition of our nationhood, one which liberates us from the parochialism of race and religion, and one which severs patriotic devotion from the cult of national power'.[42] To redeem this high ideal of patriotism, Schaar, like Walzer, stresses the necessity of

---

[40] Quoted ibid. 292.
[41] Quoted by G. Wills, *Lincoln at Gettysburg* (New York, 1992), 86–7.
[42] Schaar, *Legitimacy in the Modern State*, 296.

decentralizing decision-making processes and encouraging political participation in all major sectors of social life: work, education, communications, government.[43]

Both Schaar's and Walzer's ideas can be regarded as refinements of that distinctively American patriotism that was first and masterfully described by Alexis de Tocqueville. In this tradition, patriotism means democratic citizenship. It describes a love for a republic that the citizens feel as their own business and as their own creation; a love coupled with self-interest and pride, but still an essentially political love which translates not into desires for purification, but into the practices of participatory democracy.

The patriotism that flourished on the soil of American democracy, remarked Tocqueville, was a rational patriotism which 'grows by the aid of laws and the exercise of rights, and in the end becomes, in a sense, mingled with personal interest'. This patriotism is perhaps less ardent and less generous than the patriotism that springs from the attachment to the place where one was born,[44] but it is more creative and lasting:

A man understands the influence which his country's well-being has on his own; he knows the law allows him to contribute to the production of this well-being and he takes an interest in his country's prosperity, first as a thing useful to him and then as something he has created.[45]

Direct participation in the public life of the community, remarks Tocqueville, is the 'only remaining way' to make the citizen feel part of the republic. Civic spirit is the outcome of the 'exercise of political rights'.[46] American citizens have no common culture, no common memories, no common traditions; none

---

[43] Ibid. 307.

[44] *Democracy in America*, ed. J. P. Mayer (New York, 1969), 235. Tocqueville contrasts rational patriotism with the patriotism which 'mainly springs from the disinterested, undefinable, and unpondered feeling that ties man's heart to the place where he was born. This instinctive love is mingled with a taste for old habits, respect for ancestors, and memories of the past; those who feel it love their country as one loves one's father's house'. This patriotism however often goes together with devotion to the monarch as the personification of the nation.

[45] Ibid. 235–6.   [46] Ibid. 236.

the less they are interested in the affairs of their township, of their canton, of their state, because each of them 'takes an active part in the government of society' and is accustomed to regarding the general prosperity and the common good as his own.[47]

In Tocqueville's analysis, American patriotism is love of country that comes from duty, pride, and even greed; it has little in common with the generous, embracing, encompassing, charitable love of country theorized by republican thinkers. And yet, though sober and full of self-interest, it still is a love based on the identification with the republic obtained through political means; that is, through good laws and political participation. The republican prescription for civic virtue seems to have worked in nineteenth-century America: if the *patria* treats the citizens justly, if it allows them to participate in public life, they are likely to consider her as their own common good and love her with passion and reason.

Republican patriotism, at least on American soil, is a lively intellectual tradition. It was republican patriotism, writes Charles Taylor, that fuelled 'the sense of outrage' that motivated Americans to react against Nixon's violations. It was a sense of outrage, he specifies, that was based neither on calculation of long-term interests, nor on general commitment to the principle of liberal democracy, but on a particularistic attachment, that is, a widespread identification with 'the American way of life' defined 'by a commitment to certain ideals, articulated famously in the Declaration of Independence and Lincoln's Gettysburg address'.[48] Republican patriotism has not only been an important ideological support for freedom in the past, Taylor remarks, but 'will remain unsubstitutably so for the future'.[49] As the example of Watergate shows, a 'patriotism of the right' on the part of the citizens is essential to preserve the rule of law; that is, the very foundation of a liberal democracy. However, Taylor argues, a 'patriotic liberal regime' leaves out another equally fundamental requirement of republican patriotism and of the good republic, namely participatory self rule. Though it recognizes it, it regards

[47] Ibid. 236–7.
[48] 'Cross-Purposes: The Liberal-Communitarian Debate', 174.
[49] Ibid. 175.

self-rule as 'purely instrumental to the rule of law and equality'. In a procedural liberal society patriotism is therefore unlikely to reach its full potential.[50]

Republican patriotism, remarks Taylor, places the main emphasis on political participation. It was not primarily concerned with freedom in the modern sense of negative liberty and equal protection of individual rights, but with 'participatory self-rule'. Political participation reinforces bonds of civic friendship, a sense of common history, and the feeling of belonging to a common political entity which constitutes the essence of patriotism. Though differently argued, and based upon a different evaluation of the theoretical and cultural relevance of republicanism, Taylor's prescription is close to that of Walzer and Schaar: patriotism grows in a republic that allows for and encourages democratic self-government.

All the theorists that have argued in favour of a patriotism based on the idea that to love one's country means to love the republic as a political community based on the principle of common liberty, with its own culture and way of life, are in fact indicating the possibility of a patriotism without nationalism. It is a patriotism that stresses that the citizens' love can and must be obtained primarily by political means; that is, through the practice of good government and through justice. And by justice they mean the protection of civil rights and the political rights of the citizens. To be loved by its citizens, the republic must not tolerate discrimination and privileges and must allow the citizens to participate in public life. To love the republic they must feel close to it; they must feel it as theirs, which means to feel their fellow-citizens dear, worthy of respect and compassion. The emphasis on citizenship is not only motivated by the argument that popular sovereignty guarantees that laws aim at the common good, but also that direct political participation reinforces attachment to the republic.

This sort of patriotism makes possible the civic virtue that a good republic needs. Properly understood, civic virtue is a love of the republic or the fatherland expressed as a moral vigour that

---

[50] Ibid. 175–8.

permits the citizens to act for the common good and to resist the enemies of common liberty. Like all virtues, civic virtue also demands an effort; it asks to enrich private life, not to dissolve it into public commitment. The deeds that civic virtue requires the citizens to accomplish are greater than the achievements of private life; but only in the sense that they sustain the liberty of each and every citizen. Although civic virtue expresses itself in the public realm, it deeply affects the customs and private life of a people. Understood as love of common liberty, it cannot be a threat to civility, orderliness, and decorum. In fact, civic virtue is a weapon against the powerful or the licentious who do not want to accept the self-restraint and moderation that civil life requires.

As I have argued, patriotism of liberty does not need social, or cultural, or religious, or ethnic homogeneity. If the fatherland is less than a republic in the classical sense, citizens cannot be virtuous: they cannot love a state that treats them unjustly (though in fact they sometimes do). If the fatherland is more than a good republic—if it is a good republic and a religious or cultural or social community—civic virtue will probably reach its maximum. It may also, however, degenerate into the zealot's love of oneness, not the citizen's political love. This implies that to see the right sort of patriotism grow, we need not strengthen homogeneity and oneness but work to strengthen the practice and the culture of citizenship.

The cultural, religious, or social unity of ancient republics (whether or not these ancients republics were really as virtuous as political writers believed is a question unimportant for our purposes) cannot be reproduced in the modern world. But this does not mean that civic virtue is unattainable. Modern citizens too can love their republic, if the republic loves them, if it protects their liberty, encourages political participation, and helps them to cope with the inevitable hardships of the human condition. Though less ardent, the political love of modern citizens might be sufficient to sustain the republic and common liberty.

Understood as love of common liberty, political virtue is not a dangerous virtue. The observation that patriotism is inevitably bound to produce bigotry, intolerance, and militarism, is correct for other types of patriotism, but does not apply to the patriotism of liberty that I have been advocating in this book. A charitable love of liberty produces only liberty. Bigotry, intolerance, and war are the products of another love; that is, love or longing for oneness or uniqueness. There seem to be two distinct, though partially overlapping, pathways to civic virtue: the path of homogeneity and that of liberty. Our way should be that of liberty; that is, a political way. We do not need more citizens attending national festivals with great fervour; nor do we need more citizens willing to offer their lives to protect their country's religious or ethnic or cultural unity. We need, instead, more citizens willing and capable of mobilizing when one or more citizens are victims of injustice or discrimination, when unfair laws are passed or constitutional principles are violated.

Patriotism is different from heroic self-abnegation. The former requires us to do something more than attending to our private business; the second demands the sacrifice of our personal concerns and even our life for the common good. The virtuous citizen goes to the public square or the meeting room when he or she has to, but then he or she goes back home, or to his shop, or to join his friends. The hero sacrifices all to the republic. His love of the republic is more than a political love; it is a love enhanced by religious identification or passion for glory. But republics, except for extraordinary circumstances need less than that; they need citizens who can practise civic virtue as a completion of private life and private interest.

What Rousseau said to the citizens of Geneva applies also to us: we are neither Spartans, Athenians, nor Romans. And yet we are, or should be, concerned with liberty. We need civic virtue to prevent and to rebut the challenges to liberty that occur in our societies. The conception of patriotism and political virtue that I advocate in this book seems to me to be within our reach. However, it may not be: maybe modern citizens are no longer capable of committing themselves to 'more generous objects' and 'nobler interests', to use John Stuart Mill's words;[51] maybe

---

[51] *De Toqueville on Democracy in America*, ii, in *Collected Works*, ed. J. M. Robson (Toronto, 1977), xvii. 168–9.

we are too culturally, socially, and religiously divided and too inclined to identify with our own tribe to be able to commit ourselves to the common liberty.

In many cases, we can in fact protect our individual liberty and our welfare and the welfare of our family by not fighting for the common liberty, or otherwise sacrificing for the common good. We can surely protect our liberty without helping to protect the liberty of all members of society. By virtue of class, race, and gender, we are often insulated from violations of liberty committed against others belonging to a different class, race, or gender. We neither see nor feel the connection between our liberty and the liberty of others. We are no longer capable of compassion.

One can reply that to believe that we can protect our individual liberty without being concerned with common liberty is imprudent because it allows ambitious and arrogant men to impose their power over the laws and corrupt public institutions, thereby putting us at their mercy. Though perfectly rational, this argument is not sufficient to mobilize a passion like the love of liberty nor, more importantly, to defeat passions like avarice and cowardice which are the most powerful obstacles to civic virtue.

A more powerful drive to civic virtue is, perhaps, necessity: when corruption and oppression become unbearable, citizens sometimes retrieve a sense of public commitment. In times of extreme decay of public life, a sense of national or patriotic dignity or honour may also come to sustain virtue. We have, however, many examples of endless endurance of and adaptation to corruption and oppression: there are no sure roads that lead to a renaissance of civic virtue.

The best way to help the rebirth of civic virtue—the best way for political philosophers—is to outline a conception of patriotism that is acceptable and within our reach. The conception of patriotism as love of common liberty is, I believe, both morally sustainable and a reflection of current practices in our own times. In our own societies there are citizens defending other citizens who have been victims of injustice; citizens mobilizing against corruption and crime; citizens of different tribes invoking justice for all. They indicate for us the shape of a possible virtue and of patriotism at its best. What makes it possible is its political nature. We need more of them, and a better theory may do some good: to change our understanding of patriotism may help us to reinforce the sort of virtue that democracy needs and, more importantly, not to waste political and intellectual energies searching for an impossible or dangerous virtue.

Bibliography

ABBT, THOMAS *Vom Tode für dass Vaterland* (Berlin, 1770).

ALBERTI, LEON BATTISTA, *I primi tre libri della famiglia*, in *Opere volgari*, ed. C. Greyson (Bari, 1960).

ALTAN, CARLO TULLIO, 'Identità etnica e religione civile', *Storia contemporanea in Friuli*, 22 (1992), 9–26.

ANDERSON, BENEDICT, *Imagined Communities: Reflections on the Origin and Spread of Nationalism* (London, 1991).

ANTONI, CARLO, *La lotta contro la ragione* (Florence, 1942).

AQUINAS, THOMAS, *Summa theologiae*, in *Sancti Thomae Aquinatis opera omnia* (Rome, 1897).

AUGUSTINE, SAINT, *Enarrationes in Psalmos*, in *Opera Omnia*, ed. J. P. Migne (*Patrologia Latina*, 36–7; Paris, 1845).

—— *De Civitate Dei*, ed. George E. McCracken (London, 1957).

BATTAGLIA, FELICE, *L'opera di Vincenzo Cuoco e la formazione dello spirito nazionale in Italia* (Florence, 1925).

BERLIN, ISAIAH, *Vico and Herder* (New York, 1976).

BIANCHI, DANIELA, and RUTTO, GIUSEPPE, *Idee e concezioni di patria nell'Europa del Settecento* (Turin, 1989).

BOCCALINI, TRAJANO, *Ragguagli di Parnaso e pietra del paragone politico*, ed. G. Rua (Bari, 1910), 2 vols.; Eng. trans. *The New-found Politicke*, ed. W. Vaughan (London, 1626).

BODEI, REMO, *Geometria delle passioni* (Milan, 1991).

BOLINGBROKE, HENRY ST JOHN, FIRST VISCOUNT, *The Spirit of Patriotism*, in *The Works of Lord Bolingbroke* (London, 1967), xi. 352–71.

—— *The Idea of a Patriot King*, in *Works*, xi. 372–438.

BONANATE, LUIGI, 'Abbiamo più doveri verso i più vicini? Universalismo patriottico', *Teoria politica*, 9 (1993), 7–29.

BRUNI, LEONARDO, 'Oratio in funere Johannis Strozzae', in E. Baluze and G. Manzi, *Miscellanea novo ordine digesta... et aucta* (Lucca, 1764); Eng. trans. in G. Groffith, J. Hankins, D. Thompson, *The Humanism of Leonardo Bruni* (Binghamton, NY, 1987).

—— 'Laudatio florentinae urbis', in Hans Baron (ed.), *From Petrarch to Leonardo Bruni* (Chicago, 1968); Eng. trans. in G. Groffith, *et al.*, *The Humanism of Leonardo Bruni*.

CARTWRIGHT, JOHN, *Give us our Rights! Or, A Letter to the present electors of Middlesex and the Metropolis* (London, n.d. [1782]).

CHABOD, FEDERICO, *L'idea di nazione* (Bari, 1962).

CICERO, *De inventione*, ed. H. M. Hubbell (London, 1949).

—— *De officiis*, ed. W. Miller (London, 1947).

—— *De partitione oratoriae*, ed. H. Rackham (London, 1948).

—— *De republica* and *De legibus*, ed. Clinton W. Keynes (London, 1970).

—— *In Catilinam*, trans. L. E. Lordin *The Speeches* (London, 1937).

COLLEY, LINDA, *Britons. Forging the Nation 1707–1837* (London, 1994).

CONSTANT, BENJAMIN, 'Of the Liberty of the Ancients compared with that of the Moderns', in *Political Writings* ed. Biancamaria Fontana (Cambridge, 1988).

COYER, ABBÉ, *Dissertations pour être lues, la première sur le vieux mot patrie, la seconde sur la nature du peuple* (Paris, 1755).

CROCE, Benedetto, *Una parola desueta: L'amor di patria*, in *L'idea liberale: Contro le confusioni e gl'ibridismi* (Bari, 1944).

CUNNINGHAM, HUGH, 'The Language of Patriotism, 1750–1915', *History Workshop*, 12 (1981), 8–33.

CUOCO, VINCENZO, *Saggio storico sulla rivoluzione napoletana del 1799*, ed. Fausto Nicolini (Bari, 1929).

DERATHÉ, ROBERT, 'Patriotisme et nationalisme au XVIIIᵉ siècle', *Annales de philosophe politique*, 8 (1969), 69–84.

DEUTSCH, KARL, *Nationalism and Social Communication: An Inquiry into the Foundations of Nationality* (New York, 1953).

DIETZ, MARY G., 'Patriotism', in Terence Ball, James Farr, Russell L. Hanson (eds.), *Political Innovation and Conceptual Change* (Cambridge, 1989).

DORIA, PAOLO MATTIA, *La vita civile* (Naples, 1729).

DRIVER, CECIL, *Tory Radical: The Life of Richard Oastler* (New York, 1946).

ERGANG, ROBERT R., *Herder and the Foundations of German Nationalism* (New York, 1931).

FICHTE, JOHANN GOTTLIEB, *Reden an die deutsche Nation*, in *Schriften zur Gesellschaftsphilosophie*, ed. Hans Riel (Jena, 1928); Eng. trans. *Addresses to the German Nation*, ed. George A. Kelly (New York, 1968).

—— *Philosophie der Mauerei (Briefe an Konstant)*, ed. W. Flitner (Leipzig, 1923); Eng. trans. in H. C. Engelbrecht, *Johann Gottlieb Fichte: A Study of his Political Writings with Special Reference to his Nationalism* (New York, 1933).

FILMER, ROBERT, *Patriarcha*, ed. Peter Laslett (Oxford, 1959).

FREND, WILLIAM, *Patriotism; or Love of our Country* (London, 1804).

FUSTEL DE COULANGES, *The Ancient City*, ed. Willard Small (Boston, Mass. 1882).

GELDEREN, MARTIN VAN (ed.), *The Dutch Revolt* (Cambridge, 1993).

GERBI, ANTONELLO, *La politica del romanticismo* (Bari, 1932).

GODECHOT, JACQUES, 'Nation, patrie, nationalisme et patriotisme en France au XVIIIᵉ siècle', in *Annales historiques de la Révolution Française*, 43 (1971), 481–501.

—— *La Grande Nation: L'Expansion révolutionnaire de la France dans le monde 1789–1799* (Paris, 1956).

GOOCH, G. P., *Germany and the French Revolution* (New York, 1966).

GRAZIA, SEBASTIAN DE, *Machiavelli in Hell* (Princeton, 1990).

GREENFELD, LIAH, *Nationalism: Five Roads to Modernity* (Harvard, Mass., 1992).

GUARINI, BATTISTA, *Trattato della politica libertà*, in *Opere*, ed. M. Guglielminetti (Turin, 1971).

GUICCIARDINI, FRANCESCO, *Del modo di riformare il Governo, per meglio assicurare lo Stato alla Casa dei Medici*, in *Opere inedite*, ed. F. Canestrini (Florence, 1858), ii.

—— *Dialogo del reggimento di Firenze*, in *Dialogo e discorsi del reggimento di Firenze*, ed. R. Palmarocchi (Bari, 1932).

GUICCIARDINI, NICCOLÒ, *Quemadmodum civitas optime gubernari possit*, in Rudolf von Albertini, *Firenze dalla repubblica al principato* (Turin, 1970).

HABERMAS, JÜRGEN, 'Cittadinanza e identità nazionale', *Micromega*, 5 (1991), 123–46.

—— *Die Nachholende Revolution* (Frankfurt, 1990).

—— *Faktizität und Gektung* (Frankfurt, 1992).

HALLER, W. (ed.), *Tracts on Liberty in the Puritan Revolution* (New York, 1934), iii.

—— *The Levellers Tracts* (New York, 1944).

HAYES, CARLTON J. H., *Essays on Nationalism* (New York, 1926).

HEGEL, GEORGE WILHELM FRIEDRICH, *Grundlinien der Philosophie des Rechts*, ed. Helmut Reichelt (Frankfurt, 1972); Engl. trans. *Hegel's Philosophy of Right*, ed. T. M. Knox (Oxford, 1967).

HERDER, JOHANN GOTTFRIED, *Kleine Schriften 1791–1796*, in *Sämmtliche Werke*, ed. Bernard Suphan (Berlin, 1889), xviii.

—— *Idee zom ersten Patriotischen Institut für den Allgemeingeist Deutschlands*, in *Sämmtliche Werke*, ed. Suphan (Berlin, 1887), xvi. 600–16.

—— *Ueber den Fleiss in mehreren gelehrten Sprache*, in *Frühe Schriften 1764–1772*, ed. Ulrich Gaier (Frankfurt am Main, 1985).

—— *Ueber die neure deutsche Litteratur* (1767), in *Sämmtliche Werke*, ed. Suphan (Berlin, 1877), i. 131–456.

—— *Schulbücher* (1787–98), in *Sämmtliche Werke*, ed. Suphan (Berlin, 1889), xxx. 293–394.

—— *Kritische Wälder*, in *Sämmtliche Werke*, ed. Suphan (Berlin, 1878), iii.

—— *Selected Early Works 1764–1767*, ed. Ernest A. Menze and Karl Menges (Pennsylvania, 1992).

—— *Auch eine Philosophie der Geschichte zur buildung der Menschheit* (1774), in *Sämmtliche Werke*, ed. Suphan (Berlin, 1891), v. 475–586.

—— *Journal meiner Reise im Jahr 1769*, in *Sämmtliche Werke*, ed. Suphan (Berlin, 1884), iv.

—— *Idee zur Philosophie der Geschichte der Menschheit*, in *Sämmtliche Werke*, (Berlin, 1887), xiii. 3–441.

—— *Briefe zu Beförderung der Humanität* (Berlin, 1971), 2 vols.

—— *Briefe zu Beförderung der Humanität*, in *Sämmtliche Werke* (Berlin, 1883), xviii.

—— *Haben wir noch jetz das Publikum und Vaterland der Alten?*, in *Frühe Schriften 1764–1772*, Eng. trans. 'Do We Still have a Public and a Fatherland of Yore?', in *Selected Early Works 1764–1767*.

—— *J. G. Herder on Social and Political Culture*, ed. F. M. Barnard (Cambridge, 1969).

HEYNDRIX, JACOB, *Political Education* (1582), in Gelderen (ed.), *The Dutch Revolt*, 167–226.

HOBSBAWM, ERIC J., *Nations and Nationalism since 1870* (Cambridge, 1992).

JAUCOURT, CHEVALIER DE, 'Patrie', in *Encyclopédie*, xii (Neuchatel, 1765).

KANTOROWICZ, ERNST, *The King's Two Bodies* (Princeton, 1957).

KEDOURIE, ELIE, *Nationalism* (London, 1960).

KNIGHT, FRIDA, *University Rebel: The Life of William Frend 1757–1841* (London, 1971).

KOHN, HANS, 'The Genesis and Character of English Nationalism', *Journal of the History of Ideas*, 1 (1940), 69–94.

—— *Prelude to Nation-States, the French and German Experiences 1789–1815* (New York, 1968).

—— 'Arndt and the Character of German Nationalism', *American Historical Review*, 54 (1949), 787–803.

—— *The Idea of Nationalism* (New York, 1944).

LAPO OF CASTIGLIONCHIO, 'Oratio domini Andreae magistri Hugonis de Senis', in *Reden und Briefe italienischer Humanisten* (Munich, 1970).

LASSERRE, PIERRE, *Les Origines du Pangermanisme*, in *Le Germanisme et l'esprit humain* (Paris, 1915).

LÉON, XAVIER, *Fichte et son temps* (Paris, 1922–7), 2 vols. in 3.

LEPSIUS, REINER M. *Nation und Nationalismus in Deutschland*, in *Interessen, Ideen und Institutionen* (Opladen, 1990).

LESSING, GOTTLOB EPHRAIM, *Sämmtliche Schriften*, ed. Wendelin von Maltzahn (Leipzig, 1857), xii.

LESTOCQUOY, JEAN, *Histoire du patriotisme en France des origines à nos jours* (Paris, 1968).

LIPSIUS, IUSTUS, *De constantia*, ed. Lucien du Bois (Brussels, 1873); Eng. trans. *Two Books of Constancie*, ed. R. Kirk (New Brunswick, NJ, 1939).

LIVY, *Ab urbe condita*, ed. B. O. Foster (London, 1922).

LOMONACO, FRANCESCO, *Rapporto al cittadino Carnot*, in Cuoco, *Saggio storico*.

LUKACS, JOHN, 'Nationalism and Patriotism', *Freedom Review*, 25 (1994), 78–9.

MACHIAVELLI, NICCOLÒ, *Opere di Niccolò Machiavelli*, ed. Franco Gaeta (Turin, 1984), iii.

—— *Discorso o dialogo intorno alla nostra lingua*, in *Opere letterarie*, ed. L. Blasucci (Milan, 1964).

—— *Istorie fiorentine*, in *Opere di Niccolò Machiavelli*, ed. A. Montevecchi (Turin, 1986).

—— *Il principe e i Discorsi*, ed. S. Bertelli (Milan, 1983).

—— *Discursus florentinarum rerum post mortem iunioris Laurentii Medice*, in *Arte della guerra e scritti politici minori* (Milan, 1961).

—— *Arte della guerra*, in *Arte della guerra e scritti politici minori*.

—— *The Prince*, ed. Q. Skinner and R. Price (Cambridge, 1988).

—— *Florentine Histories*, trans. L. Banfield and H. C. Mansfield (Princeton, 1988).

—— *The Discourses*, ed. B. Crick (London, 1970).

MACINTYRE, ALASDAIR 'Is Patriotism a Virtue?', *Lindley Lecture*, University of Kansas, 26 Mar. 1984.

MAZZINI, GIUSEPPE, *Dell'amor patrio di Dante*, in *Scritti editi e inediti di Giuseppe Mazzini* (Imola, 1906), i.

—— *Dei doveri dell'uomo*, in *Scritti politici*, ed. Terenzio Grandi and Augusto Comba (Turin, 1972).

—— *Mazzini's letters*, ed. Bolton King (Westport, Conn., 1979).

MAZZINI, GIUSEPPE, *Storia della letteratura antica e moderna di Federico Schlegel*, in *Scritti editi ed inediti*, i.

—— *Fede e avvenire*, in *Scritti politici*.

—— *The Duties of Men and Other Essays by Joseph Mazzini*, with introd. by Thomas Jones (London, 1936).

—— *Life and Writings of Joseph Mazzini* (London, 1905), 6 vols.

—— *Mazzini's Letters*, ed. Bolton King, (Westport, Conn. 1979).

MEINECKE, FRIEDRICH, *Cosmopolitanism and the National State* (Princeton, 1970).

MICHELET, JULES, *Le Peuple* (Paris, 1974); Eng. trans. *The People*, ed. C. Cocks (London, 1846).

MILL, JOHN STUART, *De Toqueville on Democracy in America*, ii, in *Collected Works*, ed. J. M. Robson, (Toronto, 1977), xvii.

MILTON, JOHN, *Commonplace Book*, in *The Works of John Milton*, (New York, 1938), xviii.

—— *Samson Agonistes*, in *The Complete English Poetry of John Milton*, ed. John T. Shawcross (New York, 1963).

—— *Defence of the People of England*, in *The Works of John Milton*, (New York, 1932), vii.

—— *The Readie and Easie way to Establish a Free Commonwealth* (1660), in *Complete Prose Work of John Milton* (New Haven, 1980), vii.

MONTESQUIEU, *Mes pensées*, in *Œuvres complètes*, ed. Roger Caillois, i (Paris, Gallimard, 1949).

—— *L'Esprit des lois*, in *Œuvres complètes*, ii (Paris, 1951).

—— *Considérations sur les causes de la grandeur des romains et de leur décadence*, in *Œuvres complètes*, ii.

MOSER, FRIEDRICH KARL VON, *Beherzigungen* (Frankfurt, 1761).

NAMIER, L. B., *Nazionalità e libertà*, in *La rivoluzione degli intellettuali e altri saggi sull'Ottocento europeo* (Turin, 1957).

ORWELL GEORGE, 'Notes on Nationalism', in *The Collected Essays, Journalism and Letters of George Orwell* (New York, 1968), iii.

PALMIERI, MATTEO, *Vita civile*, ed. G. Belloni, (Florence, 1982).

PARUTA, PAOLO, *Della perfezione della vita politica*, in *Opere politiche di Paolo Paruta* (Florence, 1852).

PASSERIN D'ENTRÈVES, ALESSANDRO, 'Il patriottismo di Alfieri', in *Dante politico e altri saggi*, (Turin, 1955).

PAVONE, CLAUDIO, *Una guerra civile* (Turin, 1991).

PISACANE, CARLO, *La rivoluzione*, in Franco della Peruta, *Scrittori politici dell'Ottocento*, (Milan, s.d.), i.

PLUMYÈNE, JEAN, *Les Nations romantiques* (Paris, 1979).

POCOCK, J. G. A., *The Varieties of British Political Thought, 1500–1800* (Cambridge, 1993).

Post, Gaines, 'Two Notes on Nationalism in the Middle Ages', *Traditio*, 9 (1953), 281–320.

Price, Richard, *A Discourse on the Love of our Country* (London, 1790).

Ptolemy of Lucca, *De Regimine Principum ad regem Cipry*, in R. Spiazzi (ed.), *Divi Thomae Aquinatis, opuscula philosophice* (Turin, 1954).

Putnam, Robert, *Making Democracy Work* (Princeton, 1993).

Pyta, Donate Kluxen, *Nation und Ethos: Die Moral des Patriotismus* (Freiburg, 1991).

Quintilian, *Institutio Oratoria*, ed. H. E. Butler (London, 1921), 4 vols.

Remigio de Girolami, *Tractatus de bono communi*, in Maria C. De Matteis, *La teologia politica comunale di Remigio de' Girolami* (Bologna, 1977).

Renan, Ernest, 'Qu'est-ce qu'une nation', in *Œuvres complètes*, ed. Henriette Psichiari (Paris, 1947), i. 887–906; Eng. trans. 'What is a Nation?' in *The Poetry of the Celtic Races, and Other Studies by Ernest Renan* (Port Washington, 1970).

Rinuccini, Alamanno, *Dialogus de libertate*, in *Atti e memorie dell'Accademia toscana di scienze e lettere La Colombaria*, 21 (1956), 265–303; Eng. trans. in Renée Neu Watkins, *Humanism and Liberty* (Columbia, SC, 1978).

Rorty, Richard, 'The Unpatriotic Left', *New York Times*, 13 Feb. 1994.

Rosselli, Carlo, *Socialismo liberale*, (Turin, 1979); Eng. trans. *Liberal Socialism*, ed. Nadia Urbinati (Princeton, 1994).

—— *Scritti dell'esilio* (Turin, 1992), ii.

Rousseau, Jean-Jacques, *La Nouvelle Héloïse*, in *Œuvres complètes* ed. B. Gagnebin and M. Raymond (Paris, 1964), ii.

—— *Lettres écrites de la montagne*, in *Œuvres complètes*, iii.

—— *Du contrat social*, in *Œuvres complètes*, iii.

—— *Discours sur les sciences et les arts*, in *Œuvres complètes*, iii.

—— *Économie politique*, in *Œuvres complètes*, iii.

—— *Émile*, in *Œuvres complètes*, iv.

—— *Considérations sur le gouvernement de Pologne*, in *Œuvres complètes*, iii.

—— *Discours sur l'origine de l'inégalité*, in *Œuvres complètes*, iii.

—— *Discours sur la vertu du héros*, in *Œuvres complètes*, ii.

—— *Lettre à d'Alembert*, ed. L. Brunel (Paris, 1922).

—— *Dernière réponse de J.-J. Rousseau de Genève*, in *Œuvres complètes*, iii.

ROUSSEAU, JEAN-JACQUES, *The Basic Political Writings*, ed. D. A. Cress (Indianapolis, 1987).

—— *The Government of Poland*, ed. W. Kendall (Indianapolis, 1985).

RUSCONI, GIAN ENRICO, *Se cessiamo di essere una nazione* (Bologna, 1993).

RUSSO, LUIGI, *Tramonto del letterato* (Bari, 1960).

SALLUST, *De coniuratione Catilinae*, ed. Charles Anthon (New York, 1836).

SAMUEL RAPHAEL, *Patriotism: The Making and Unmaking of British National Identity*, i. *History and Politics* (London, 1989).

SANDEL, MICHAEL, 'Morality and the Liberal Ideal', *New Republic* (7 May 1984), 15–17.

—— 'The State and the Soul', *New Republic* (10 June 1985), 37–41.

SCHAAR, JOHN, *Legitimacy in the Modern State* (New Brunswick, NJ, 1981).

SCHLEGEL, AUGUST WILHELM, *Vorlesungen über Schöne Litteratur und Kunst*, iii. *Geschichte der Romantischen Litteratur* (Stuttgart, 1883).

SCHOCHET, G. J., *Politics, Politeness and Patriotism* (Washington DC, 1993).

SETON-WATSON, HUGH, *Nations and States: An Inquiry into the Origins of Nations and the Politics of Nationalism* (London, 1977).

SHAFER, BOYD, *Faces of Nationalism: New Realities and Old Myths* (New York, 1972).

—— *Nationalism: Myth and Reality* (New York, 1955).

—— 'Bourgeois Nationalism in the Pamphlets on the Eve of the French Revolution', in *Journal of Modern History*, 10 (1938), 31–50.

SHAFTESBURY, ANTHONY, THIRD EARL OF, *Characteristics of Men, Manners, Opinions, Times* (Gloucester, Mass., 1963).

SKINNER, QUENTIN, 'Ambrogio Lorenzetti: The Artist as a Political Philosopher', *Proceedings of the British Academy*, 72 (1986), 1–56.

—— 'The Principles and Practice of Opposition: The Case of Bolingbroke versus Walpole', in Neil McKendrick (ed.), *Historical Perspectives* (London, 1974), 93–128.

—— 'Machiavelli's *Discorsi* and Pre-Humanist Origins of Republican Ideas', in G. Bock, Q. Skinner, M. Viroli (eds.), *Machiavelli and Republicanism* (Cambridge, 1993), 121–41.

SMITH, ANTHONY, *The Ethnic Origins of Nations* (London, 1986).

SNYDER, LOUIS, *German Nationalism: The Tragedy of a People* (Harrisburg, Ill., 1952).

STERBERGER, DOLF, *Verfassungspatriotismus* (Frankfurt am Main, 1990).

TAGUIEFF, PIERRE-ANDRÉ, *Théories du nationalisme* (Paris, 1991).

TAMIR, YAEL, *National Liberalism* (Princeton, 1994).

TAYLOR, CHARLES, 'Cross-Purposes: The Liberal-Communitarian Debate', in Nancy L. Rosenblum, *Liberalism and the Moral Life* (Cambridge, Mass., 1989).

TOCQUEVILLE, ALEXIS DE, *Democracy in America*, ed. J. P. Mayer (New York, 1969).

TODOROV, TZVETAN, *On Human Diversity* (Harvard, Mass., 1993).

TOLAND, JOHN, *The Oceana and other Works of James Harrington Esq. Collected, Methodiz'd and Review'd, with an Exact Account of his Life Prefix'd by John Toland* (London, 1747).

—— *A Letter concerning the Roman Education*, in *A Collection of Several Pieces of Mr. John Toland* (London, 1726).

—— *The Life of John Milton* (London, 1699).

VAIR, GUILLAUME DU, *De la sainte philosophie: Philosophie morale des stoïques* (1599), ed. G. Michaut (Paris, 1946).

VENTURI, FRANCO, *Utopia and Reform in the Enlightenment* (Cambridge, 1971).

VICO, GIAMBATTISTA, *Principi di una scienza nuova* (1725), ed. Giuseppe Ferrari (Naples, 1859).

—— *Seconda scienza nuova* (1744), ed. Giuseppe Ferrari (Naples, 1859); Eng. trans. *The New Science of Giambattista Vico*, ed. Th. G. Bergin and M. H. Fisch (Ithaca, NY, 1968).

VIERKANDT, ALFRED, 'Patriotismus', in *Handwörterbuch der Soziologie* (Stuttgart, 1931).

VILAR, PIERRE, 'Patrie et nation dans le vocabulaire de la guerre d'Indépendance espagnole', in *Annales historiques de la Révolution Française*, 43 (1971), 503–34.

VILLARI, ROSARIO, *Per il re o per la patria* (Bari, 1994).

VIROLI, MAURIZIO, *From Politics to Reason of State* (Cambridge, 1992).

VOLTAIRE, *Dictionnaire philosophique*, in *Œuvres complètes* (Paris, 1826), lvii.

WALZER, MICHAEL, *Obligations: Essays on Disobedience, War and Citizenship* (Harvard, Mass., 1970).

—— *What it Means to be an American* (New York, 1993).

—— 'Civility and Civic Virtue in Contemporary America', in *Radical Principles* (New York, 1980).

WEIL, SIMONE, *L'Enracinement: Prélude à une déclaration des devoirs envers l'être humain* (Paris, 1949); Eng. trans. *The Need for Roots* (New York, 1952).

WIELAND, CHRISTOPH MARTIN, *Ueber deutschen Patriotismus*, in

Gesammelte Schriften, ed. Wilhelm Kurrelmeyer (Berlin, 1987), 586–95.

—— *Kosmopolitische Addresse an die französische Nationalversammlung*, in *Gesammelte Schriften*, 316–35.

WILLS, GARRY, *Lincoln at Gettysburg* (New York, 1992).

WOLFE, D. M. (ed.), *Leveller Manifestoes of the Puritan Revolution* (New York, 1944).

ZERNATTO, GUIDO, 'Nation: The History of a Word', *Review of Politics*, 6 (1944), 351–66.

Index